MAKING Soft furnishings

MAKING Soft furnishings

p

This is a Parragon Book
First published in 2002

Parragon
Queen Street House
4 Queen Street
Bath BA1 1HE, UK

Created and produced for Parragon by
THE BRIDGEWATER BOOK COMPANY LIMITED

CREATIVE DIRECTOR Stephen Knowlden
ART DIRECTOR Michael Whitehead
EDITORIAL DIRECTOR Fiona Biggs
EDITOR Sarah Yelling
DESIGNER Alistair Plumb
PHOTOGRAPHY Steve Tanner and Karl Adamson
STYLIST Jack Britton
PICTURE RESEARCH Lynda Marshall
INDEX Indexing Specialists

Hardback ISBN: 0-75258-271-2
Paperback ISBN: 0-75258-272-0

Printed in China

contents

how to use this book

Making Soft Furnishings is a useful book for the complete beginner and the experienced needleworker alike, as it takes you step-by-step through a variety of projects for the home. Clearly written text, informative photographs and diagrams lead you efficiently through the projects, guaranteeing successful results.

This book can be used in several ways: it can be read from cover to cover and treated as a complete needlework manual, or it can be dipped into and specific projects picked out and completed. Either way, it is an invaluable volume if you want to make soft furnishings for your home.

The first chapter, **Getting Started**, is just that. All the tools of the trade are introduced, as are the different types of fabrics that are suitable for making soft furnishings. The text then moves on to the different projects. **Window Treatments** introduces the art of curtain and blind making, and describes the method clearly and easily. **Take A Seat** shows you how to

cover chairs and sofas – always useful as these items are expensive to replace. **Top Tables** shows you how to make your tables a talking point and **Storage Solutions** describes clever ways to tidy up your clutter. **And So To Bed** demonstrates how easy it is to make your own sheets, duvet covers, pillow cases and quilts, while **Finishing Touches** introduces charming additions – such as bows and rosettes – that can be used to enhance any decorating scheme. There is also a useful compendium of patterns and an informative **Glossary**. *Making Soft Furnishings* offers you everything you need to make your home a cosy and inviting place.

It is vital that you choose the right fabric for the soft furnishing project that you want to complete. This section displays all the typical fabrics that are used for soft furnishings and describes their appearance, suitability and laundering instructions. There are handy samples of each fabric too, so you can see what, for example, brocade or crewelwork look like. Soft furnishing fabrics are usually quite expensive, so you must make your choice carefully, especially if you are planning on buying large amounts of material – for curtains, for example. Always check the laundering requirements too.

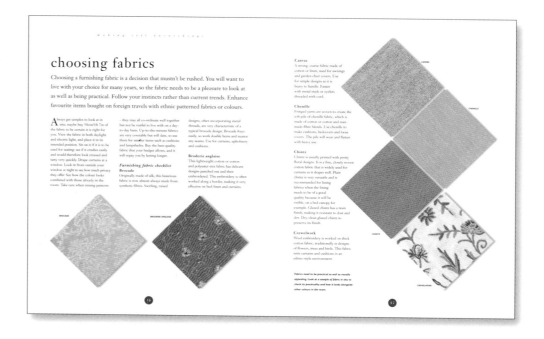

The basic techniques section describes all the likely techniques that will be needed for the projects that feature in the book. There are instructions for sewing different types of seam, making bias binding and attaching it, making piping and applying it, and matching the patterns on a fabric. There are also hints and tips, such as how to finger-press and how to make a cord tidy to keep your curtain cords neat and out of the way. This is a vital section for all readers.

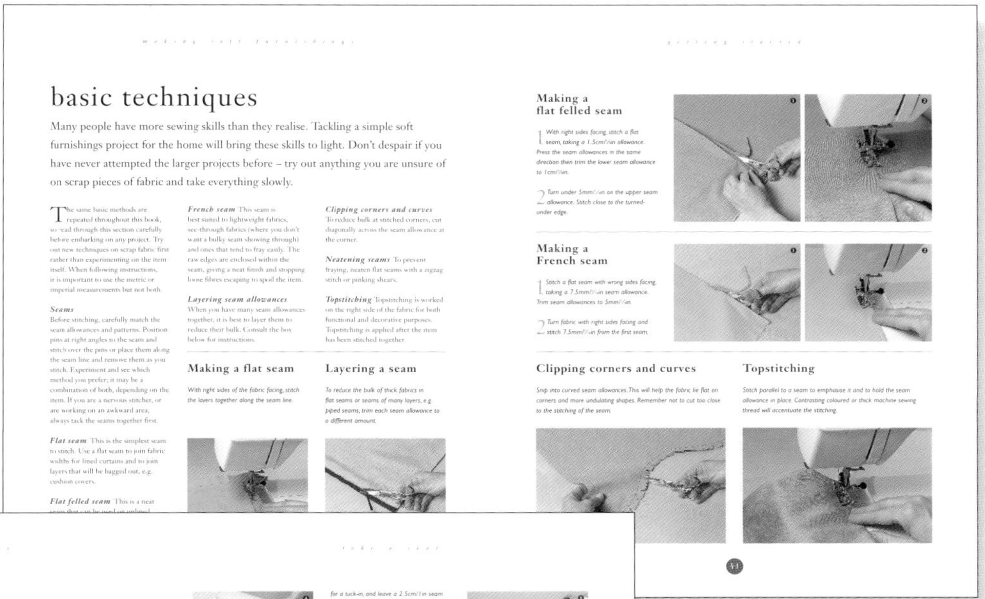

basic techniques

Many people have more sewing skills than they realise. Tackling a simple soft furnishings project for the home will bring these skills to light. Don't despair if you have never attempted the larger projects before – try out anything you are unsure of on scrap pieces of fabric and take everything slowly.

The same basic methods are repeated throughout this book, so wail through this section carefully before embarking on any project. Try out new techniques on scrap fabric first rather than experimenting on the item itself. When following instructions, it is important to use the metric or imperial measurements but not both.

Seams
Before stitching, carefully match the seam allowances and patterns. Position pins at right angles to the seam and stitch over the pins or place them along the seam line and remove them as you stitch. Experiment and see which method you prefer; it may be a combination of both, depending on the item. If you are a nervous stitcher, or are working on an awkward area, always tack the seams together first.

Flat seam This is the simplest seam to stitch. Use a flat seam to join fabric widths for lined curtains and to join layers that will be bagged out, e.g. cushion covers.

Flat felled seam This is a neat

French seam This seam is best suited to lightweight fabrics, see-through fabrics (where you don't want a bulky seam showing through) and ones that tend to fray easily. The raw edges are enclosed within the seam, giving a neat finish and stopping loose fibres escaping to spoil the item.

Layering seam allowances
When you have many seam allowances together, it is best to layer them to reduce their bulk. Consult the box below for instructions.

Making a flat seam
With right sides of the fabric facing, stitch the layers together along the seam line.

Layering a seam
To reduce the bulk of thick fabrics, e.g. piped seams, trim each seam allowance to a different amount.

Clipping corners and curves
To reduce bulk at stitched corners, cut diagonally across the seam allowance at the corner.

Neatening seams To prevent fraying, neaten flat seams with a zigzag stitch or pinking shears.

Topstitching Topstitching is worked on the right side of the item, for both functional and decorative purposes. Topstitching is applied after the item has been stitched together.

Making a flat felled seam
1 With right sides facing, stitch a flat seam, taking a 1.5cm/½in allowance. Press the seam allowances in the same direction then trim the lower seam allowance to 1cm/⅜in.

2 Turn under 5mm/¼in on the upper seam allowance. Stitch close to the turned-under edge.

Making a French seam
1 Stitch a flat seam with wrong sides facing, taking a 7.5mm/¼in seam allowance. Trim seam allowances to 3mm/⅛in.

2 Turn fabric with right sides facing and stitch 7.5mm/¼in from the first seam.

Clipping corners and curves
Snip into curved seam allowances. This will help the fabric lie flat on corners and more undulating shapes. Remember not to cut too close to the stitching of the seam.

Topstitching
Stitch parallel to a seam to emphasise it and to hold the seam thread will accentuate the stitching.

armchair cover

Bring new life to an old and tatty armchair with a loose cover. A removable cover is not only an economical alternative to having furniture reupholstered – which can be an enormously expensive undertaking – but it is practical too, as it can be removed as often as you like for laundering.

Make sure that the chair is in reasonably good condition before you start. Piping will define the shape and give a professional finish, and a discreet zip fastening at one side of the back will enable the cover to be removed easily. The cover fits snugly under the chair with a drawstring. Loose covers for sofas are made in exactly the same way as for a chair, but the fabric

for the inner back will need to be joined. A centre seam is unsightly, so have a seam toward the side edges on each side of the inner back and the outer back of the sofa. The zip opening can be in one of these seams on the outer back.

Re-covering an armchair or sofa gives a dramatic new look. Fitting a loose cover also means it can be removed and washed easily.

Making the pattern
Time and care spent preparing the pattern will reward you with a perfect fit. The cover should sit smoothly but not be tight. The pattern must be made from fabric, as paper will not follow the chair's contours. An old sheet will do. If you do not have any old fabric to hand, buy a cheap remnant, such as calico, to use. Of course, if the chair already has a loose cover, simply take it apart and press flat to use as a pattern.

1 Remove any loose cushions. Mark the exact centre of the chair on the front and back with chalk; measure this accurately as the pattern will only be made for one half

for a tuck-in, and leave a 2.5cm/1in seam allowance on all other edges. Snip the seam allowance around the arm to help the fabric lie smoothly.

2 Pin the fabric to the seat, matching a straight edge to the chalk line. Extend the fabric up the back and arm, and mark a 10cm/4in allowance at the back edge and taper it along the arm to 2.5cm/1in at the front. Trim to fit, allowing a 2.5cm/1in seam allowance on the front edge.

3 Pin the inner arm over one arm of the chair. Extend the fabric onto the seat. As before, mark a 10cm/4in allowance at the back edge and taper along the seat to 2.5cm/1in at the front. Trim to fit, snipping the curves and allowing a 2.5cm/1in seam allowance on the other edges.

4 Now pin the fabric to the outer arm, allowing 10cm/4in on the lower edge and 2.5cm/1in on the other edges.

5 Look at the position of seams and grain lines on the chair and note them when making the pattern. So that the pattern-making fabric is not too bulky to handle, roughly cut it into pieces about 20cm/8in longer and wider than the area you are working on. Use T-pins to pin the fabric to the chair, as they are easier to see on the wide expanse of a piece of furniture than dressmaking pins.

6 Pin the fabric to an arm gusset and again, matching to the chalk line. Trim, allowing 10cm/4in on the lower edges and 2.5cm/1in on the other edges.

7 Pin a straight edge to the chalk line on the back of the chair. Smooth the fabric outwards and trim it so it lies flat, allowing 10cm/4in at the lower edge and a 2.5cm/1in seam allowance on the other edges.

8 Pin fabric to the back gusset, trim to fit, adding a 2.5cm/1in seam allowance at all edges. Snip the curves at the lower edge.

9 Make patterns for the shaped cushions.

This is one of the general projects that feature throughout the book. Here, an armchair re-cover is illustrated with photographic steps and described in numbered text steps. There are simpler projects featured too, such as making a floor cushion and a blind to hide a shelving unit.

There are also feature projects too, such as this squab cushion project. These are generally projects that add a special touch to your home, such as a beaded table runner and a jolly wall tidy for your child's room. These projects can be made in any suitable fabric of your choice and you can decorate and embellish them to match your own colour and decorating scheme.

FEATURE PROJECT 1

squab cushion

A tie-on cushion filled with a thin layer of foam adds some padding to a hard kitchen chair seat. Make a feature of the ties at the back of the cushion by binding them around the chair legs. You could use contrasting coloured ribbons for this if you wanted.

Making a squab cushion

1 To make a pattern, cut a piece of pattern paper or brown parcel paper larger than the seat. Place it on the seat with a weight or tap. Fold the edges of the paper over the seat to define the shape. If necessary, snip the paper around the rails so it lies flat.

2 Remove the pattern. Add 1.5cm/⅝in seam allowance on all edges. Use the pattern to cut two chair covers from fabric. Cut the seam allowance off the pattern. Tape the pattern to 1.2cm/½in thick foam with masking tape. Draw around the pattern with an on-erasable pen. Remove the pattern and cut out the foam.

3 Make up a length of piping for the side and front edges using the cover fabric (see page 46). Pin and tack the piping to the side and front edges on the right side of one cover, starting and finishing 1.5cm/⅝in from the back edges. With right sides facing, stitch the covers together, taking a 1.5cm/⅝in seam allowance and leaving a 27cm/11in opening to turn on the back edge.

4 Layer the seam to reduce the bulk. Snip the curves and corners. Lay the foam cushion on top of the cover, matching the seam. Reach inside the cover and pin the foam to the top cover. Turn the cover right side out and slipstitch the opening closed. Remove the pins.

5 Cut four 3.5cm/1½in wide bias strips 45cm/18in long for the ties. Fold the ties lengthwise in half with the right sides facing. Stitch, taking a 5mm/¼in seam allowance. Use a bodkin to turn the ties right side out. Turn in the ends and slipstitch closed. Place the cushion on the seat and pin the ties each side of the back rails. Sew securely in place then tie around the legs.

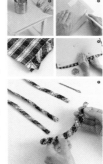

introduction

The world of fabrics, textiles and needlework is rich and varied, and once entered it is very difficult to leave. Many people did sewing at school and have never picked up a needle since – so this is the book for you if you want to get back into sewing again. This book is packed full of fascinating soft furnishing projects, which range from the simple to the more complex, and they are fully described and photographed throughout. There is advice on choosing fabric, basic techniques and vital information on colour and texture. So, pick up your needle and thread, set up your sewing machine, and prepare to enter the luxurious and cosy world of *Making Soft Furnishings*.

introduction

Soft furnishings can really enhance a room and provide an attractive decorative atmosphere. You don't need to be an accomplished needleperson to attempt many of the projects in this book – there are simple makeovers that even the beginner can attempt.

There is a wonderful choice of fabrics from all over the world readily available to us nowadays, and modern, easy-to-use fixings make soft furnishing a craft accessible to everyone. Having such a choice, however, makes it difficult to know where to begin making such an important and potentially expensive decision regarding your home and lifestyle.

Fantastic home features in glossy magazines can be frustrating if they have inspired you to create a certain look or individual item for your own home, but you do not know how to achieve it. This book is designed to lead you through the different options available, from creating a colour scheme and room style and selecting fabrics, to making up soft furnishings, and recycling or making over the furnishings you have already. It is economical to make the major soft furnishings that are

used daily, such as curtains, blinds, table linen, seating and bed-linen, and it is great fun to create the more decorative elements, such as cushions and lampshades.

The book has projects for both the novice and the accomplished needleperson. You could have a theme running throughout your home or change the mood for each room, but take care that you do not overdo this, as too much contrast in the home can be unsettling. You are likely to be attracted by certain colour schemes and styles which will bring together the overall look of your home. Consider also the architectural style of the rooms, as creative window treatments can show beautiful period windows at their best, or disguise characterless ones.

Colour in the home
Colour within the home affects our moods quite considerably. Different people benefit from different colours, depending upon their personalities.

Unless you really want to go over the top, use red sparingly in the home. It is a very strong colour and can overpower its surroundings if used in large expanses, but a touch of red here and there can be stimulating.

Orange is another vibrant colour, but it also has earthy associations too. Orange will add warmth to a north-facing room. Use terracotta shades if you want to suggest warmth but prefer less vitality in a room than a bright orange.

In many countries, yellow represents the power of the sun. It is a stimulating colour which can overpower a small room, but its links to longevity and happiness make it a popular choice for family-oriented rooms.

Changing the covers of chairs is an easy way to transform the decorative atmosphere of a room (left). Creative treatments can make the most of period windows and doors (right).

Brown is literally a grounding colour. It gives a sense of well-loved antiquity and has a stabilising effect.

Green has obvious associations with the natural world around us. It is thought to calm the nerves and invoke feelings of safety, and so is used internationally for safety codes. As it is such a balancing colour, it can be used in most situations, but avoid it for offices and other work-related rooms as too much calm does not induce one to work!

Blue represents the energy derived from water. It is a tranquil and serene colour that is a popular choice for bedrooms, as it is believed to suggest sleep. Blue is also often used in rooms where many people gather, as it can deter conflict and stress. Those prone to low moods should avoid too much blue in the home, as it may may literally give them the 'blues'.

Introspection, dignity and artistry are all associated with the colour purple. It is a regal colour that is great for opulent styles in grand rooms. Purple is said to inhibit bad behaviour and is often chosen for meditative locations, as it has very strong links with spirituality.

Pink is a gentle shade of red. It is a feminine and romantic colour, and is a popular shade for bedrooms because it is calm and nurturing and is thought to be sedating.

Being colourless, white is a superb backdrop to other colours, and a white room or sofa emphasises the people that are there, rather than their surroundings. Shades of white and cream are comfortable to live with, whereas brilliant white can often be too barren and stark.

Grey is a neutral colour that can be regarded either as harmonious or depressing, depending upon your mood. It should be used thoughtfully, as it can appear dull.

Black absorbs all other colours and can be a stunning backdrop to any other colour. Obviously, it can be depressing to live with a lot of black, but careful touches of black add a mysterious atmosphere of drama.

Inspiration board

When deciding upon a colour scheme for your home, consider whether you want to make a room seem larger or smaller. Pale colours appear to enlarge a room, and dark colours make it

seem smaller. Consider when the sun hits the room: is it all day long or just for a short time during the day? Colours look very different during the day compared with the night, as sunlight and artificial light have different effects.

Study fabric swatches, magazine tear sheets and manufacturer's brochures, and collect together your favourites. Pin these to a board for inspiration, and you are likely to find a certain style and colour choice running through your selection. Imagine your own possessions among them, and a clear vision of your personal style will soon become clear. Add other sources of inspiration: a paint sample, seed packet or the colour of an item of junk mail can set you off on a whole new scheme, so don't rush into a decision that you may have to live with for a long time.

Your favourite swatches and pictures may be of a style you have always loved and lived with, but you may also find colours and items cropping up that you initially thought were not 'you'. This may be sending you the unexpected message that now is the time for change, so follow the instinct started by the inspiration board and say 'out with the old and in with the new'.

Be brave and do not stick to one colour. Choose shades of different colours that blend together well and seem easy to live with. Different textures add interest, and there is a large choice of interesting, tactile fabrics available nowadays. Some, such as velvet, are problematic for a beginner to sew, but they can be used where minimal sewing is needed, and textured fabrics are shown at their best when worked in simple styles.

Modern techniques mean that many fabrics once regarded as difficult to work with are now more stable to use yet still retain their effect. Alternatively, replace a tricky fabric with a slightly more robust one. Chiffon, for example, is difficult to work with, but there are many sheer fabrics available that give a similar effect but are much easier to handle.

Creating your own fabric

You may have a beautiful fabric in mind for a particular project, but cannot find it in the shops or find that it is too expensive to buy. Do not despair – it is simple to create your own fabrics. The range of fabric paints available today is easy to use and hard-wearing, so you can apply your own designs to fabric or decorate it with trimmings. It is possible to create an all-over pattern quickly with readymade stencils and stamps. Pick a design motif from your wallpaper or other soft furnishings and apply it to your fabric with paints or fabric pens. You can dye a light-coloured fabric to match a new colour scheme, and even large items can be dyed successfully in a washing machine.

A few personal possessions added to your favourite fabric swatches, magazine tear sheets or manufacturer's brochures will soon create a clear vision of your personal style.

getting started

There are many practical considerations to think about when embarking upon a soft furnishing project. This chapter outlines the fabrics and trimmings that are most commonly used. Basic equipment and haberdashery are also explained concisely. You may have many of the most regularly used tools and standard haberdashery already and will find that you do not need to invest in specialist equipment and extras.

Experiment with different techniques to find out what you like doing; you may lean towards detailed needlework, such as patchwork and appliqué, or prefer to work on straightforward clean lines like making blinds or curtains. Simple upholstery can instantly alter the look of a tatty piece of furniture, and while specialist equipment is not needed for a beginner you may be inspired to experiment further with this rewarding craft. This book will lead you through the areas of soft furnishings that most appeal to you and you will soon pick up new skills, whether you are a novice or already a keen needleworker.

choosing fabrics

Choosing a furnishing fabric is a decision that mustn't be rushed. You will want to live with your choice for many years, so the fabric needs to be a pleasure to look at as well as being practical. Follow your instincts rather than current trends. Enhance favourite items bought on foreign travels with ethnic patterned fabrics or colours.

Always get samples to look at in situ; maybe buy 50cm/1ft 7in of the fabric to be certain it is right for you. View the fabric in both daylight and electric light, and place it in its intended position. Sit on it if it is to be used for seating: see if it crushes easily and would therefore look creased and tatty very quickly. Drape curtains at a window. Look in from outside your window at night to see how much privacy they offer. See how the colour looks combined with those already in the room. Take care when mixing patterns

– they may all co-ordinate well together but not be restful to live with on a day-to-day basis. Up-to-the-minute fabrics are very covetable but will date, so use them for smaller items such as cushions and lampshades. Buy the best-quality fabric that your budget allows, and it will repay you by lasting longer.

Furnishing fabric checklist
Brocade
Originally made of silk, this luxurious fabric is now almost always made from synthetic fibres. Swirling, raised

designs, often incorporating metal threads, are very characteristic of a typical brocade design. Brocade frays easily, so work double hems and neaten any seams. Use for curtains, upholstery and cushions.

Broderie anglaise
This lightweight cotton or cotton and polyester-mix fabric has delicate designs punched out and then embroidered. The embroidery is often worked along a border, making it very effective on bed-linen and curtains.

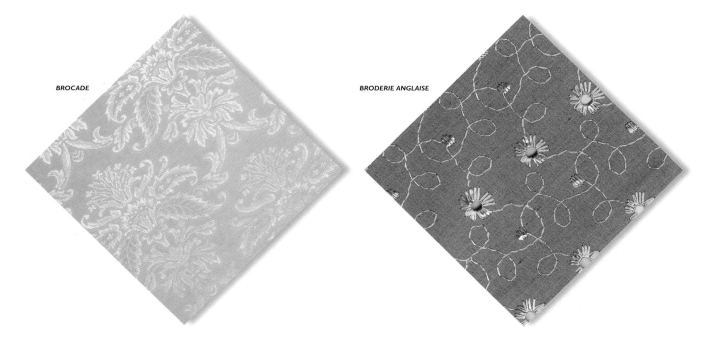

BROCADE

BRODERIE ANGLAISE

Canvas

A strong, coarse fabric made of cotton or linen, used for awnings and garden chair covers. Use for simple designs as it is heavy to handle. Fasten with metal studs or eyelets threaded with cord.

Chenille

Fringed yarns are woven to create the soft pile of chenille fabric, which is made of cotton or cotton and man-made-fibre blends. Use chenille to make cushions, bedcovers and loose covers. The pile will wear and flatten with heavy use.

Chintz

Chintz is usually printed with pretty floral designs. It is a fine, closely woven cotton fabric that is widely used for curtains as it drapes well. Plain chintz is very versatile and is recommended for lining fabrics when the lining needs to be of a good quality because it will be visible, on a bed canopy for example. Glazed chintz has a resin finish, making it resistant to dust and dirt. Dry-clean glazed chintz to preserve its finish.

Crewelwork

Wool embroidery is worked on thick cotton fabric, traditionally in designs of flowers, trees and birds. This fabric suits curtains and cushions in an ethnic-style environment.

Fabrics need to be practical as well as visually appealing. Look at a sample of fabric in situ to check its practicality and how it looks alongside other colours in the room.

CANVAS

CHENILLE

CHINTZ

CREWELWORK

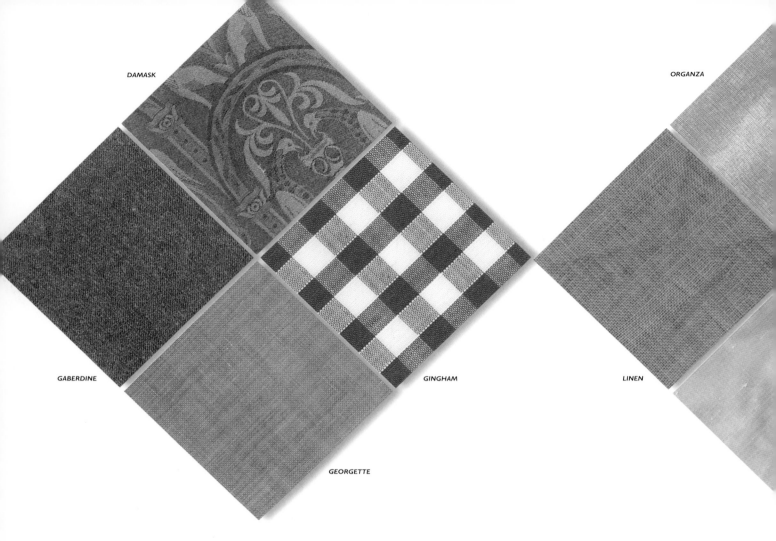

DAMASK

ORGANZA

GABERDINE

GINGHAM

LINEN

GEORGETTE

Damask

Damask, a very popular choice for soft furnishings, originates from fourteenth-century Damascus. The woven surface designs usually feature flowers, fruits or figures, and are mostly self-toned, meaning that the design is the same colour as the background. Linen damask is traditionally used for tablecloths as it is very elegant but also hard-wearing and can be boiled to get rid of any stains and starched. When calculating fabric quantities, bear in mind that damask designs are usually one-way.

Gaberdine

A hard-wearing, closely woven ribbed fabric made of cotton or wool and sometimes man-made fibres. Use gaberdine for upholstery.

Georgette

This fine, floaty fabric is made in a variety of fibres. It does not crease easily and can be used to make sheer curtains and soft blinds. It frays easily, so make double hems and neaten any seams.

Gingham

This colourful and hard-wearing fabric is reminiscent of schooldays. Gingham is usually white with woven checks and sometimes stripes of another colour. It is a classic fabric for soft furnishings in children's rooms, for kitchen curtains and tablecloths.

Linen

This strong natural fabric is available in different weights. It is expensive and creases very easily, but drapes well and feels luxurious. It can be blended with polyester, which makes it easier to handle but of poorer quality. Linen is machine-washable. Iron it damp on the wrong side with a hot iron.

Organza

This stiff, lightweight fabric is made from silk, polyester or viscose. Metallic and hand-painted organzas can be used for dramatic effects. It creases easily, and the creases are difficult to remove. Use organza for sheer curtains, or lay it over another fabric and treat both as one to make cushion covers.

PVC

PVC is a thermoplastic material. Most fabrics called PVC are knitted or woven cotton that has been sprayed with polyvinyl chloride, making it water-resistant. PVC is firm to handle, does

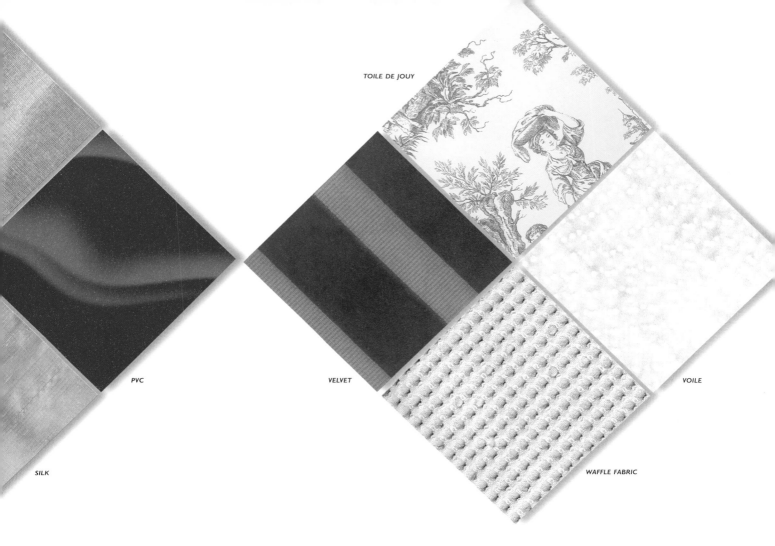

TOILE DE JOUY

PVC

VELVET

VOILE

SILK

WAFFLE FABRIC

not fray and can be used for simple blinds, tablecloths and outdoor furnishings. To clean, wipe over with a damp cloth.

Silk

Silk will bring a touch of glamour and luxury to a room. It is not a hard-wearing fabric, so use it decoratively rather than for items in regular use. It drapes well, but colours fade quickly in sunlight.

Toile de Jouy

Although this fabric originated in India, it has been made for the last two centuries in Jouy, France. Pastoral engraved designs are printed in one colour on natural-coloured cottons. This is one of the few designs that works well when used entirely in a room, as a wallcovering, curtains and upholstery or bed-linen.

Velvet

Velvet is available in a superb range of rich and luxurious colours, and has a wonderful pile which must always be used in the same direction. This fabric is difficult to handle when making soft furnishings and should not be tackled by a beginner. If possible, tack and stitch all seams in the direction of the pile. If the fabric puckers, slip tissue paper between the layers. Dralon velvet rather than a dressmaking velvet is recommended for soft furnishings, especially for upholstery as it is harder-wearing and resistant to fading in sunlight. Never wash or spot-clean velvet, instead hang it on a rail and steam-clean it instead. Do not fold velvet or hang it on a clothes hanger, as this will create creases and break the pile; roll it instead.

Certain fabrics are suited to particular functions. Georgette is a sheer, decorative fabric and, like silk, is not suitable for any items in regular use. Linen and gaberdine, on the other hand, are strong and hard-wearing.

Voile

Made from cotton, man-made fibres and sometimes silk, voile is a soft, fine fabric used for sheer curtains and soft blinds. Cotton voile can be starched to add body.

Waffle fabric

The threads in waffle or honeycomb fabric form ridges and valleys on both sides of the cloth, making it very absorbent. It is therefore a practical choice for soft furnishings that can be used in the bathroom or kitchen.

19

utility fabrics

A utility fabric has a functional purpose, but many of these fabrics are handsome enough to be used as attractive fabrics in their own right. Hardwearing canvas and ticking come in many bright colourways and can be used to make cushions and curtains, and can cover items of furniture as well.

Brushed cotton
A soft, warm cotton fabric with a slightly fluffy brushed surface. It is used to interline curtains.

Buckram
Cotton cloth that is made firm with size to stiffen pleats on curtain headings. It is available in strips or by the metre/yard.

Bump
A mediumweight interlining for curtains, pelmets and bedcovers, bump is a thick, fluffy cotton fabric.

Calico
This inexpensive, all-purpose cotton fabric was first produced in Calcutta, from where it gets its name. Calico is closely woven and available in various weights and widths. It washes and wears well but does tend to crease easily. Unbleached calico is cream-coloured with occasional dark flecks. For practical purposes, use calico for undercovers and mattress covers, as it is very hardwearing, but it can also be used for any soft-furnishing purpose. It has become very popular nowadays because it harmonises well with other fabrics, dyes efficiently and is very cheap to buy.

BRUSHED COTTON

COTTON SATEEN

HESSIAN

CALICO

Cotton sateen

This is a cotton fabric woven with a satin weave, making it very smooth to the touch and with a pleasant sheen. Because it comes in wide widths, cotton sateen is often used both to line curtains and to make curtains. Allow extra fabric for shrinkage.

Domette

A soft and fluffy open-weave fabric made of wool or wool and cotton and used to interline lightweight curtains and bedcovers.

Hessian

Usually a coarse, loosely woven jute fabric used for upholstery. It is available in finer weaves and can be used for sturdy curtains, blinds and wallhangings. Hessian frays easily. Dampen it to pull into shape, as the grain can become distorted.

Interfacing

Use interfacing to stiffen curtain headings, pelmets and tiebacks. There are woven and non-woven varieties in different weights to match your fabric. They are sold in packs or by the metre/yard, 82cm/32¼in wide. Iron-on (fusible) interfacing is pressed to the wrong side of the fabric with an iron.

Muslin

Use a piece of natural-coloured muslin as a pressing cloth. Muslin is also a popular choice for sheer curtains as it is cheap to buy and drapes well, so it can be used in volume.

Self-adhesive stiffening

This is a self-adhesive card that is cut to shape for pelmets, tiebacks and lampshades. Its backing is then peeled off revealing its adhesive surface, which is stuck to the fabric.

Ticking

This strong fabric is traditionally used for mattress and pillowcovers because its close weave makes it featherproof. Its distinctive coloured stripes on a white background are very striking, making it a popular fabric for soft-furnishing purposes.

Wadding

Place wadding between fabrics to pad them for making quilts. Cotton wadding is sandwiched between two layers of papery fabric. Polyester wadding is more commonly used; it is much springier than cotton wadding and comes in different weights, such as 56g/2oz, 113g/4oz and 226g/8oz per metre/yard.

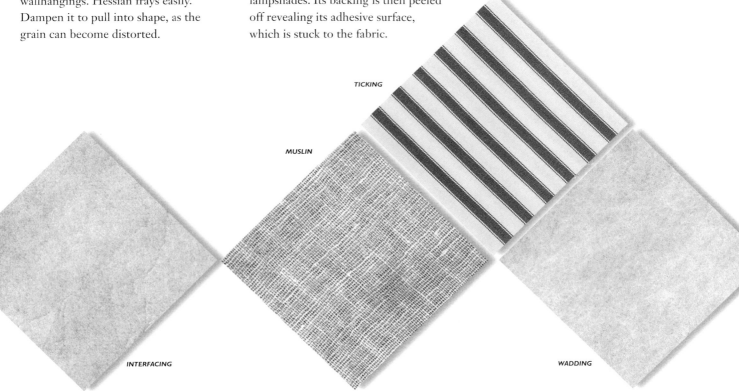

TICKING

MUSLIN

INTERFACING

WADDING

fabric care

Care for your soft furnishings regularly, and they will repay you by lasting for much longer. Gently vacuum-clean them on a light setting with a soft-upholstery attachment, paying particular attention to crevices between curtain pleats or swags and seating where dirt and dust can gather.

Plump up pillows and cushions regularly to maintain their shape and shake off dust. Most soft furnishings must be dry-cleaned; washing will break up loosely woven interlinings and wreck special finishes on fabrics. Remove pet hairs with a de-fluff mitt or a wet rubber glove. Make a note of the fabric content and any cleaning instructions when you buy fabric, then you will know how to care for it and deal with any stains.

Stain removal
Deal with spills promptly. Read instructions on specialist cleaning preparations carefully before use, and test them on a discreet area or scrap of left-over fabric first. If possible, work on stains from the wrong side of the fabric.

Crevices between curtain pleats collect dust and dirt. Use the soft-upholstery attachment of a vacuum cleaner to gently remove any dirt.

Candle wax
If spilt, scrape off as much as possible with a palette knife, then sandwich the fabric between layers of brown paper and iron it to melt the wax onto the paper. Keep replacing the paper until all the wax is gone. When coloured wax is removed, some colour will remain on the fabric; dab this off with a little alcohol.

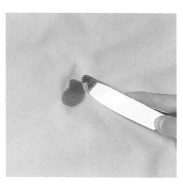

Tea

If possible, soak the stain on washable fabrics with hot water before it dries. Dab dry-cleanable fabrics with a wet pad or have the item dry-cleaned. Dried-in stains can sometimes be removed with glycerine, which can loosen them.

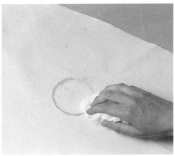

Blood

If you prick your finger whilst sewing and drop blood on the fabric, immediately roll a small ball of thread from the fabric between your fingers and moisten it. Rub the ball of thread on the drops of blood to remove them. If the stain is large, apply salt to the surface to soak it up, then soak a washable fabric in cold water; hot water will set the stain. Sponge dry-cleanable fabrics with cold water containing a little liquid detergent. Resist the temptation to rub at the stain.

Coffee and milk

Dab with liquid detergent diluted in warm water.

Fruit juice

On washable fabrics, stretch the stain over a bowl and pour warm water through it. Cover stains on silk and wool with borax, then wash in warm water.

Grease and oil

Slip a clean cloth under the stain and apply a proprietary stain remover. Dab washable fabric with liquid detergent.

Ink

Use a proprietary stain remover to suit the type of pen used. Use undiluted liquid detergent on washable fabrics, and methylated spirit on dry-cleanable fabrics.

Mildew

Spots of mildew can develop on fabric in a damp environment – particularly on curtains if they rest against a window covered with condensation. Mildew can sometimes be removed by soaking in bleach and water; always test on scrap fabric first, as the bleach may fade the material.

Scorch marks

Brush off as much of the scorching as possible with a stiff brush. Mix salt and lemon juice and apply to the marks. Allow the item to dry in the sun.

Water marks

Lightly sponge the entire surface evenly, then press. Carefully shake silk and velvet over steam from a kettle, covering the spout with a cloth to prevent it spluttering.

Wine

Dabbing spilt red wine with white wine will thin it and make it easier to wash out. Sprinkle the stain with salt to soak as much of it up as possible then launder the item, ideally before the stain has time to set.

decorative trimmings

A well-chosen trimming can make all the difference to an item of soft furnishing, and shows that thought has gone into the finishing touches. Always check to see whether the trimming has the same wash-care instructions as the fabric it is to be attached to; some trimmings are not colour-fast.

Ribbons

Pompoms

Eyelet lace

There are whole shops devoted to beautiful beads, ribbons, braids, feathers and trimmings of all kinds, so you will be spoilt for choice if decorative trimmings are your thing. A plain cushion or a lampshade edge can be transformed into a work of art with an exotic beaded trim, for example, or you can experiment with jolly pompoms and ribbons.

Beads

There are masses of inspirational beads that can be used to trim soft furnishings. Tiny rocaille and bugle beads can be handsewn at random or to a definite design. Drop beads have a hole across the top or centrally along their length for sewing. Check the washing instructions, and avoid using glass beads, which may break or splinter.

Braid

This straight-edged woven trimming can be sewn, glued, nailed or stapled in place, either purely as decoration or to hide seams or cover raw edges of fabric.

Buttons

Use buttons for decorative as well as practical use. There is a huge choice available, and the price range is just as huge. Don't forget self-cover buttons which you can cover with your choice of fabric. Sew-through buttons have flat backs with two or four holes. Shank buttons have a loop underneath to sew through, and are best for thick fabrics and rouleau loop fastenings.

Cord

Handsew colourful woven and twisted cords as decoration, or use cord as a drawstring to fasten storage bags. Inexpensive white piping cord is also very effective when used uncovered.

Edging lace

This lace has a straight edge to insert in a seam. Some edging laces are gathered to give a readymade frill.

Eyelet lace

Broderie anglaise is often used for eyelet lace. Both edges of this narrow lace have a fancy finish. There is a row of eyelets along the centre which can be threaded with ribbon, either purely for decoration or as a drawstring.

Fold-over braid

This flat nylon braid is folded slightly off-centre. The raw edge of the fabric is slotted inside, with the wider half of the braid underneath. The layers are then stitched together. It is available in a range of colours and can be used to neaten tablecloths and throws.

Tassel

a metal back with grooves in for sewing through. Some stones are attached with a separate metal back that goes under the fabric. The back has prongs to hold the stone in place.

Piping
Ready-made piping is available in a limited range of colours. It is easy to make by covering piping cord with bias strips of fabric. Piping gives definition and a professional finish to a seam.

Pompom edging
This retro-style edging suspends a row of small pompoms, which are very effective on lampshades and curtains.

Pompoms
It is very simple to make your own pompoms, and they make a lively addition to cushions and throws.

Ribbon
Colourful ribbons come in all sorts of widths, materials and finishes. They can be stitched in stripes and checks, used as ties or as drawstrings for storage bags.

Rickrack braid
This wavy woven braid suits the decor of many children's rooms.

Plain curtains, lampshades and cushions can be transformed into works of art by adding a decorative trimming. Some trimmings can be practical as well as decorative.

Russia braid
This is a fine silky braid that comes in lots of glossy colours. Stitch it in place along its central groove.

Sequins
Strings of sequins can be sewn by hand or stitched along the centre by machine. Single sequins can be sewn by hand.

Tassels
Readymade tassels are often expensive, but they do give a satisfying finishing touch to cushions, table runners and many other applications. It is economical to make your own tassels in exactly the colour you want.

Fringing
Most fringings have a flat edge so they can be inserted in a seam, and a zipper or piping foot is used to stitch it. If the fringe edge has a row of stay stitching, leave it in place until the item you are making is finished, otherwise stray threads will get caught in the seams.

Gimp
Similar in use to braid, gimp has a scalloped edge rather than a straight one. It is easier to fit around corners than braid.

Insertion cord
Here, decorative cord has a flat flange woven into it to be inserted in a seam. Apply it in the same way as piping.

Jewellery stones
Made from glass or plastic, jewellery stones are for decorative purposes only, such as on lampshades. Sew-on jewellery stones have holes drilled or

Gimp

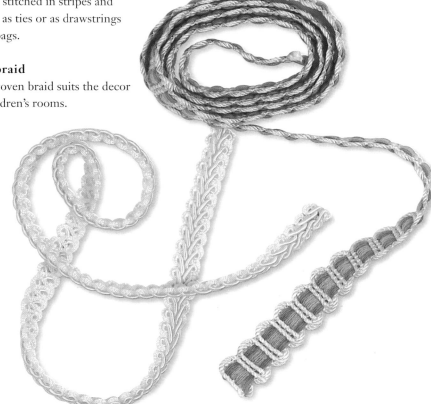

utility trimmings

Some of the extras needed to fasten fabrics and neaten edges are very appealing in their own right, and as well as being concealed, they can be used to make a feature in themselves. All of these trimmings are available in the haberdashery sections of most department stores.

The style for utility furnishings has recently taken off, as designers constantly search for new fabrics and trimmings to create the newest trend. Buttons, hooks and eyes, touch-and-close tape and different types of cord have all been called into service on the decorative front. These trimmings are also particularly useful if you are planning a nautical theme in a room. Thick cord ties and eyelets can give a vigorous air of salty tradition to a modern decorating scheme.

Bias binding

This is a strip of bias-cut fabric with the edges pressed under for binding curved and straight edges. It is available by the metre/yard or in prepacks in different colours and widths in cotton or satin. It is easy to make your own, to match or contrast with the main fabric.

Blind cord

This strong, narrow cord is used for drawing Swedish and Roman blinds open, and for drawstrings.

Curtain weights

Most curtains will hang better if weights are attached inside the hems. Weights are available as button-shaped discs or as a chain. Both types come in different weights.

Eyelets

Metal eyelets have a nickel or gilt finish and come in a kit with a fixing tool. They come in a few sizes, 1.5cm/⅝in being the most widely available diameter. Use eyelets for hooking up blinds, as a curtain heading and for assembling garden canopies. 6mm/¼in diameter metal eyelets are available in a limited range of enamel colours and are fixed with a tool rather like a pair of pliers.

Hook and eye tape

Metal hooks and eyes are attached to cotton tape to fasten duvet covers and cushion covers.

Binding and webbing

Choose from different widths and colours of binding for curved or straight edges.

Piping cord

Available in different thicknesses, this inexpensive white cotton cord is used for making your own piping.

Poppers

Like press fasteners, poppers are ball-and-socket fasteners, but are held in place with pronged rings. They are available in kits and are suitable for heavyweight fabrics.

Seam binding

This straight woven tape of cotton or nylon is used for finishing single hems where a double hem would be too bulky.

Press fasteners

These are two-part metal or transparent plastic ball-and-socket fasteners which can be used to fasten cushion covers. There are self-cover press-fastener kits available in different sizes for covering in your own fabric when you want to make a feature of them, for fastening a duvet cover for example.

Press-fastener tape

This two-part tape is sold by the metre/yard and has press fasteners along its length. It is ideal for fastening duvet covers and cushion covers.

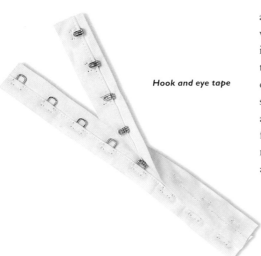

Hook and eye tape

Piping cord is inexpensive to work with. You can add your own tassels or pompoms as a lively addition to soft furnishings.

Touch-and-close tape

This is a two-part tape, one tape with a looped mesh surface and the other with a hooked surface. The two layers interlock when pressed together. The tapes are available for sewing, ironing on, or with an adhesive backing for sticking. Use them to fix loose covers and attach blinds to battens. The fastener is available in a limited number of widths and colours, and as small discs.

Twill tape

This firmly woven cotton tape is used to strengthen seams and for ties to attach bed valances, and for unobtrusive drawstrings.

Upholstery tacks

1.2cm/½in long upholstery tacks are the most versatile size to use.

equipment

It is vital to have the right equipment when you are contemplating beginning a new soft furnishing project: there is nothing worse than getting part of the way through and discovering that you have to go out to buy something vital! Go through what equipment you do have and add and replace as necessary from the list below.

Even a newcomer to sewing will probably already have some of the equipment needed. Keep your tools together and use them only on fabrics and their trimmings, so they do not get dirty or blunted. Work on a clean, flat and well-lit surface, and keep sharp tools beyond the reach of young children and pets. An area lit by a daylight-simulation bulb is kind to the eye and does not alter the colour of fabrics, which other light bulbs can do.

Web stretcher

Air-erasable pen
This pen can be used on fabric, as any marks will gradually disappear. Always test on a scrap of fabric first.

Bias binding maker
This small metal tool is threaded with strips of fabric which are pulled through and pressed to form bias binding.

Tailor's chalk

Dressmaking shears
Bent-handled dressmaking shears are the most comfortable and accurate to use for cutting fabric, as the angle of the lower blade allows the fabric to lie flat. They are available in different lengths, so test the size before buying. A top-quality pair is expensive but will last a lifetime and it is worth paying that extra bit in the long run.

Embroidery scissors
A small pair of sharp scissors is indispensable for snipping threads and cutting into intricate areas. Keep them in a small cloth case when not in use.

Hammer
Used to hammer tacks, eyelets and poppers in place.

Ironing board and iron
Use a sturdy ironing board, because you will find that you will be handling very large and weighty pieces of cloth and the board will need to be able to take the strain. Invest in the best iron you can afford, preferably a steam/dry iron with a reliable heat setting.

Metre/yard stick
Made from wood or metal, this measure can be used on curtains and for drawing cutting lines on fabric.

Pattern paper
This lightweight paper is faintly marked with a grid to aid the drawing of patterns. Brown parcel paper is also suitable for this purpose. Never use newspaper as it will dirty the fabric.

Pencil
Always keep a sharp pencil and paper to hand in the planning stages to make notes and record measurements. A propelling pencil or sharp HB pencil is recommended. Use a chinagraph pencil on PVC and vinyl fabrics.

Pinking shears
These cut a zigzag fray-resistant edge and are used to neaten seams and cut out fabrics that fray easily.

Pressing cloth
Use a piece of inexpensive cheesecloth or muslin about 1m/3ft 3in square to protect the fabric you are ironing from becoming shiny.

Screwdriver
Use this to fix screws to walls for curtain tracks, pelmets and battens for blinds.

Seam ripper
This small implement has a sharp, inner curve for cutting seams open

Steam iron

when mistakes have occurred, and a point for picking out threads.

Set square
Use a set square for making accurate angles when drawing patterns on paper and fabric.

Sewing gauge
This 15cm/6in long ruler has a slider that can be set at different levels for marking hems and seams, and as a quilting guide.

Sewing scissors
One blade is pointed and the other rounded so fabric can be trimmed without getting snagged.

Spirit level
Use this to position curtain tracks and battens for blinds.

Staple gun
This is a fast way of attaching fabric in upholstery, and for fixing swags and tails.

Steel measure
Use a retractable steel measure to measure windows and beds.

Tailor's chalk
This coloured chalk, available in wedge and pencil forms, is used to mark fabric as it can be brushed off.

Tape measure
A plastic-coated or cloth tape measure is useful for measuring around curves.

Thimble
A thimble protects your finger when handsewing. Thimbles come in different sizes and are made of leather, metal or plastic: an open-topped leather thimble is recommended. Wear a thimble on the middle finger.

Transparent ruler
A 30.5cm/12in ruler is a useful size for drawing against on paper and fabric, and for checking measurements.

Web stretcher
This is only necessary if you do a lot of upholstery, otherwise it's probably not worth buying. It is used to stretch webbing across the frame of a chair.

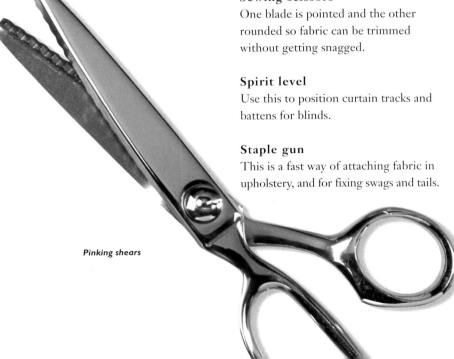

Pinking shears

haberdashery

Haberdashery items are the real nuts and bolts of the whole sewing and making soft furnishings process. It is vital that you have the right kind of needles for the fabrics you are sewing, and you can never have too many pins. A good range of different coloured threads is also a necessity.

Gather together a selection of needles, pins and threads when you are planning your next soft furnishings project. They are inexpensive, and having the correct ones for a project will make it easier to work on and give a better finish when making soft furnishings.

Handsewing needles
Needles for handsewing come in different sizes. The higher the number, the shorter and finer the needle.

Ballpoint needle
This needle is for knitted fabrics. The rounded point slips between the yarns instead of piercing them. The size range is 70–100 (9–16).

Betweens needle
This short-length needle should be used in quilting projects.

Bodkin
This thick, blunt needle has a large eye for threading cords, ribbon or elastic through casings, and for turning fabric

Curved needle

tubes right side out. Use a safety pin if you do not have a bodkin.

Curved needle
A curved needle is for sewing around curves on upholstery and lampshades, and for getting into tight corners.

Machine-sewing needles
Needles for sewing machines come in different sizes with different-shaped points. The lower the number, the finer the point. For example, size 70 (9) is the finest and should be used on fine, lightweight fabrics and size 110 (18) is the thickest. Sizes 70–90 (9–14) are the most commonly used.

Sailmaker's needle
This needle has a sharp, triangular point for inserting through strong canvas. Use it to sew heavy-duty fabrics for the garden.

Sharp-point needle
This is the most versatile needle. Use it to stitch woven fabrics.

T-pins

The size range for sharp-point needles is 70–110 (9–18).

Sharps needle
This long, general-purpose needle is useful for tacking and sewing hems.

Wedge-point needle
Stitch leather and vinyl with a wedge-point needle to lessen the chance of splitting the material. The size range is 80–110 (11–18).

Pins
Corkscrew pins
These small upholstery pins fix loose covers unobtrusively in place; just screw them into the upholstery.

Dressmaker's pins
There are different thicknesses of pins for different fabrics. Household pins are the most versatile. Use lace or

Beeswax

Button thread

Button thread
This is a thick, tough thread for handsewing heavy fabrics that need to be strongly secured. It has a glazed finish to help it slip through closely woven, heavy fabrics.

Cotton-covered polyester thread
This is a strong, coarse thread for heavyweight fabrics and vinyl.

General-purpose mercerised cotton thread
Use this to sew lightweight and mediumweight cotton, linen and rayon. Smooth, silky mercerised thread is available in a large choice of colours. Do not use on stretchy fabrics, as the stitches will snap if stretched.

General-purpose polyester thread
This works well on woven synthetics, knitted and other stretchy fabrics.

Tacking thread
Use this weak thread in a contrasting colour to the fabric so it is easy to see when you want to remove it.

bridal pins on silk and other delicate fabrics, as other pins will mark the surface. Coloured glass-headed pins are easy to see on a large expanse of fabric. Pins made from stainless steel are hardwearing: nickel-plated pins may leave black marks on fabric.

T-pins
Use sturdy T-pins instead of dressmaking pins to fix fabric temporarily to upholstered items when making patterns and re-covering.

Threads
Sewing thread should be strong and durable and have some 'give' in it. Choose thread to match the fabric weight and colour. If an exact colour match is not possible, choose a darker rather than a lighter shade.

Beeswax
Pull thread through beeswax to strengthen it and stop it twisting.

Sewing thread

patterns

Squares and rectangles are the shapes most often cut to make soft furnishings, and these are best marked directly onto the fabric. You will need to make a pattern for shaped items such as curtain tiebacks, lampshades and seating, especially if you need to cut out more than one piece at a time.

Patterns can be easily made from brown parcel paper or special pattern-making paper, which is available from haberdashery suppliers. Do not use newspaper, as it will dirty the fabric, the work surface and your hands. Draw the pattern piece on the paper, adding a seam allowance. Mark the grain line and any fold lines, and balance marks such as dots on the seam or notches on the seam allowance; these marks are essential if you are matching one piece of fabric to another. To make a symmetrical pattern piece, fold the paper in half and draw one half of the piece against the fold, then cut out through both layers and open the pattern out flat to use.

If you have made a pattern from fabric – to re-cover a chair, for example – press it flat and mark the seam lines. If you have a set of old loose covers that you wish to use as patterns, check the fit on the piece of furniture in question and make any alterations that are necessary. Carefully undo all the seams, marking balance marks as you part the pieces. Label the pieces clearly and mark the top, bottom and side edges so you know what goes where when you put them on the furniture. Roughly repair any tears or sew patches over large worn holes so the pattern keeps its shape. Press the patterns flat.

Layouts

Carefully work out how much fabric to buy and the most economical way to arrange the pattern pieces on the paper. Cut down on wastage as much as you can. Note whether the fabric has a nap – this means a pile that runs in one direction – or a design that works in one direction only, in which case the patterns need to lay in the same direction. Allow extra for matching patterned fabrics (see page 37).

Use the width of the fabric to calculate how much fabric to buy. If most of the pieces are to be cut from measurements, e.g. squares or rectangles, take a sheet of paper to represent the fabric, the side edges being the selvedges. Draw the pieces on the paper, marking their dimensions and adding them up so they fit across the width. Mark on their dimensions and grain lines, and butt the edges together to lessen wastage. Check that seam allowances and hems are included. Next, add the dimensions along the side selvedge edges to the amount of fabric. Keep the layout diagram for positioning when cutting.

For shaped pattern pieces, use long rulers and tape measures on a large table or the floor to mark out an area that is the width of the fabric, or half the width of the fabric if you need to cut patterns in pairs. Arrange the patterns within the space, keeping grain lines level with the marked edges that represent the selvedges or a selvedge and fold. If the fabric has a nap, make sure all the pieces lie in the correct direction. Check that you have included all the pattern pieces, as some may need to be repeated. The length of the table or floor area taken up by the patterns is the length of fabric needed. Make a rough sketch of the layout to refer to when positioning for cutting.

Make patterns for shaped items such as curtain tiebacks, lampshades and seating. Use brown parcel paper or special pattern-making paper, but not newspaper.

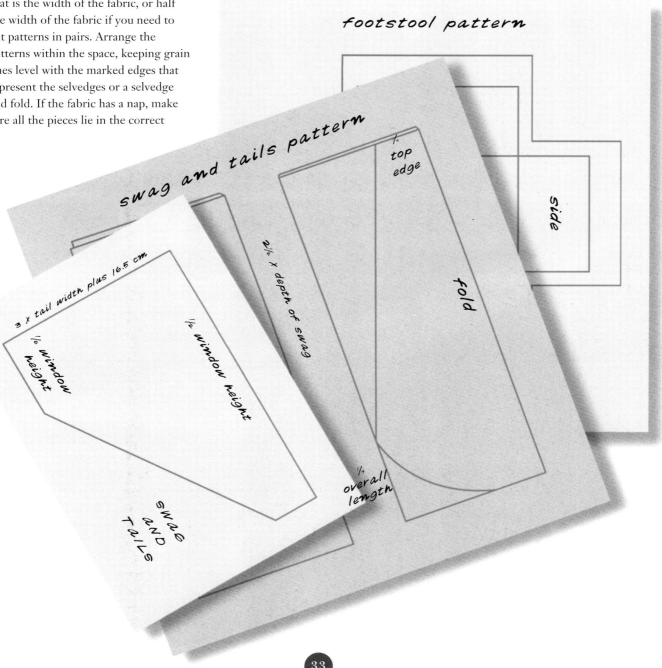

footstool pattern

top edge

side

fold

swag and tails pattern

2½ x depth of swag

3 x tail width plus 16.5 cm

½ window height

½ window height

½ overall length

SWAG AND TAILS

preparing the fabric

Fabrics for larger projects, such as curtains and covering sofas and chairs, can be very expensive, and it is worth handling the fabric properly so it doesn't spoil. Check whether a fabric will shrink or not, and always test for washability. Finding the grain line is also vital, and will save you a lot of time and frustration.

Many fabrics shrink. Ask the retailer when you buy a fabric if this is likely to happen. If it is liable to shrink, add an extra 10 per cent to the fabric quantities, then wash the fabric before cutting. To test washability, dampen a corner of the fabric to see if water marks the surface; if it does, do not wash it but dry-clean when necessary.

Grain lines
Woven fabrics stretch differently if pulled in different directions, and this affects the way a fabric hangs. The lengthwise grain, called the warp, runs the length of the fabric parallel to the selvedges. The warp has less stretch, making it easier to sew in this direction without stretching or puckering the fabric. The crosswise grain is called the weft and runs from selvedge to selvedge. It has a little more stretch than the lengthwise grain.

The bias is any line that is not the lengthwise or crosswise grain. The bias will stretch and the true bias, which is at 45 degrees to the lengthwise or crosswise grains, stretches the most. Take care when stitching along the bias, as seams will stretch.

Some woven fabrics have obvious grains. In others they are harder to see.

Finding grain lines

There are two ways to find the crosswise grain. The first method is suited to lightweight and loosely woven fabrics. First, snip into the selvedge and carefully pull out a crosswise thread. Cut along the channel that is left in the weave. Alternatively, on firmly woven fabrics snip into the selvedge and tear across the fabric to the other selvedge.

If the fabric has a woven stripe or check, this will be the grain line. This method does not work on printed stripes and checks, as they are unlikely to be printed exactly on the grain.

Once the crosswise grain has been found and torn or cut across, fold the fabric in half lengthwise. The layers should lie smoothly together with the selvedges matched. If they do not match, dampen the fabric and pull it diagonally to stretch it gently back into shape. Leave it to dry flat with the corners and all edges aligned.

Pressing and ironing

Pressing is a vital part of sewing and should be done throughout a project and not just at the final stage. The difference between pressing and ironing is that in pressing, the iron is pressed down onto the fabric, lifted up and moved onto the next section, and in ironing, the iron glides over the surface of the fabric. Use a light pressure, allowing the weight and heat of the iron to do the work.

Iron out any wrinkles and creases on the fabric before cutting out. If the fabric has a definite fold line, press it out before cutting. If a faint line is left along the fold, this must be avoided when laying out the pattern pieces.

Smooth and straighten the fabric, removing pins and tacking as these will leave indentations if pressed. Press each

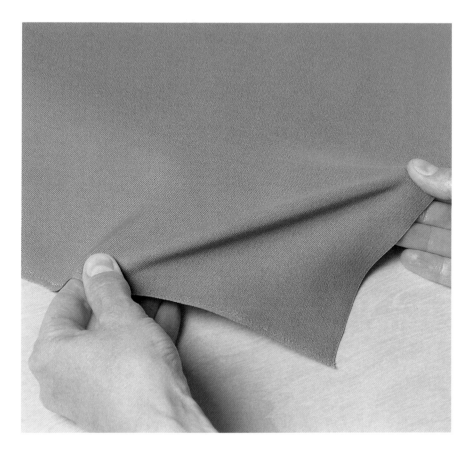

seam after it is stitched. Do not press in any sharp creases until you are sure they are in the correct position, as they may be difficult to remove. In general, press from the wrong side of the fabric.

Set the iron to the correct heat setting for the fabric and test on a scrap or discreet corner of the fabric. Wool needs a warm setting and benefits from a lot of steam when pressing. Great care must be taken when pressing velvet: lay the fabric pile side down on a towel and hold the iron over, but not touching, the fabric on a steam setting.

Always use a pressing cloth when pressing the right side of the fabric, to stop the fabric becoming shiny. Cheesecloth or muslin are the most versatile fabrics to use, as you can see through them. Use a lightweight

Woven fabrics stretch differently if pulled in different directions, according to the crosswise and lengthwise grains. The grains affect the way a fabric hangs and stretches.

cotton for heavyweight fabrics. Do not use calico or a tea towel, as they hold too much water, which will produce a lot of steam and ruin some fabrics. Use a dry cloth with a steam iron and a damp cloth with a dry iron. Wring the cloth out well to use it damp. The seam allowances on some fabrics can make an indentation, so cut a strip of brown parcel paper and slip it under the seam allowance before pressing.

When dealing with embroidered fabrics, lay them face down on a soft fabric such as interlining to protect the raised surface when pressing.

cutting out

Cutting out the fabric is a major part of creating soft furnishings. Do not rush this stage – cutting mistakes can be costly, as most cannot be rectified. Although it is tempting to rush right in and get started, take your time to position the pattern pieces correctly and economically as this will save you time later on.

Cutting selvedges

It is often advisable to cut off selvedges (the neatened edges that run the length of the fabric), as they are woven tighter than the fabric, sometimes causing it to pucker. If you join fabric widths with the selvedges on, cut into the seam allowances at 10cm/4in intervals to release any tightness.

Lay the fabric out flat on a large table or the floor, depending upon the size of the fabric: ideally, the cutting area should be accessible from at least three sides. To cut pairs of patterns, fold the fabric in half lengthwise or widthwise if that suits your layout better; otherwise keep the fabric single.

How to cut out

1 *Pin the pattern pieces on top, matching the grain lines, or draw the dimensions of the pieces with an air-erasable pen or tailor's chalk. Use a ruler and set square to draw straight lines and right angles.*

2 *Cut out the pieces, cutting thick fabrics one layer at a time and patterned fabrics the same so you can match the designs accurately. Save fabric scraps for testing stitches and the heat of the iron.*

3 *On vinyl or leather, stick pattern pieces in place on the wrong side with masking tape, and draw around the piece with an air-erasable pen or tailor's chalk. Remove the pattern and cut out the fabric one layer at a time.*

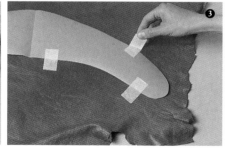

Matching patterned fabrics

1 Use an air-erasable pen or tailor's chalk to draw a line across the fabric selvedge to selvedge. Avoid placing the line through a design motif, as this will disrupt the overall effect. Cut off excess fabric above an upper seam or hem allowance. Lay the fabric out flat right side up on a large table or the floor. Measure the length of the curtain including allowances, and cut off the excess fabric.

2 Lay the remaining fabric selvedge to selvedge with this first piece, matching the level of the pattern. Cut across the fabric to match the first piece. Cut any remaining pieces in the same way. Cut off the selvedges.

3 Fold under a 1.5cm/⅝in seam allowance along one long edge. Lay the folded edge over the adjacent edge of the other length of fabric, matching the pattern. Pin and ladder stitch the pieces together.

4 Now fold over the top fabric so the right sides are together. Stitch the seam, using a flat felled seam for unlined curtains and a flat seam for lined curtains.

Matching pattern repeats

Extra fabric must be allowed for matching patterned fabrics. In general, add one pattern repeat for each fabric width. The pattern repeat is usually marked on the fabric label; if not, ask the retailer to measure the repeat.

Widths of fabric usually need to be joined to make curtains, but this is also sometimes necessary when making bedcovers and re-covering sofas.

Extra fabric may also be needed for positioning an element of the fabric design to show it whole and at its best, on the centre of a cushion for example. Although this means extra expense, it will give a satisfying end result. Make a pattern from greaseproof or tracing paper so you can see through it. Fold it into quarters to find the centre, open out flat and mark the fold lines and grain line. Lay the pattern over a motif on the fabric, matching the grain lines and the centre of the pattern to the centre of the design. Pin in place and cut out.

the sewing machine

Although some people prefer the method of handsewing (and this always has an important place in the needleperson's skillbase) you will find that you cannot do without a sewing machine if you want to tackle larger soft furnishing items, such as bulky curtains or a set of loose covers. It is a vital piece of equipment.

A sewing machine is the biggest and most important investment to be made for the sewing room. There are many considerations when choosing one, most importantly, for what do you intend to use it? A machine that does straight stitch, zigzag stitch and neat buttonholes is the most basic in terms of requirements, and is enough for most people's needs. If you have considered experimenting with machine embroidery and fancy stitches, choose a machine with push-button controls or a computerised system. An overlocking machine or serger is useful if you intend to sew a lot, as it neatens seams quickly and efficiently.

Research the market and buy from a reputable dealer. Ask for demonstrations of the machine's functions, and test-run a few machines yourself for comparisons and to see if you like the feel of a particular machine. Do not overlook secondhand machines, as you may find a bargain. A secondhand machine should have been well maintained and come with its original instruction manual.

When researching the best sewing machine for your requirements, check that the speed controls and bobbin winding mechanism are easy to operate. The machine should be simple to thread. Work a buttonhole – are you pleased with the result, and was it simple to do? Can the machine be left set up in position with the lid on when not in use, or will it need to be moved each time and packed away in its case? In the latter scenario, consider the size and weight of the machine. Ask friends and family for recommendations, as every home sewer will have his or her favourite make of machine.

How it works

There is a huge range of sewing machines to choose from, but they are all fairly similar in operation. In all sewing machines, the presser foot holds the fabric in place; the needle, threaded with the upper thread, penetrates the fabric and goes into the bobbin area to pick up the lower thread to form a stitch. Read your sewing machine manual carefully to familiarise yourself with the machine's features and operating techniques.

Power supply

Turn the power supply off before setting up the machine. Check that the electrical voltage of the machine is the same as your power supply. Plug in the cord socket, then insert the plug into the power supply. Switch on the power. Switch off the machine when it is not in use, and pull out the plug.

Foot control

The harder you press the foot control, the faster the machine will run. The sewing speed can be varied on most machines.

Sewing light

The sewing light is especially helpful when you are sewing dark colours. When the bulb goes replace it immediately, following the manufacturer's instructions.

Presser foot

The presser foot holds the fabric in place. Most machines have a basic foot and a few extra feet for special purposes, such as a zipper or piping foot, buttonhole foot, blind stitch foot and darning foot. Presser feet can be changed by either being snapped off and on, or unscrewed and screwed on.

Feed

The feed moves the fabric backwards as you stitch. The distance the fabric is moved is controlled by the stitch length regulator, which must be set carefully for each type of fabric.

Stitch length regulator

The numbers on the regulator represent either the stitch length metrically in millimetres or the number of stitches per inch. The two are compatible: for example, if each stitch length is 2.5mm, there are ten stitches per inch.

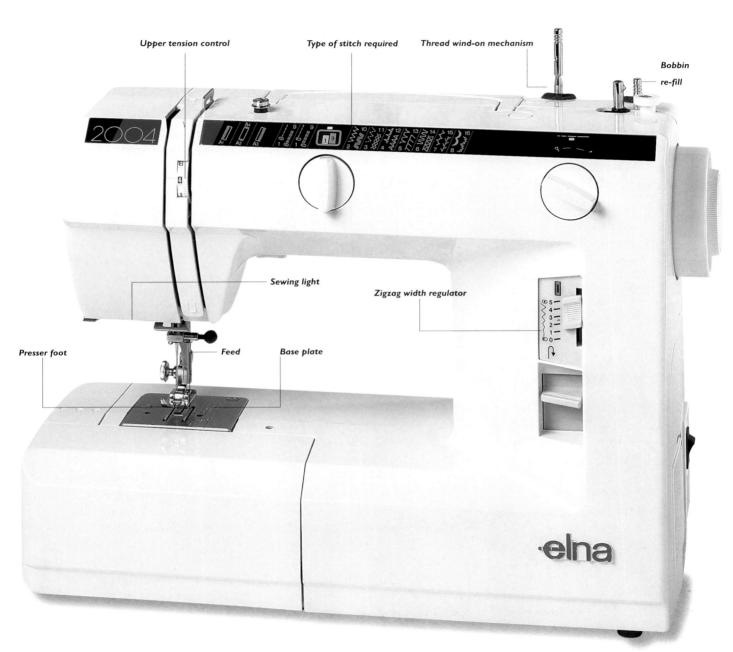

Upper tension control

Type of stitch required

Thread wind-on mechanism

Bobbin re-fill

Sewing light

Zigzag width regulator

Presser foot

Feed

Base plate

Bobbin and bobbin case The bobbin is wound with the lower thread. The bobbin is slotted anticlockwise into the bobbin case, which then slots into the machine bed below the feed. When the bobbin runs out, it can be refilled using the main thread and wound on by the machine.

After use Store the machine with a scrap of fabric under the foot to soak up any leaking oil. Using a stiff brush, regularly brush out any fluff from around the base plate and the feed dogs, and from the bobbin holder. Keep an eye on the belt which drives the machine, and replace it regularly.

The sewing machine is a vital piece of equipment for larger items of soft furnishings such as loose covers or curtains. Choose a machine that does the type of stitches you intend to use.

basic techniques

Many people have more sewing skills than they realise. Tackling a simple soft furnishings project for the home will bring these skills to light. Don't despair if you have never attempted the larger projects before – try out anything you are unsure of on scrap pieces of fabric and take everything slowly.

The same basic methods are repeated throughout this book, so read through this section carefully before embarking on any project. Try out new techniques on scrap fabric first rather than experimenting on the item itself. When following instructions, it is important to use the metric or imperial measurements but not both.

Seams
Before stitching, carefully match the seam allowances and patterns. Position pins at right angles to the seam and stitch over the pins or place them along the seam line and remove them as you stitch. Experiment and see which method you prefer; it may be a combination of both, depending on the item. If you are a nervous stitcher, or are working on an awkward area, always tack the seams together first.

Flat seam This is the simplest seam to stitch. Use a flat seam to join fabric widths for lined curtains and to join layers that will be bagged out, e.g. cushion covers.

Flat felled seam This is a neat seam that can be used on unlined curtains and other items where both sides of the fabric will be visible as the raw edges are enclosed.

French seam This seam is best suited to lightweight fabrics, see-through fabrics (where you don't want a bulky seam showing through) and ones that tend to fray easily. The raw edges are enclosed within the seam, giving a neat finish and stopping loose fibres escaping to spoil the item.

Layering seam allowances When you have many seam allowances together, it is best to layer them to reduce their bulk. Consult the box below for instructions.

Clipping corners and curves To reduce bulk at stitched corners, cut diagonally across the seam allowance at the corner.

Neatening seams To prevent fraying, neaten flat seams with a zigzag stitch or pinking shears.

Topstitching Topstitching is worked on the right side of the fabric for both functional and decorative purposes. Topstitching is applied after the item has been stitched together.

Making a flat seam

With right sides of the fabric facing, stitch the layers together along the seam line.

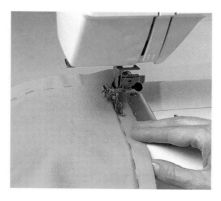

Layering a seam

To reduce the bulk of thick fabrics in flat seams or seams of many layers, e.g. piped seams, trim each seam allowance to a different amount.

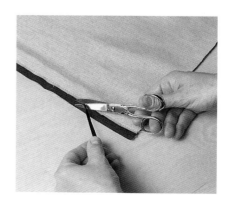

Making a flat felled seam

1 With right sides facing, stitch a flat seam, taking a 1.5cm/⅝in allowance. Press the seam allowances in the same direction then trim the lower seam allowance to 1cm/⅜in.

2 Turn under 5mm/¼in on the upper seam allowance. Stitch close to the turned-under edge.

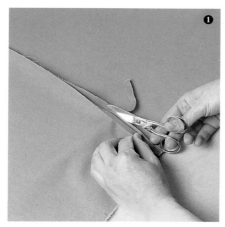
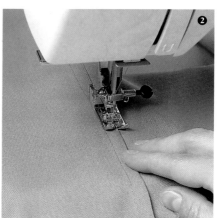

Making a French seam

1 Stitch a flat seam with wrong sides facing, taking a 7.5mm/⅜in seam allowance. Trim seam allowances to 5mm/¼in.

2 Turn fabric with right sides facing and stitch 7.5mm/⅜in from the first seam.

Clipping corners and curves

Snip into curved seam allowances. This will help the fabric lie flat on corners and more undulating shapes. Remember not to cut too close to the stitching of the seam.

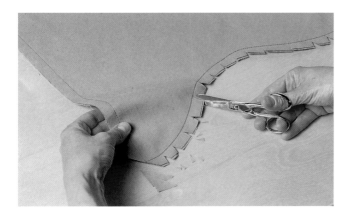

Topstitching

Stitch parallel to a seam to emphasise it and to hold the seam allowance in place. Contrasting coloured or thick machine sewing thread will accentuate the stitching.

Hand stitches

Hand stitching is an essential part of any sewing process, and soft furnishing projects are no exception. Some fabrics lend themselves to being hemmed by hand, for example, and tacking is vital.

Tacking The more you stitch, the more confident you will become and therefore less reliant on tacking before stitching. (However, it is often a good idea to do so.) Tacking is useful for tricky areas or joining many layers of fabric. Work the tacking stitches in a contrasting coloured thread so they are easy to see when you come to remove them later. Tacking thread comes in a limited range of colours but any sewing thread will do.

Slipstitch Slipstitching is used to join two folded edges or one folded edge to a flat surface, such as to close openings in seams, to secure bindings in place or to hem light to mediumweight fabric. The stitches should be almost invisible. Working from right to left, bring the needle out through one folded edge. Pick up a few threads of the adjoining fabric and then a few threads on the folded edge. Repeat along the length.

Herringbone stitch Herringbone stitch is used to hem heavyweight fabrics and to join the butted edges of wadding together. The stitches are worked from left to right with the needle pointing to the left. Bring the needle to the right side.

Finger-pressing It is not always possible to get the tip of the iron into intricate corners to press the seam. *See below for more details.*

Cord tidy Cords on curtain tapes should not be cut off once the heading has been drawn up. Make a small bag to slip the excess cord into to allow the heading to be opened out flat again for laundering or hanging at a different sized window.

Temporary tacking This is a practical way of fixing fabric to a solid frame whilst working. Even if you intend to staple the fabric with a staple gun, in many instances it is helpful to use temporary tacking first.

How to tack

Pin the layers together then work a long running stitch by hand. Set the machine to a long stitch length for tacking by machine.

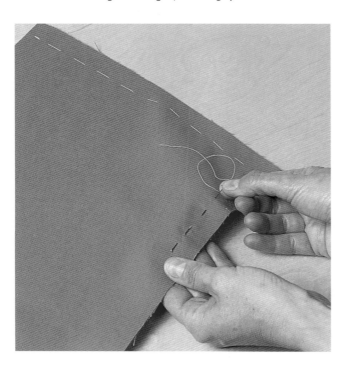

How to finger-press

If you can't reach the seam with the iron, simply moisten your finger and run it along the seam to finger-press.

Making a cord tidy

1 *Cut a rectangle of fabric such as calico 12 x 10cm/4¾ x 4in. Fold widthwise in half, with the right sides facing. Stitch the raw edges taking a 1cm/⅜in seam allowance and leaving a 3cm/1¼in gap in the short upper edge.*

2 *Clip the corners and turn right side out. Slip the cords into the bag and sew it to the top of the curtain on the underside.*

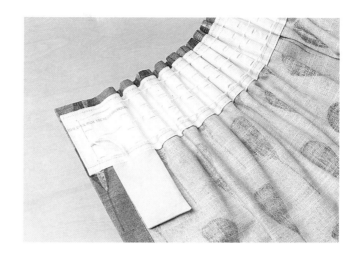

How to herringbone stitch

1 *Make a small stitch through the fabric above and 5mm–1cm/¼–⅜in to the right.*

2 *Make the next stitch below and 5mm–1cm/¼–⅜in to the right. Continue to alternate stitches and space them evenly apart.*

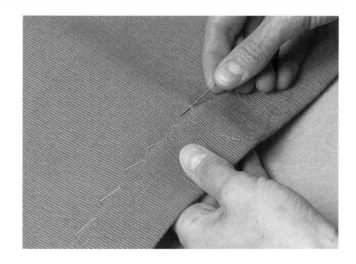

Temporary tacking

1 *Lever off old tacks with a tack lifter, which is a traditional upholstery tool, or use the blade of a screwdriver. If the head snaps off a tack, hammer the shaft into the wood to prevent it snagging the fabric.*

2 *Drive the tack halfway home with a hammer; it is then easy to remove for repositioning. A tack hammer with a magnetic tip will hold a tack in place. Hammer the tack in straight; if it starts to lie crooked, remove it and start again or knock it upright. If it does not lie straight, the head may snag the fabric and you.*

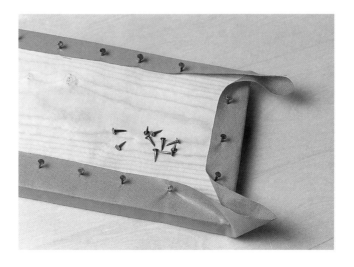

Bindings

Curved raw edges should be bound with bias-cut binding. The binding can be manipulated to follow the contours of the fabric but will still lie flat. This is because the bias grain is the stretchiest part of the fabric.

Cutting bias strips Although ready-made bias binding is inexpensive and widely available, it is very economical to make your own and it has many uses, such as binding raw edges, covering piping and making ties. When working out what the width of the strips should be, use a tape measure to measure around the front and back of the fabric edge to be bound. Generally, cut strips for bias binding are double the finished width to allow for seam allowances and stretching. The seam allowance should match that of the item when cutting strips to make piping.

Joining bias strips Once cut, bias strips can be easily joined and then sewn together securely with the machine. *See text opposite for more details.*

Making bias binding A bias binding maker is very useful for making single bias binding and you will find the whole process very satisfying. This handy gadget is available in most haberdashery departments and stores. *See text opposite for using one.*

Some fabrics are easier to handle double when applying a binding. Make sheer fabric bindings double. A bias binding maker is not needed to make a double binding. Simply press the strip lengthwise in half with the right sides facing.

Attaching double bias binding Double bias binding is useful when you are working with sheer or lightweight fabrics. *See text opposite for more details of this process.*

Cutting bias strips

1 Measure the length of the edge that is to be bound with the bias strips, adding 10cm/4in for ease and turning under the ends. Extra fabric will need to be added for joining lengths.

2 Fold the fabric diagonally, at a 45-degree angle to the selvedge. This diagonal fold is the true bias. Press along the fold then open out flat. With tailor's chalk or an air-erasable pen and ruler, draw lines the width of the binding that are parallel with the fold line. Cut out along these lines.

Attaching single bias binding

1 *Open out one folded edge of the bias binding. With right sides facing and matching the raw edges, pin the binding to the fabric. Stitch along the fold line.*

2 *Turn the binding to the underside and slipstitch the fold along the seam line.*

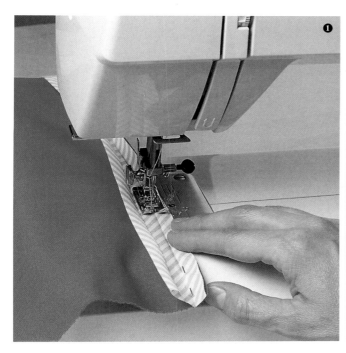

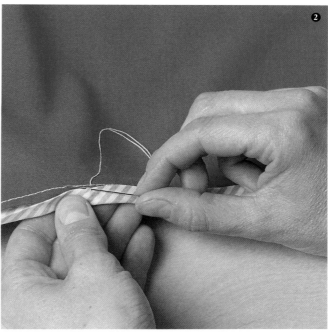

Joining bias strips

Position one end of two strips at right angles, with the right sides facing and the raw ends matched. Stitch the bias strips together, taking a 5mm/¼in seam allowance. Press the seam open then cut off the corners.

Making bias binding

Push the strip through the wide end of the binding maker with the wrong side of the fabric face up. If the fabric is thick, a pin is useful to ease it out of the narrow end. As the strip emerges through the narrow end, the edges will be turned under, press them in place.

Attaching double bias binding

Pin double bias binding on the right side of the fabric, matching the raw edges. Stitch the bias binding in place then turn the folded edge to the underside and slipstitch along the seam.

Piping

Piping gives a nicely finished look to
many handsewn items, from the edges
of cushions to lampshades and throws.
You can buy quite a wide range
of different kinds of piping in
haberdashery stores but it is very
easy to make your own. Then you can
be sure that you will get your piping
either to match or contrast with the
fabric of your finished item.

Making piping Although piping is
available readymade by the metre/yard,
the colour range is limited. Make your
own piping by covering piping cord,
which comes in various thicknesses.
Wash it first to preshrink.

**Applying piping and turning
corners** Piping should be tacked into
place and then machine stitched.
Turning corners can be daunting, but it
is just a question of taking it slowly.
(*See text opposite for more details.*)

Joining the piping ends Piping
cord can be slightly frustrating because
it can fray amazingly easily. Joining it
smoothly is easier than you think, and
always leaves a very pleasing (and
hopefully invisible!) result. (*See text
opposite for more details.*)

Stitching piping Lay the second
piece of fabric on top of the tacked
piped fabric with right sides facing.
Tack through all the layers. With a
zipper or piping foot on the sewing
machine, stitch the piping in position.

Attaching cord If cord is to be sewn
along a seam, leave a 3cm/1¼in gap in
the seam in an unobtrusive place, such
as the lower edge of a cushion, or
carefully cut a gap in a stitched seam.

Making piping

1 Measure the circumference of the cord and add a 3cm/1¼in seam allowance – this is the
width of the bias strip needed to cover the cord. Cut a bias strip of fabric in this width and
to the length needed. Join the bias strips if necessary. When measuring an item to calculate how
much piping is needed, add 10cm/4in for ease and joining ends.

2 Lay the cord along the centre of the strip on the wrong side. Fold the strip lengthwise in
half, enclosing the cord. Pin the raw edges together. Set the sewing machine to a long length
stitch for machine tacking. Using a zipper or piping foot, stitch close to the piping.

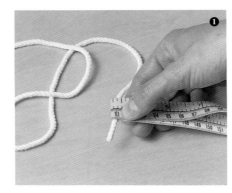

Joining the piping ends

1 To join the ends of the piping neatly, allow a 2.5cm/1in overlap and pin the piping in place
to 5cm/2in each side of the overlap. Unpick the piping tacking for 5cm/2in each side of the
overlap to reveal the cord. Cut off half the strands at each end of the cord to thin it.

2 Twist the ends of the cord together and bind with thread. Wrap one end of the piping fabric
around the cord again. Turn under 5mm/¼in on the other end and wrap it around the cord.
Tack the cord in place ready for stitching.

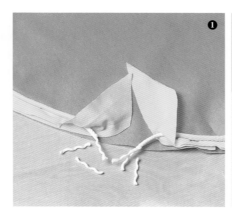
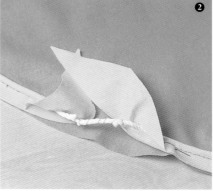

Applying piping and turning corners

Pin the piping to the right side of the fabric. Snip the seam allowance of the piping at curves and corners. Tack in place by hand or machine using a zipper or piping foot.

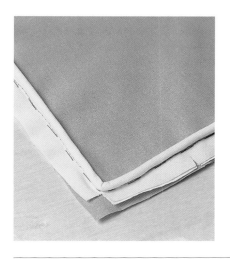

Mounting fabric

There are many beautiful sheer fabrics available today and it may often seem that their application is rather limited because they are quite delicate and slippery. Sheer or unstable fabrics can be mounted onto denser fabrics, however, to give them some stability then the two fabrics can be treated as one. This technique is not suitable for large areas of fabric or areas prone to lots of wear but it is ideal for smaller cushion covers and table runners. Consider the colour of the underlying fabric carefully as it will be visible and will be affected by the colour or loose weave of the fabric on top.

Bonding web Bonding web is a fusible webbing used to apply fabric to fabric. It is ideal for appliqué work. It is simply ironed on.

How to mount fabric

Pin the sheer fabric to a background fabric, starting at the centre and smoothing the layers outwards. Tack the fabrics together along the outer edges.

Attaching cord

Unravel one end of the cord so it is not so bulky and poke it into the hole. Lay the cord along the seam and catch it in place with small stitches. Unravel the other end and poke it into the hole, sewing the gap closed securely.

Applying bonding web

1 *Draw your design on the paper backing side of the bonding web. Be aware that a mirror image of the design should be drawn. Roughly cut out the shape and iron it onto the wrong side of the fabric.*

2 *Cut out the design. Peel off the backing paper and position it right side up on the background fabric. Iron the motif to fuse it in place.*

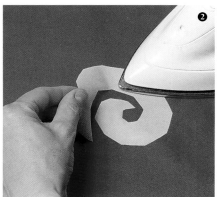

window treatments

Dressing windows is practical as well as decorative. Curtains and blinds offer privacy, cut out unwanted light, reduce outside noise and conserve heat. As they are the source of natural light in a room, windows are often a focal point and deserve a treatment that will display them at their best, whether that is to highlight their elegant shape, emphasise a glorious view or to hide an unattractive window or outlook.

This chapter outlines a variety of superb styles to set off your windows, ranging from using modern styles, such as tab-top curtains, to traditional swag and tails. All the important stages are covered, from choosing a style and measuring windows to creating beautiful drapes and blinds.

Remember that curtains and blinds are not just for windows; many of the innovative ideas shown here can be used to make bed curtains and drapes for doorways and screens.

calculating measurements

Before taking the plunge into making curtains, loose covers and bed-linen, it is vital that you take all the measurements you need. This is a part of the process that must not be rushed – you don't want to spend hours working on a pair of curtains then find that they are too short when you hang them at your window, for example.

Ideally, have the curtain or blind fittings in place before measuring for fabric. If this is not possible, lightly mark their intended position on the wall or window frame. Slip a few hooks or rings onto the track or pole. To make a window seem larger and to let in more light, extend curtain tracks or poles beyond the frame so that curtains can be pulled right back to the edges of the frame.

Measuring the length

For gathered headings on a track and for curtains with casings, measure the length from the top of the track or pole. For tab-top curtains or curtains hanging from rings, measure from the bottom of the tab or ring. For case-headed curtains, measure from below the pole. For blinds, measure from the top of the batten.

Consider what is in front of the window when deciding upon the length of a curtain or blind. If there is furniture in front, a sill-length curtain may be the best option so that the curtain is easy to draw and does not interfere with the furniture. If there is a radiator in front of the window, below-sill-length curtains that finish just above the top of the radiator will allow heat from the radiator to warm the room well when the curtains are closed.

Floor-length curtains can finish just above the floor surface or flow onto the floor for a more elaborate effect; soft fabrics work best for this type of window dressing – if the fabric is thick, it will just pile up unattractively on the floor and look as if the curtains have been made to the wrong length!

Add an allowance for the heading and lower hem to the length. For a standard heading and pencil pleats, add 3.8cm/1½in to the upper edge. For curtains with a casing, use a cloth tape measure to measure the circumference of the pole, adding 1cm/⅜in for ease plus 2cm/¾in seam allowance; extra will be needed for a frill at the top, so allow twice the height of the frill. Add a 1.5cm/⅝in seam allowance to the top of tab-top or tie curtains. The depth of the hem will vary according to the fabric, but generally add 15cm/6in for unlined curtains and 10cm/4in for lined curtains. See individual blind instructions for hems and allowances.

Measuring the width

Measure the width of the track or pole with a steel tape or long wooden ruler. For overlapping curtain tracks in two halves, add the length of the overlap.

Multiply this measurement by 1½–3 for a gathered heading, by 2–2½ for a pencil-pleated heading, and by 2 for triple and cylindrical-pleated headings. Add a 2.5cm/1in hem at each side for unlined curtains, and a 3.8cm/1½in hem to each side for lined curtains.

Fabric widths

Unless a window is extremely narrow, widths of fabric must be joined to make curtains. Divide the total width measurement by the width of your chosen fabric for the number of fabric widths required. Round up the fabric widths to the largest amount, as 3.2cm/1¼in seam allowances are also needed for each join. (See page 37 for pattern repeats and joining widths.) If you have an uneven number of fabric widths and there will be a pair of curtains at the window, cut one width lengthwise in half and place it at the outer edge of the curtains.

Lining

The same amount of lining is needed as for the curtain fabric, but do not allow extra for matching patterns.

The length of a curtain will depend on what lies in front of the window. Floor-length curtains are ideal for windows without furniture in front or radiators below. Sheer-fabric curtains that flow onto the floor give an elaborate effect.

curtain fabrics and poles

Curtains are a big investment if you decide to buy them readymade, and the situation is the same even if you make them yourself. Assess your windows carefully and make sure that you select the right kind of fabric for them. Bear in mind the fact that sunlight fades textiles and that curtains need washing or dry-cleaning too.

Choosing fabrics

When choosing fabrics for windows, bear in mind how the fabric hangs and drapes, whether its colour is likely to fade in sunlight, and if it is washable or will need to be dry-cleaned. Buy linings with the same washing instructions as the curtain fabric, and remember to buy extra fabric if it is likely to shrink.

Consider how much privacy is needed. A bathroom with a clear glass window will need a sheer fabric to let in daylight but maintain privacy, and something denser for when the light is on in the evening, whereas other rooms may just need a curtain or blind that can be drawn at night. A heavyweight lined curtain is advisable in a bedroom that gets the early morning sun.

The window treatment must fit in with the other furnishings and decor in the room. Patterned wall coverings, flooring and upholstery need a plain area to rest the eye. Alternatively, if the walls and other furnishings are plain, boldly patterned curtains or blinds can add interest to the room.

A kitchen window above a sink is prone to splashes of water or steam, so choose a hard-wearing fabric. A blind is often a better option than a curtain in this situation because it can fit smoothly against the window and be rolled up when not needed. Fabrics that are specially treated to inhibit the growth of mildew and mould are ideal for well-insulated kitchens and bathrooms that have a lot of steam.

Drapes and swags require soft, pliable fabrics, whereas formal curtains and blinds need a heavier weight of fabric to hang vertically. Stiff fabrics hold a pleat well and are a good choice for Roman blinds.

Firm fabrics with a close weave are excellent for roller blinds. Spray-on fabric stiffener can be applied to many fabrics to make them suitable for making such blinds; ready-stiffened fabrics are also available.

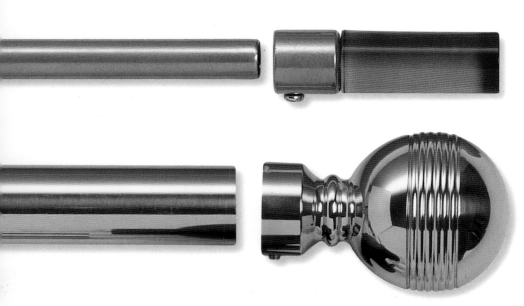

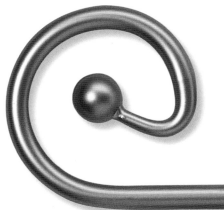

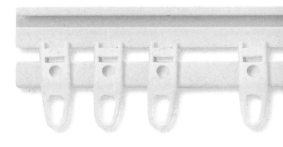

metal poles are adjustable or can be extended, while others can be bent to fit the shape of a bay window.

Lightweight curtains, such as those made from sheer fabrics and café curtains, can be threaded onto metal or plastic rods which are usually expandable and do not need fixings but can be extended to fit within a window recess. Sheer fabrics can be hung from a length of sprung plastic-covered wire that has screw eyes screwed into the ends; these are hooked onto screw hooks fixed within a recess.

Finials

Finials are the decorative ends that slot onto or into the end of curtain poles. Most have a small screw that is tightened to secure it to the pole. There is a large range available nowadays, made from metal, wood, plastic, pottery, glass and Perspex. You can also model your own finials from clay or papier-mâché and paint them to match your decor.

Curtain poles and finials (decorative ends) are always visible so they play a significant part in the decorative scheme of a room. If you want something more discreet, choose a curtain track.

Tracks and poles

In general, a curtain track is discreet and hidden from view when the curtains are closed, and a curtain pole is always visible and therefore part of the decorative scheme in a room.

Tracks

Curtain tracks can be fixed on brackets to the wall, window frame or ceiling. Most are made of plastic, but more expensive metal tracks are available to hang large,

heavy curtains that need extra support. Tracks can have a pelmet or valance in front to hide them. Some tracks are bendable to fit within a bay window. Tracks are also available in two halves so that a pair of curtains can be overlapped. Corded tracks allow the curtains to be opened and closed by pulling a cord.

Poles and rods

Curtain poles are available in different thicknesses of wood and metal. Many

curtain headings

If you thought that curtain tape was the only way to head a curtain, then think again! There are many different finishes that can be applied to the tops of curtains, and many of these can be decorative in their own right. Assess the type of decorating scheme that you have and design your headings accordingly.

Most gathered headings are created with curtain tape, which is available by the metre/yard and has 1–3 rows of fine cord running along its length. The tape is sewn to the back of the curtain and the cords are drawn up to the required width to gather or pleat the curtain. There are 1–3 rows of slots on the tape to insert hooks through. Having a choice of rows of slots allows you to hang the curtains at the level that is right for you and to conceal the hooks. Tapes are available in different widths and weights; lightweight mesh tapes are for use on sheer curtains. Curtains can also be attached with casings, tabs, ties and eyelets.

Standard heading
This tape produces a simple, gathered heading which works well on small curtains, lined or unlined, in any weight of fabric.

Pencil pleats
Here, a row of neat, upright pleats is created. This heading can be used on light to mediumweight fabrics, either unlined or lined.

Triple pleats
Cordless tape or buckram is first sewn to the top of the curtains, then the triple pleats are made by dividing one large pleat into three smaller ones and handsewing them in place. Use medium to heavyweight fabric for these so they keep their shape.

Goblet or French pleats
Cordless tape or buckram is applied to the top of the curtains, then deep pleats are stitched at regular intervals. The pleats are padded out with a roll of stiff interfacing. This style is best suited to medium to heavyweight fabric.

Casing
This treatment works best on fine fabrics. A fine rod or wire is inserted through a channel stitched in the curtain.

Hooks and runners
Hooks are made from plastic or metal. Use metal hooks on heavyweight curtains and on handsewn headings. Plastic hooks are slotted through the curtain tape and then onto runners that slot onto the track. Hooks are usually placed at 7.5cm/3in intervals. Some hooks are combined with runners as a single unit. Runners are usually supplied with a track. The runners at the outer ends of the track are known as end-stops because they literally stop the curtain falling off the track.

If the curtain heading is to cover the track, position the hooks in the lower row of slots; if the curtain is to hang below a pole, place the hooks in a row of slots close to the top of the tape but not so that they show above the curtain. Apply hooks to uncorded tape by slipping them behind each pleat and handsewing them securely with a strong button thread.

Rings

Wooden, plastic or metal curtain rings slot onto curtain poles; make sure the ring is large enough to slide comfortable along the pole. Remove the screw eye from the bottom of the rings and handsew the rings securely to the top of the curtains, or attach them to the curtain by inserting the curtain hook through the heading tape and onto the screw eye. Alternatively, clip a curtain clip onto the curtain then fix it to the screw eye.

Dressing curtains

To help your curtains to drape attractively, it is advisable to 'dress' them for a few days, which will help to set the pleats or gathers. Hang the curtains and arrange the folds to look their best. Pin the folds in place at the bottom, then loosely tie soft tapes or ribbon around them, holding the tapes in place with pins. Remove the tapes and pins after a few days.

Many different finishes can be applied to the tops of curtains, from simple, gathered headings to more elaborate goblet pleats. Certain styles are suited to particular fabric weights.

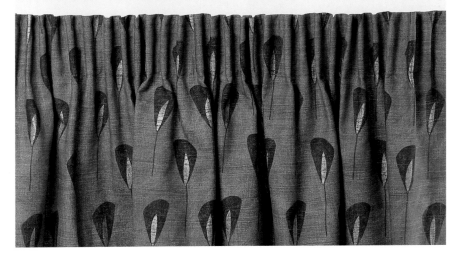

making curtains

Curtains can be daunting to make – especially if you have never made them before. Start with a simple pair of unlined curtains and work your way up to lined curtains as you get more confident. Make sure you have done all your measuring accurately and are using the correct type of fabric for your chosen curtain.

Unlined curtains

Unlined curtains are quick and easy to make, but do not hang as well as lined curtains. They are not usually light-fast, so may not be suitable for a bedroom or bathroom. (See page 50 to calculate fabric quantities.) If you want the fabric to stand above the tape, add double the height of the stand to the length measurements. You will also need standard or pencil-pleat tape the entire width of the curtain.

Loose-lined curtains

A detachable lining is very versatile, as it can be removed from the main curtain for laundering. This is useful if the curtain and lining have differing washing instructions. Even if they have the same washing procedure, if a curtain is very bulky it may not fit into a domestic washing machine with the lining, and a detachable lining can be washed separately to lighten the load.

Making a detachable lining

Less fabric is needed for a detachable lining than for the curtain. Make up the curtain following the instructions for an unlined curtain on the opposite page. Cut the lining in the same way as the unlined curtain, using 1½ times the length of the track. Detachable lining tape has two 'skirts', which are applied to either side of the lining. If you are making a pair of curtains, the knotted ends of the cord should be on the meeting edges of the curtains.

1 Cut out the lining and join the widths with flat felled seams if necessary. Turn 1cm/⅜in of the fabric under, then 1.5cm/⅝in on the long side edges. Machine stitch close to the inner folds. Cut a length of lining tape the width of the lining plus 10cm/4in. Unthread the cords at one end and knot them together.

2 Cut the tape 1cm/⅜in from the knotted end. Part the skirts and slip the top of the lining between them, with the corded side on the right side of the lining and with the knotted end of the tape extending 1cm/⅜in beyond the curtain. Pin the layers together.

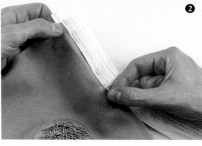

3 Unthread the cords at the other end of the tape level with the edge of the lining. Cut the tape 1cm/⅜in beyond the lining, but leave the ends of the cord free. Turn the tape ends to the back of the lining in a double hem and pin in place.

4 *Stitch close to the ends and lower edge of the tape, enclosing the lining.*

5 *Pull up the cords so the lining is the same width as the curtain heading. Roll up the tape and sew to the top of the curtain. Insert the hooks 7.5cm/3in apart through the lining tape. With the wrong sides facing, slip the hooks through the curtain tape so that both hang from the same hooks. Machine stitch a double hem so the lining is 1.5cm/⅝in shorter than the curtain.*

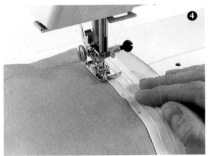

Making unlined curtains

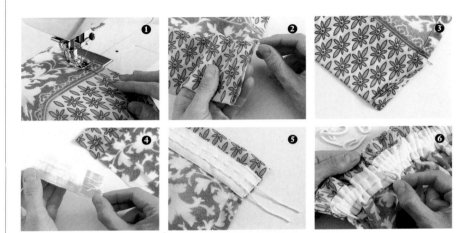

1 *Cut out the curtain and join the widths with flat felled seams if necessary. Turn 1cm/⅜in under then 1.5cm/⅝in on the long side edges. Slipstitch or machine stitch in place close to the inner folds.*

2 *Press 7.5cm/3in twice to the underside on the lower edge to form a double hem. Mark the corner and the point where the lower hem meets the inner edge of the side hem with a pin.*

3 *Unfold the hem once at the corner. Fold the corner at an angle between the pins. Refold the hem. Slipstitch the hem and mitres in place.*

4 *Press 3.8cm/1½in to the underside at the upper edge, or, if you want the curtain to stand above the tape, turn the fabric down that amount plus 3.8cm/1½in. Knot the cord ends together at one end of the tape. Turn under the knotted ends.*

5 *Pin the tape 2.5cm/1in below the top of the curtain, covering the turned-under edge, or, if the curtain is to stand above the tape, turn the fabric down that amount plus*

2.5cm/1in. *Stitch close to the long edges and ends of the tape, taking care not to catch in the cords. Stitch both long edges in the same direction so you do not drag the fabric in opposite directions.*

6 *Pull up the cords to gather the fabric to the required width. Knot the free ends of the cord. Adjust the gathers evenly. Slip the hooks through the slots in the tape, placing one at each end then at 7.5cm/3in intervals. Roll up the excess tape and sew to the top of the curtain or slip the cord into a cord tidy (see page 43).*

making curtains

Lined curtains

Lining curtains gives protection from dust and sunlight, and cuts down on heat loss and noise. A locked-in lining gives a very professional finish and helps the curtain to hang well.

Interlined curtains

Interlining within a curtain gives body and provides insulation. With this in mind, you could line the curtain in a warmer fabric, such as brightly coloured brushed cotton. This would

be particularly effective if the main curtain was made in a figured chenille fabric or a cosy fleece. Don't use a lining fabric that is too bulky, however: you do want the curtains to fall nicely when they are hanging at the windows.

Making lined curtains

1 Measure and cut out the fabric (see page 50). Include 3.8cm/1½in top and side hems and a 10cm/4in lower hem. Cut the lining the same size, omitting the lower hem allowance. Join the curtain and lining widths with flat seams. Press 3.8cm/1½in to the wrong side on the side edges. Secure in place with herringbone stitch (see page 42–3), finishing 15cm/6in above the lower edge.

2 Turn up a 2cm/¾in hem then a 8cm/3¼in deep hem on the lower edge. Make a mitred corner (see page 57), slipstitch the mitre and hem the lower edge with herringbone stitch. Turn up 1.5cm/⅝in then 3.5cm/1⅜in on the lower edge of the lining. Machine stitch the lining in place.

3 Lie the curtain out flat, wrong side uppermost, on a large table or the floor. Place the lining on top with wrong sides facing and the lower edge 5cm/2in above the lower edge of the curtain.

4 On a single-width curtain, turn back one third of the lining, aligning the fabric grains and the top edges. To join the layers together, use a double length of thread to pick up two threads of the lining fabric, then the

same of the curtain fabric. Leave a gap of about 10cm/4in and repeat, catching the fabric together along its length. Keep the thread loose so it does not pull at the fabric. Fold the lining out flat again and smooth over its surface, then repeat on the opposite edge of the curtain. This is known as locking in. On curtains using more than one width of fabric, start at the seam nearest the centre, locking the seams together, then work outwards from the seam, joining the layers at approximately 40cm/1ft 4in intervals across the curtain. When locking seams

together, stitch through the seam allowance and not the surface of the curtain or the lining.

5 Trim the side edges of the lining level with the curtain, then turn 3.2cm/1¼in under. Pin then slipstitch in place, turn the corner at the lower edge and slipstitch for 3.8cm/1½in, leaving the remainder of the hem free. Check the length and press down the upper edge and attach the heading tape (see steps 5–6 on page 57).

Making interlined curtains

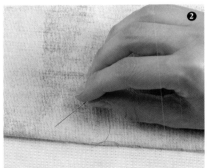

1 To join widths of interlining, overlap the edges by 1.2cm/½in and stitch through the layers with a zigzag stitch. If you do not have this facility on your sewing machine, butt the edges together and join them with a herringbone stitch. Take care not to stretch the interlining when joining it. Cut the interlining the same size as the curtain.

2 Join the interlining, curtain and lining widths, using flat seams for the curtain and lining. Lie the interlining out flat on a large table or the floor. Lie the curtain smoothly on top, right side uppermost. Fold back the curtain and join the layers together with a locking stitch in the same way as locking in the lining. Work two rows of locking on each width of fabric and along the seams.

3 Gently turn the curtain over so the interlining is facing upwards. Turn a 3.8cm/1½in hem under along the side edges, and herringbone stitch in place. Turn up a 10cm/4in single hem, mitre the corners and herringbone stitch in place.

4 Lie the lining right side uppermost on top, matching the lower edges. Lock the lining to the interlining. Trim the side edges level with the curtain. Turn 3.2cm/1¼in under on the side and lower edge, and slipstitch to the curtain. Check the length, turn down the upper edge and attach the heading to the curtain.

making curtains

Case-headed curtains
Lightweight curtains look very good with cased headings threaded onto rods or sprung wire. Cut out the curtain (see page 50). For a 2.5cm/1in frill to stand above the rod or wire, add double the height of the frill to the length measurements, e.g. 5cm/2in. For the width, allow 1½–3 times the width of

the pole, depending on how much fullness you require.

Double-layer curtain
A pretty valance can easily be incorporated into a simple case-headed curtain. To the length of the curtain, add an allowance for the hem, the circumference of the rod plus

6mm/¼in, and the depth of the valance plus 1.5cm/⅝in.

Flat-headed curtains
Flat-headed curtains are an economical use of fabric as they are generally no more than 1½ times the width of the window. They can be fixed in place with ties, tabs, rings or eyelets.

Making case-headed curtains

1 Join the fabric widths, using a French seam on sheer fabrics. Hem the sides and lower edge with double hems, either with a machine stitch or slipstitch.

2 Press 1cm/⅜in under at the upper edge. Next, press 2.5cm/1in under plus half the rod circumference plus 6mm/¼in for ease. Stitch 6mm/¼in above the lower pressed edge, then 2.5cm/1in below the upper pressed edge to form a channel to thread the rod through. Insert the rod through the channel and adjust the gathers.

Making scalloped café curtains

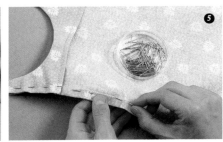

Fix the rod in position. Measure the drop of the curtain from the bottom of the rod to sill length. Add a 10cm/4in hem and a 1.5cm/⅝in seam allowance. Measure the width of the rod. You will need 1½ times the width plus 1.5cm/⅝in for each side hem.

1 *Cut out an 8.5cm/3⅜in wide strip of paper, which is half the curtain width less 1.5cm/⅝in. Label one end as the centre fold. Use a pair of compasses to describe a 10cm/4in diameter semicircle on paper and cut it out as a template for the scallops. Fold the scallop in half and draw around it on the centre fold end of the strip, matching the corners.*

2 *Open out the scallop. Move the scallop 2cm/¾in along the template strip and*

lightly mark its position. Continue along the template to about 2cm/¾in from the other end. If the end scallop does not fit well, adjust the size of the gaps between the scallops. Cut out the template.

3 *Cut out the curtain and a 10cm/4in wide strip of fabric for the facing that is the width of the curtain. Join the curtain widths with a flat felled seam if necessary. Stitch a 5mm/¼in deep hem on the long lower edge of the facing. Pin the facing to the upper edge of the curtain, right sides facing and matching the raw edges.*

4 *Pin the template on one half of the facing 1.5cm/⅝in from the upper and side raw edges. Draw around the template with tailor's chalk. Flip the template to continue on the other half. Stitch along the*

drawn lines. Trim the scallops, leaving a 5mm/¼in seam allowance. Snip the curves and clip the corners. Turn right side out and press.

5 *Press under 5mm/¼in then 1cm/⅜in on the side edges. Slipstitch in place. Turn a double hem on the lower edge and stitch.*

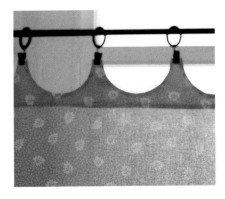

Making double-layer curtains

Make a double hem on the lower edge. Make 1.5cm/⅝in double hem on the upper edge on the right side of the fabric. Fold the upper edge to the right side for the depth of the valance plus half the rod circumference measurement plus 6mm/¼in. On one edge, mark a point with a pin half the rod circumference measurement plus 6mm/¼in below the pressed edge. Stitch across the

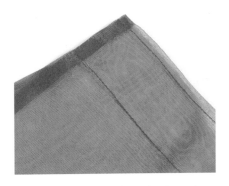

curtain at this point to form the channel. Insert the rod.

shower curtains

There is a large range of shower curtains available on the market, but they are expensive for what they are and the colours and designs aren't always exactly what you want. There really is nothing simpler than making a shower curtain yourself, and you can choose an outer fabric curtain that matches your room scheme.

Apart from preventing water escaping when showering, a shower curtain can bring a welcome touch of colour to a plain bathroom. And there is nothing nicer than being able to pick out the fabric that matches your colour scheme and taste. Shower curtain rails are expandable with a suction pad at each end, so do not need to be screwed into tiled walls. Chunky plastic rings that clip onto eyelets in the top of the curtain are then threaded onto the rail. (These are readily available at many DIY outlets and other home stores.) Eyelets are also available in a kit with a fixing; choose large eyelets that are at least 1.2cm/½in in diameter. If the choice of curtaining for showers seems limited, remember that an outer curtain, that does not need to be waterproof, can be added instead.

Choosing fabric

Obviously, a shower curtain must be waterproof. Department and furnishing fabric shops stock 100 per cent nylon, 100 per cent PVC and 100 per cent vinyl in many colours and designs. In general, waterproof fabrics are available in widths of 1.3m/51in. This is too narrow for most showers, so the fabric widths will need to be joined. Position the join at the centre of the curtain,

and join the widths with a French seam. Kite shops and chandleries stock rip-stop nylon, which is a lightweight material that comes in bright colours and large widths.

Pull a wet shower curtain flat to allow it to dry, otherwise mildew will form in the creases. Waterproof fabrics are not machine washable; to clean them, wipe down with a soft cloth and non-abrasive cleaner.

Measuring up

Standard shower curtains are 1.8m/70in square, but it is important to measure your own site as circumstances vary greatly. The curtain must be long enough to tuck inside the bath or shower tray. Fix the shower rail in position. Measure the drop from the rail to at least 20cm/8in inside the bath or just above the floor of the shower tray. Measure the length of the fixed rail; the curtain can be made to the rail measurement or 25 per cent wider – do not make the curtain any wider than that, as this will gather the curtain, trapping moisture that cannot dry out.

Shower curtains are simple to make and can be chosen to match a bathroom scheme. Make sure the curtain is long enough to tuck inside the bath or just above the floor of a shower tray.

Making a basic shower curtain

Hold layers of waterproof fabric together with paper clips or masking tape, as dressmaking pins will leave permanent holes. Use a wedge-pointed needle in the sewing machine.

1 *Cut out the shower curtain, adding 6cm/2½in to the width and 12.5cm/5in to the length for hems. Fold a 1.5cm/⅝in double hem on each side edge, and stitch close to the inner edges. Fold a 3cm/1¼in double hem on the top edge. Stitch close to the inner edges.*

2 *On the wrong side, use a chinagraph pencil to mark the position of the eyelets along the centre of the hem on the upper edge about 15cm/6in apart, starting and finishing 2cm/¾in in from the side edges. Fix the eyelets at the marks. Fold a double hem on the lower edge and stitch close to the inner fold. When hanging the curtain, the right side faces outwards.*

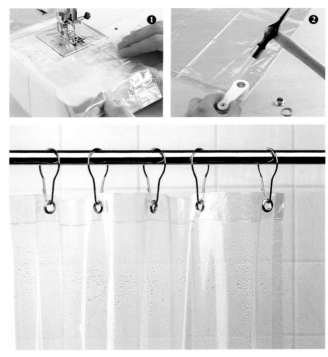

Making a lined shower curtain

There are two methods of making a lined shower curtain. The simplest way is to follow the basic method above to make one shower curtain from waterproof fabric and one from your chosen outer fabric. Hang both curtains from the same rings, with the waterproof curtain facing into the shower and the outer curtain facing into the room.

For a more lavish style, make the basic waterproof curtain then make an unlined curtain (see page 56) using synthetic curtain tape. Pull up the tape to fit the rail and fasten the ends securely. Slip a plastic curtain ring onto each shower rail ring. Fix the curtain tape to the rings with plastic curtain hooks.

When using the shower, have the outer curtain outside the bath or shower.

recycled curtains

Good-quality curtains last for many years, and it is a shame to discard them because your windows are a different shape when you move house. Curtains can be adapted in many stylish ways, however – if they are too short they can be lengthened with an attractive border in a contrasting colour, and hemmed if they are too long.

Curtains do not suffer a lot of wear and tear, so they last for many years. You may bring curtains with you to a new home, and although they do not always fit your new windows, there are quite a few ways of adjusting them. Good-quality second-hand curtains can be found at auctions and car boot fairs.

It is simple to cut down curtains that are too large. To extend curtains, let down a deep hem to add length, and make a false hem with seam tape if you are left with a very narrow hem allowance. Adding tabs at the top of the curtain or hanging them on rings will also gain you extra length.

It is not only conventional curtains and blinds that can be used at windows. Hang a colourful tablecloth or lightweight ethnic bedcover or throw. Add tabs at the top for hanging, or fix to clips to hang from curtain rings.

Adding borders can be an excellent way of recycling curtains to fit bigger windows. They can also create an attractive design, as shown by these decorative floral borders.

Curtains with borders
A border gives a smart finishing touch to curtains and is an excellent way of recycling curtains to fit bigger windows. A border can be added to all four edges or just one edge. Bagging the curtain out with lining is quick to do, although it is only suitable for small curtains that use no more than one width of fabric, for example. For best results, use fabrics of similar weight.

Drapes and swags
Beautiful fabrics do not have to be cut and sewn to create stunning window dressings. It is often the simplest treatments that work best. A swathe of fine fabric draped around a curtain pole looks very dramatic and can be used alone or with curtains or blinds.

Swedish swags
Create a soft yet flamboyant effect around your windows with Swedish swags. Hardly any sewing is necessary to achieve a stunning result using only a single length of fabric. Use a lightweight or sheer fabric: a colourful sari would be ideal.

Making a curtain with borders on all edges

1 Unpick the curtain heading and hems. Launder and press flat. Decide upon the border width and add 3cm/1¼in. Cut a strip of fabric this width for each edge of the curtain, that is, the length of the cut curtain edge plus twice the finished border width. Press under each end of the borders at right angles to create mitres. The pressed line will be the seam line. Open the seams out flat.

2 Starting 1.5cm/⅝in from the inner edges, stitch along the seam lines with the right sides facing. Trim the seam allowance to 1.5cm/⅝in. Press seams open.

3 With right sides facing, stitch the inner edges of the border to the curtain, pivoting the seam at the mitred border seams. Press the seam open.

4 Cut a piece of lining the same size as the bordered curtain. Lay the curtain flat, right side up. Lay the lining on top with right sides facing and pin together, smoothing the layers outwards from the centre. Stitch the outer edges, taking a 1.5cm/⅝in seam allowance and leaving a gap in the upper edge to turn through. Clip the corners and turn right side out. Press and slipstitch the opening closed. Add a heading to the top edge.

Making a Swedish swag

1 Fix a large cup hook into the wall at each side of the window, approximately 7.5cm/3in beyond the corners of the window. Lay the length of fabric across the hooks, allowing it to dip in the centre. Cut the tails shorter if you wish, but allow 25.5cm/10in at each side for the rosette. If the fabric is too bulky to drape nicely, cut it narrower.

2 Press 1cm/⅜in under twice on all edges to make a double hem. Stitch in place. If using a sari, hem only the ends of the fabric. Starting at each end, measure the chosen length of the tail plus 12.5cm/5in. Mark with a pin at the centre of the strip.

3 Pick up the fabric at the pin mark and bunch it into a point with your other hand. Slip an elastic band over the bunched fabric. Repeat at the other end.

4 Insert the hooks into the bunched rosettes, with the tails hanging at each side. Adjust the swag and the tails so they drape in regular folds.

attic curtains

Attic curtains can make a room feel cosy and intimate. Many attic windows are the slanting skylight kind, so it is important to adjust your curtain style to match this. Panels, blinds and shutters can all be used for this purpose, and these types of blinds and window panels can be made in a whole variety of different materials.

Angled windows, such as those in attic rooms, need careful planning. These windows are often smaller than usual, but can be emphasised by painting the frames a stronger colour than the walls. A simple but effective treatment for angled windows is to have a pair of curtains with casings at the top and bottom with rods slipped through, fixed above and below the window.

Dormer windows are recessed windows within a sloping roof. The recess can make the windows appear further away from the room than they actually are, so an attractive curtain will accentuate them and make them into a real feature. It is usually best to attach the fittings to the window frame itself. A hinged curtain rod will minimise loss of light, and can be closed across the window at night and opened against the recess during the day. Alternatively, use a track that bends around the recess and windows; the curtains will be in front of the recess when open, thus not obscuring the window.

Skylights are set into roofs. They do not usually need a covering for privacy, but to block out light in the mornings and to create a cosy atmosphere at night. A sheer curtain with a casing at the top and bottom, as suggested for an angled window, is one solution.

Window panels

A flat-hung window panel is a good idea for a window or skylight that needs a streamlined style. The panel has eyelets that fix onto hooks at each corner. If the window is particularly wide, you will need to place more hooks and eyelets along the upper edge so the panel does not dip in the centre. If lined in a contrasting fabric, the panel will look good half-open, with the lower eyelets hooked onto the top hooks or held open diagonally onto a hook on a side edge of the frame. Alternatively,

the eyelets can slot onto dowels that are inserted into drilled holes.

Choose a firm, closely woven fabric for best results. Organza is really the only suitable sheer fabric to use, and is very effective at filtering sunlight. If you do choose to use a lightweight fabric such as organza, test the eyelets first on a scrap of fabric to make sure they are not too heavy for the fabric and do not tear out. A strip of lightweight interfacing applied to the top and bottom of the outer fabric will add strength and support the eyelets.

Making a window panel

Fix a cup or dresser hook at each corner of the window, either on the frame or beyond its edges, and in a position that will allow the panel to lay flat. Have the upper hooks pointing upwards and the lower hooks pointing downwards. Measure the distance horizontally and vertically between the hooks, then add 8cm/3¼in to the horizontal and vertical measurement to allow for the eyelets and seam allowances.

1 *Cut two panels, either from the same fabric or from two co-ordinating fabrics. Stitch together with right sides facing, taking 1.5cm/⅝in seam allowance and leaving a*

gap to turn through. Clip the corners, then turn right side out.

2 *Press the panel and slipstitch the opening closed. If you wish, apply a decorative border such as ribbon or braid*

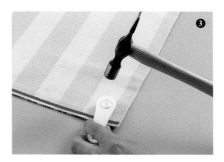

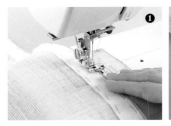

Sheer loose window panel

Instead of sheer curtains for privacy, consider a sheer loose panel for a contemporary feel. The upper edge of the panel is fixed directly to the frame, or to a batten screwed to the frame, with touch-and-close tape so it can be removed easily for laundering.

1 *Cut a single panel the window width plus 3cm/1¼in by the window length plus 6cm/2½in. Stitch a 1.5cm/⅝in hem on the side edges. Press 1cm/⅜in under at the upper edge. Stitch a length of sew-on touch-and-close tape along the upper edge, enclosing the raw edge of the fabric.*

2 *Press 1cm/⅜in under then 4cm/1¾in on the lower edge. Stitch close to both pressed edges to make a channel. Saw a length of 1.2cm/½in diameter wood dowel 6mm/¼in shorter than the width of the panel, and paint it the same colour as the panel. When dry, slip the dowel into the channel. Handsew the ends closed. Press corresponding adhesive-backed touch-and-close tape along the top of the frame or to a fixed batten, and press the top of the panel on top.*

to the outer edges. It should be no wider than 1.2cm/½in so that it does not interfere with the eyelets.

3 *Mark the eyelet position 2cm/¾in in from each corner with an air-erasable pen. Hold the panel over the hooks and check the positions, adjusting if necessary. Following the manufacturer's instructions, fix a 1.5cm/⅝in diameter metal eyelet to the upper corners. Slip onto the hooks and check the lower positions. Fix the lower eyelets in place.*

making shutters & blinds

Stretch fabric over simple wooden frames to make a very practical pair of shutters or vary the look with a Swedish blind, which is rolled by hand from the lower edge. A Swedish blind is not suitable for windows wider than 1.8m/6ft because the dowel will sag and the blind will be difficult to roll up.

Making fabric shutters

1 Decide upon the finished size of the blind (see page 50 for measuring a window). To make a pair of shutters, cut four lengths of 2.5cm/1in 'one by one' wooden strip the height of the frame, and four lengths of the same strip half the width of the frame less 5cm/2in. Use wood glue to stick the half-width strips between the top and bottom of the uprights to form the shutter frame. Make sure the corners are at right angles.

2 Clamp the joints in place whilst the glue dries. Hammer 3.8cm/1½in panel pins through the joints to secure. Fix a pair of 5cm/2in flush hinges to the shutter along the outer side edges.

3 For each cover, cut a piece of fabric the width of the shutter frame plus 3cm/1¼in by twice the height of the shutter frame plus 10.5cm/4¼in. Stitch a 1.5cm/⅝in hem along the side and lower edge.

4 Stitch 2cm/¾in wide sew-on touch-and-close tape to the right side of the lower hemmed edge. Press 1cm/⅜in under on the upper short end. Stitch the corresponding touch-and-close tape on top.

5 With wrong sides facing, wrap the cover around the shutter frame. Press the touch-and-close tapes together. Screw the hinges to the frame. Fix a handle or knob to the opening edges.

Making a Swedish blind

1 Decide upon the size of the finished blind. To make a lined blind, cut two blinds the blind width plus 3cm/1¼in by the blind length plus 3cm/1¼in. Stitch the blinds together along the side and lower edges with right sides facing, taking 1.5cm/⅝in seam allowance. Clip the corners, turn right side out and press.

2 Saw 1cm/⅜in diameter wooden dowel 1.5cm/⅝in shorter than the width of the blind. Drop the dowel into the blind. Using a zipper or piping foot, stitch across the bottom of the blind, enclosing the dowel.

3 Press 1.5cm/⅝in to the wrong side on the upper edge. Stitch touch-and-close tape to the upper edge, concealing the raw edge of the fabric.

4 Saw a 1.2cm/½in thick, 2.5cm/1in wide wooden batten 1cm/⅜in shorter than the width of the blind. Staple the corresponding touch-and-close tape to the front of the batten.

5 Slip curtain rings onto two 25.5cm/10in lengths of webbing. Pin the ends together. Staple to the top of the batten 5cm/2in in from the ends so the rings hang over the front. Insert a screw eye into the underside 5cm/2in in from the ends. Fix the batten in place, with the touch-and-close tape facing outwards.

6 Press the blind to the front of the batten, matching the touch-and-close tapes.

7 Tie the cord to the left-hand screw eye, then bring it down under the blind and up through the left-hand curtain ring. Tie the other end of the cord to the right-hand eye, and bring it under the blind and up through the right-hand curtain ring, with the cord coming from the left-hand ring (see diagram below). Fix a cleat to the wall on the right-hand side. Roll up the blind then pull up the excess cord and wind it around the cleat to hold the blind at the desired level.

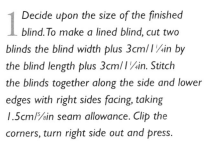

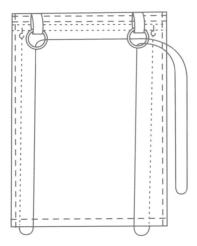

roller blinds

Roller blinds can look cool and contemporary in a modern setting, and look neat rolled up in the day. You can use a roller-blind kit – available in various widths – or you can construct your own. You can stiffen fabric with a spray-on stiffener or you can use material produced especially for making blinds.

Roller blinds are a good choice to cover a window above a radiator or item of furniture, because they cover only the glass and suit being sill-length. Roller blinds are best made using a roller-blind kit, available in various widths. If you need a different width from those available, buy the next size up and saw the roller and lower batten to size. Measure up roughly first, then again when the brackets and roller are in position, to get an exact fit. Measure the window; if you intend to hang the blind outside a window recess, allow 5.6cm/2¼in overlap. If you intend to hang the blind inside a recess, deduct 3.2cm/1¼in from the width to allow for the blind fittings.

Most roller-blind kits contain a wooden roller, a side control and dummy pin to fit into the ends of the roller, a wooden batten to keep the lower edge of the fabric straight, two brackets, cord, a cord holder which is fixed to the batten, and a cord pull.

Choosing and preparing fabric
Pre-stiffened fabric for roller blinds is available at furnishing-fabric stores. It has been treated to make it resistant to fraying and some fabrics are fade-resistant and spongeable. Pre-stiffened fabric comes in standard widths up to 2m/2¼yd wide but can be cut

narrower. Most mediumweight fabrics can be stiffened with a fabric-stiffening spray specially formulated for roller blinds, which stiffens the fabric and makes it fray-resistant. Test the spray on a scrap of fabric first to make sure it is colourfast. Spray the fabric before cutting, as it may cause shrinkage.

Roller blinds can be set in a variety of positions according to the amount of light and the need for privacy. Their simple lines make them ideal for home offices or other work environments.

Making a roller blind

1 Read the kit instructions. Fix the brackets in place. One bracket will hold the side control and should be fixed to the side of the window where the cord will be operated. They should be at least 3.2cm/1¼in from a recess outer edge if fixing to the outside of a recess, and at least 5cm/2in above the window to stop light getting in. Brackets fixed inside a recess should be as close to the recess as possible and 3.2cm/1¼in below the top of the recess to allow space for the roller. Use a spirit level to check that the brackets are level. Fix the brackets to a wall with Rawlplugs.

2 Measure the distance between the brackets with a metal or wooden ruler. If necessary, saw the roller to this length, allowing space for the side control and dummy pin. The fabric will need to be trimmed if the roller has been shortened. Lay the fabric out flat, wrong side face up. Use a metal or wooden ruler to draw a line along one side edge to narrow the fabric to match the roller. If the blind has a shaped hem, take an equal amount off each side. Cut to size with a craft knife or pair of scissors.

3 Some rollers have a straight line marked along their length for positioning fabric. If yours does not, use a metal or wooden ruler to draw a straight line. Lay the fabric flat and place the roller under the upper edge. Lift the fabric over the roller and match it to the straight marked line. Stick temporarily in place with masking tape then fix with tacks, a staple gun or strong double-sided tape.

4 Fix the side control and dummy pin into the ends of the roller. Fix the roller onto the brackets. Measure from a bracket to below the window sill for a blind hanging outside a recess and to the sill for inside a recess. Add 25cm/10in to allow for the roller and batten. If the blind needs to be shortened, cut the fabric to size. The edges must be straight and the corners at exact right angles.

5 If you have cut the blind and roller narrower, saw the batten to 1.2cm/½in narrower than the blind. Turn under 4cm/1½in on the lower edge to make a channel for the batten. Check that the batten will slot in easily, make the channel deeper if not. Stitch close to the raw edge with a zigzag stitch. Slip the batten into the channel.

6 Refer the the manufacturer's instructions to fix the cord pull and to check the tension when lowering and raising the blind.

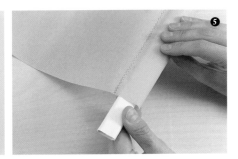

lambrequins

A pelmet that extends at least halfway down each side of a window is called a lambrequin. It is usually quite shapely, creating a dramatic silhouette against the window. A lambrequin can be used on its own in front of a small window, or can be teamed up with curtains or a blind. Avoid sheer or very lightweight fabrics.

Making a lambrequin with self-adhesive pelmet interfacing

The shape is formed from self-adhesive pelmet interfacing that is then covered with fabric. Self-adhesive pelmet interfacing has a peel-off paper backing and is available by the metre at 60cm/23¾in wide. If you want to make a lambrequin deeper than this, use buckram instead. Do not join self-adhesive pelmet interfacing because it will make a visible ridge. Buckram can be joined invisibly with carpet tape.

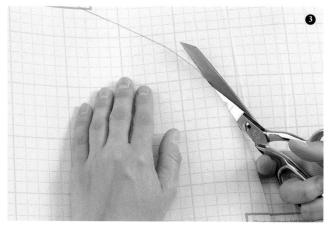

1 *Measure the intended width and depth of the lambrequin and draw a square or rectangle to size on paper. Do not make the depth more than 60cm/23¾in if you intend to use self-adhesive pelmet interfacing. Make sure that the corners are right angles, and draw straight lines against a metal or wooden ruler. Cut out and fold the paper in half, matching the side edges. Measure down the fold for the depth of the centre of the lambrequin and mark its position.*

2 *Now draw the inner edge of the lambrequin, starting at the centre. When you are happy with the shape, cut it out and open the pattern out flat. Tape the lambrequin in front of the window with masking tape, making adjustments if necessary.*

3 *Tape the pattern to the paper side of the interfacing with masking tape and draw around it. Remove the pattern and cut out the lambrequin. Use the pattern to cut one lambrequin from fabric, adding 1.5cm/⅝in allowance on all edges. Cut one lambrequin from lining, adding 1.5cm/⅝in on the curved edges.*

4 *Ease the backing paper away from the centre of the interfacing and cut it across the width. Peel back the paper a little way on each side of the cut. Carefully place the fabric, right side up, on top. Press the fabric smoothly onto the exposed adhesive. Continue peeling*

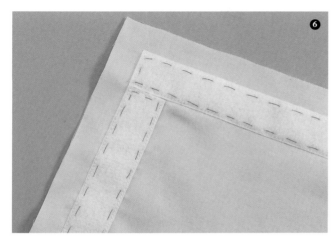

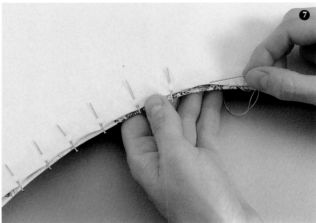

back the paper and sticking down the fabric. Smooth the fabric outwards to eliminate any wrinkles or air bubbles.

5 With the wrong side up, snip the curves and cut the corners of the fabric diagonally 5mm/¼in beyond the interfacing corners. Peel back the backing paper around the outer edges. Press the diagonal corner then the straight and curved edges to the wrong side.

6 Tack and stitch a length of the soft part of 2cm/¾in wide touch-and-close tape, 2cm/¾in below the upper edge of the lining and 2cm/¾in within the side edges on the right side. Stitch another length 2cm/¾in inside the side edges to 5cm/2in above the lower edge. Press under 1cm/⅜in on the outer edges.

7 Ease the backing paper away from the centre of the interfacing and cut it across the width as before. Peel back the paper and stick on the lining, enclosing the raw edges of the fabric. Turn under and pin the raw edges of the lining to the lambrequin about 3mm/⅛in

inside the curved edges, snipping the curves so the lining stays flat. Slipstitch the lining to the fabric.

8 Nail corresponding lengths of touch-and-close tape to the upper and side edges of the architrave. Press the lambrequin on top. Alternatively, attach a lambrequin to corresponding lengths of touch-and-close tape nailed to 2.5 x 2.5cm/1 x 1in battens.

Using a pelmet box
When making a pattern for a lambrequin that is to be applied to a pelmet box, add the depth of the box to the side edges and apply touch-and-close tape to the top edge only.

swags and tails

Swags and tails can look softly draped or formally pleated, depending on the kind of look you are trying to achieve. They suit bigger windows better as the pleating and large amounts of fabric need a certain amount of space in which to look their best. Don't choose fabrics that are too stiff or have a very busy pattern.

Swags and tails lend an element of sophistication to a room and can enhance a large window that might otherwise appear rather plain. Use good-quality fabric that will hold the drapery well. Fabrics with distinct designs are not suitable, as motifs will be lost amongst the folds and may lie at what seems an odd angle as the swag fabric is cut on the bias grain. The lining fabric will be visible on the tails, so you may wish to use a co-ordinating fabric for this.

Traditional swags and tails are constructed in three parts: the swag is fixed across the front of a shelf pelmet with a tail at each side. Try out the pattern in scrap fabric first to make sure you are happy with the effect.

These softly draped swags and tails give an informal and relaxed feel to the bathroom. The following instructions show how to create a more formal pleated look.

Making swags and tails

1 *To make a pelmet shelf to support the swag and tails, saw a length of PAR (planed all round) wood 16.5cm/6½in deep and 1.2cm/½in thick to 13cm/5¼in longer than the width of the window. Fix the shelf above the window with L-shaped brackets.*

2 *Measure the intended depth of the swag down from the centre of the shelf. This should not be more than a sixth of the height of the window. To make a pattern (see page 76), draw a rectangle that is 20cm/8in wider than the shelf width by two and a half times the swag depth. Cut out and fold the rectangle in half, having the fold parallel with the depth edges. The fold will be the centre of the swag.*

3 Mark a point on the long edge up from the lower edge that is a quarter of the overall length. Draw a curve between the point and the lower edge of the fold line. Measure along the top edge from the fold line and mark a point a quarter of the folded top edge measurement. Join the two points with a straight line. Draw the grain line at a 45-degree angle to the fold line. Refer to the diagram on the next page.

4 Cut out the pattern and open it out flat to cut a swag from scrap fabric. Ideally, this should be of a similar weight and feel to the final fabric. Pin the slanted side edges into pleats 10–15cm/4–6in deep and facing upwards.

5 To check the fit, attach the swag temporarily to the front edge of the shelf with masking tape or drawing pins; start by matching the centres and work outwards. If necessary, re-pin the pleats or adjust the pattern.

6 Decide how wide you want the tails to be; they will extend over the ends of the swag. Refer to the diagram on the next page to cut a paper pattern, and mark the grain line parallel with the long edge. Use the pattern to cut a tail from the scrap fabric. Mark the top edge 16.5cm/6½in from the long edge: this mark will match the corner of the shelf, and the long edge will be the return that goes along the side of the shelf.

7 Pleat the rest of the upper edge as far as the mark, with the pleats facing outwards. Stick the tail around one end of the shelf with masking tape or drawing pins. Check the effect and adjust if necessary. Remove the trial swag and tail, and transfer the pleat positions and any alterations to the paper pattern.

8 Use the pattern to cut a swag from fabric and lining and a pair of tails from fabric and lining, adding a 1.5cm/⅝in allowance to all edges. Stitch the swags together along the curved edge with right sides facing. Snip the curves and turn right side out.

9 Tack the raw edges together. Pin the pleats in position and stitch across them. Neaten the raw edges with a zigzag stitch.

10 Working outwards from the centre, attach the swag to the shelf using tin tacks, with 1.5cm/⅝in of the upper edge extending onto the top of the shelf. Adjust if necessary, then hammer the tacks home.

11 Pin each fabric tail to a tail lining with right sides facing. Stitch together, taking 1.5cm/⅝in seam allowance and leaving the upper edge open. Clip the corners and turn right side out. Tack the upper edges together and pin the pleats. Stitch across the pleats, then neaten the upper edge with a zigzag stitch.

12 Temporary tack one tail to the shelf with 1.5cm/⅝in of the upper edge extending onto the top of the shelf. Fold the tail neatly round the corner. Hammer the tacks home. Repeat on the other side of the shelf.

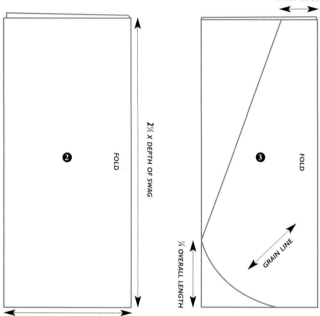

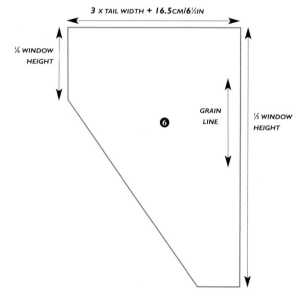

¼ TOP EDGE

2½ × DEPTH OF SWAG

FOLD

❷

FOLD

❸

GRAIN LINE

¼ OVERALL LENGTH

10CM/4IN LONGER THAN ½ SHELF WIDTH

3 × TAIL WIDTH + 16.5CM/6½IN

¼ WINDOW HEIGHT

GRAIN LINE

❻

⅓ WINDOW HEIGHT

tiebacks

The finishing touch to your curtains is a pair of co-ordinating tiebacks. As well as looking good, tiebacks allow as much daylight as possible into the room. They are usually positioned about two-thirds of the way down the curtains. In general, a tieback is 46–61cm/1ft 6in–2ft long.

Straight tiebacks are best for narrow curtains, and crescent shaped, curved tiebacks for wider curtains. Choose light to mediumweight fabrics. Only a small amount of fabric is needed, so use left-over curtain fabric for a co-ordinating look or use a remnant of contrasting fabric. The edges can be bound or have braid or fringing added by hand when complete. If you wish to bind the edges, cut two fabric tiebacks and one of pelmet interfacing, and pin the interfacing between the fabric layers with the right sides facing outwards, then bind the edges.

A metal ring is sewn to each end of the tieback and slips easily onto hooks attached either side of the curtain. If the curtains will not be drawn closed, fancy tiebacks can be used, as they will not be handled each day. A chiffon scarf fastened around the curtain in a flamboyant bow will add glamour; a string of beads will have the same effect. Specially made tasselled tieback cords are very expensive. A tasselled dressing-gown cord is an instant tieback: twist it a few times to shorten it, then wrap it once or twice around the curtain and slip it over a hook.

Holdbacks
Holdbacks have the same function as tiebacks. They are rigid, often like large

horizontal hooks that the curtain is slipped behind. A popular style of holdback is a boss, which is a disc with a short rod behind that is fixed to the wall. To make a fabric-covered boss, either in fabric to match the curtain or a contrasting design, cut a circle of fabric 5cm/2in wider than the diameter of the boss; centre any motifs on the fabric.

Run a gathering stitch around the circumference and slightly draw up the thread. Cut a circle of wadding 2.5cm/1in wider than the diameter of the boss. Place the wadding centrally on the wrong side of the fabric. Slip the fabric circle over the boss and pull up the thread tightly, enclosing the boss. Fasten the thread ends securely.

Making a lightweight straight tieback

1 Cut a strip of mediumweight fusible interfacing 46 x 6.5cm/18 x 2½in. Cut two strips of fabric 49 x 9.5cm/19¼ x 3¾in. Press the interfacing centrally to one fabric tieback.

2 Stitch the tiebacks together just outside the edges of the interfacing with right sides facing, leaving an opening on the lower edge to turn through. Clip the corners and turn right side out. Press and slipstitch the opening closed. Attach a ring as described below.

Making curved tiebacks

1 Measure around a drawn-open curtain using a tape measure, holding the tape loosely. To make a pattern, draw a rectangle on paper that is half the tieback measurement by 12.5cm/5in. One short edge will be the fold line. Draw a half-crescent shape within the rectangle.

2 Cut out the shape and hold it around the curtain to check the shape and fit; pull the curtain upwards a little so it drapes nicely over the top. Remember that if a tieback is too tight, it will crease the curtain and the creases will probably be visible when the curtain is drawn closed, so it is best to have a looser look. Mark the position for the hook on the wall.

3 Cut the tieback from fusible pelmet-weight interfacing. Cut two tiebacks from fabric, adding 1cm/⅜in seam allowance. Press the interfacing centrally to one fabric tieback. Snip the curved edges and press them over the interfacing.

4 Pin the remaining tieback on top. Snip the curves and turn the raw edges under, then slipstitch the outer edges together.

5 Sew braid, cord or piping to the outer edges. Handsew a curtain ring at each end on the wrong side, positioning the ring so half of it extends beyond the tieback.

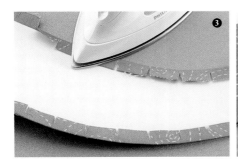

french pleat curtain

French pleat curtains look very stylish and suit most room styles. You can draw attention to the attractive rounded shape of the pleats by sewing a bright button under them (as here) or another trimming such as beads or pompoms.

A hand-pleated heading always looks very sophisticated. Rounded French pleats are also known as goblet pleats because of their curvaceous shape. It is worth investing in good-quality fabric that will hold the goblet shapes well. Here, self-cover buttons have red fabric applied and attached to each pleat, to echo the dramatic shade of the ruby red tulips on the fabric design. When buying fabric, allow twice the width plus 3.8cm/1½in for each side hem. Add 30.5cm/1ft to the length for the heading and hem. Make, line and hem the curtain as described on pages 56–57.

Making a French pleat curtain

1 Press 20cm/8in to the underside on the upper edge. Open out flat again and cut the lining level with the fold line. Cut 10cm/4in wide strips of mediumweight iron-on interfacing to fit across the top of the curtain. Place the strips on the curtain, with the lower edge of the strips level with the fold line. If the interfacing strips need to be joined, overlap them by 1cm/⅜in.

2 Press the strips to fuse them to the curtain. Fold the upper edge of the curtain over the strip.

3 Fold the upper edge again to make a double hem. Press in position and tack across the lower edge. Slipstitch the ends closed.

4 Measure the width of the curtain and take 10cm/4in off the measurement. Divide the remainder into an odd number of sections of 10–12.5cm/4–5in. Starting and finishing 5cm/2in from the ends, mark the divisions with tailor's chalk on the heading on the wrong side. Bring the chalked lines together in pairs to form rounded goblets on the right side. On the wrong side, slipstitch the edges together using a double length of thread.

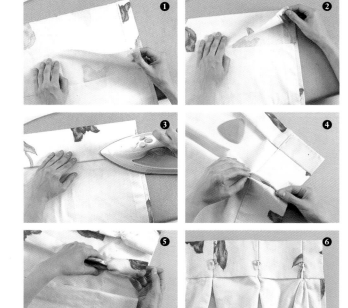

5 On the right side, make a single stitch around the pleat on the tacked line and pull up the thread to gather the base of the goblet. Repeat to secure in place. Open out the goblet at the upper edge and oversew to the top edge of the curtain to hold the goblet open.

6 Remove the tacking. Sew a button to each goblet. Check the length of the curtain. Sew a metal sew-on curtain hook to the back of each pleat.

Tip

Wadding or scrunched-up tissue paper can be slipped into the goblets to hold the shape if necessary.

tab-top curtains

Curtains hung by tabs are very popular because, as well as being easy to make, they show off the wonderful choice of curtain poles available today. Most fabrics are suitable, but smooth, lightweight or slippery fabrics are easier to draw along the pole.

Making tab-top curtains

1 To calculate fabric quantities, measure the window width and double the measurement, add 3cm/1¼in for both side hems. Measure the intended drop of the curtain from 6.3cm/2½in below the curtain pole to allow for the tabs. Add 4.5cm/1¾in to the drop measurement for the hem and seam allowance.

2 Now work out how many tabs will fit across the top of the finished curtain. The tabs are positioned 12–15cm/4¾–6in apart and are 3cm/1¼in wide. Measure the circumference of the pole with a tape measure, and add 14.5cm/5¾in to the

measurement. Cut the tabs 8cm/3¼in wide. A 5cm/2in wide strip of dupion silk the width of the curtain plus 3cm/1¼in is needed for the upper band. Dupion silk is usually only 90cm/1yd wide, so it may be economical to join the band rather than cut it in a single length. Stitch a 1cm/⅜in seam allowance throughout.

3 Cut out the curtain from voile. Press 5mm/¼in under then 1cm/⅜in on the side edges. Stitch close to the inner edges. Press 1cm/⅜in under then 2.5cm/1in on the lower edge. Stitch close to the inner edges.

4 Cut an 8cm/3¼in wide strip of dupion silk long enough to cut the number of tabs needed. Fold lengthwise in half with right sides facing. Stitch the long edges. Press the seam open. Turn right side out with a bodkin and press, placing the seam centrally. Cut into equal lengths for the tabs.

5 Fold each tab in half with the seam inside. Pin the tabs to the upper edge on the wrong side of the curtain, positioning one tab at each end and spacing the rest an equal distance apart.

6 Cut a 5cm/2in wide strip of dupion silk for the upper band, the width of the curtain plus 3cm/1¼in. Press 1cm/⅜in under on one long edge. With the right side of the band facing the wrong side of the curtain, pin and stitch the band to the upper edge, with 1cm/⅜in extending beyond the sides of the curtain.

7 Clip the corners. Turn the band to the right side, and press under the ends of the band. Tack the band to the curtain and topstitch close to the band edges.

Tip
Plastic tab-top gliders are available to fit under the tabs, to help them glide along the pole.

pelmet

A fabric-covered pelmet adds a neat border to a blind or a curtain heading. The pelmet is made from self-adhesive pelmet interfacing, which has a peel-off paper backing on one or both sides. The pelmet is attached with touch-and-close tape to a wooden pelmet shelf.

The pelmet should extend at least 6.5cm/2½in beyond each side of the window. A piece of wood about 10cm/4in deep and 1.2cm/½in thick is a versatile size for the pelmet shelf. Fix the brackets to the underside of the pelmet shelf about 20cm/8in apart, or to the top of the shelf if they would otherwise coincide with the window recess.

Closely woven mediumweight fabrics are ideal for making a pelmet but most fabrics are suitable. Use an inexpensive, closely woven fabric such as curtain lining to line it. This vibrant pelmet has a simple wavy edge. Design your own pelmet on scrap paper first. The top edge and the ends must be straight but the lower edge can be any shape you like.

Making a pelmet

1 Measure the length and depth of the pelmet shelf. To make a pattern, cut a 15cm/6in wide strip of pattern paper or brown parcel paper that is the length plus twice the depth of the pelmet shelf. Mark the centre of the pelmet and the depth. Draw a wavy line along the lower edge on one half. When you are happy with the design, fold the pattern in half and cut it out.

2 Use the pattern to cut one pelmet from self-adhesive pelmet interfacing. Cut one pelmet from fabric and lining, adding a 1.5cm/⅝in allowance to all edges. Ease the paper backing away from the centre of the pelmet interfacing and cut it across the width. Peel back the paper for about 4cm/1½in each side of the cut, exposing the adhesive. Stick the fabric centrally on top and peel away the backing paper, smoothing the fabric outwards to eliminate air bubbles.

3 Cut diagonally across the fabric 5mm/¼in from the corners of the pelmet. Snip the curves of the fabric. Peel away the pelmet backing paper from the edges and press the corners then the outer edges of the fabric to the back of the pelmet.

4 Stitch a length of the soft part of touch-and-close tape 1.5cm/⅝in within the ends and upper edge of the lining on the right side. Press under 1.5cm/⅝in on the ends and upper edge of the lining. Peel off the paper backing from the pelmet interfacing and press the lining smoothly on top.

5 Snip the curves of the lining along the lower edge. Slipstitch the pressed edges of the lining to the pelmet then slipstitch the lower edges together, turning under the snipped edges as you work. Staple the corresponding length of touch-and-close tape to the edge of the pelmet shelf and press the pelmet in place, folding it around the corners of the shelf.

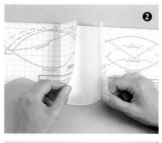

roman blind

The Roman blind is the most elegant of window treatments, particularly when a clean and neat appearance is required. When raised, the blind lies in flat, horizontal pleats which are kept in shape by wooden dowels threaded through narrow channels.

Making a Roman blind

1 Measure the intended width and drop of the blind. Add 6cm/2¼in to the width for hems and 15cm/5¾in to the drop for the channels and hems. Cut out the blind and a 7cm/2¾in wide strip for the lower band that is the blind width plus 3cm/1¼in. Press under 1cm/⅜in then 2cm/¾in on the side edges. Stitch close to both pressed edges.

2 Press under 1.5cm/⅝in on the upper edge. Pin the soft half of a length of sew-on touch-and-close tape over the pressed edge. Stitch close to the edges of the tape. Fix a 2.5cm/1in high x 1.2cm/½in deep batten in position above the window. Use a staple gun to staple the corresponding length of touch-and-close tape to the front of the batten. Screw a screw eye into the underside 5cm/2in in

from each end. Fix another screw eye 1.5cm/⅝in in from one end on the side of the window you want the cleat to be. Fix the cleat in place.

3 Press under 1.5cm/⅝in on one long edge of the band. With the right side of the band facing the wrong side of the blind and with 1.5cm/⅝in of the band extending at each end, stitch the band to the lower edge taking a 1.5cm/⅝in seam allowance. Press under the ends. Press the band to the right side along the seam. Stitch close to both long edges.

4 Divide the blind drop measurement into seven equal amounts for the pleats. Working down from the upper edge, mark the following measurements on one side edge with a pin: twice the pleat measurement plus 4cm/1½in, twice the pleat measurement plus 4cm/1½in, twice the pleat measurement plus 4cm/1½in. Repeat on the opposite edge. With right sides facing, bring the pins at one set of 4cm/1½in marks together on each side edge and press the fold.

5 Stitch 2cm/¾in from the fold, forming a channel for the dowel. Repeat on the other 4cm/1½in marks to form three channels. Cut four lengths of 1cm/⅜in diameter wooden dowel 1cm/⅜in shorter than the blind width. Insert the dowels into the channels and the band. Slipstitch the ends closed.

6 On the wrong side of the blind, sew a plastic blind ring to the channels 5cm/2in in from the side edges. Tie a length of blind cord to the lower ring on each side. Thread it up through the rings. Press the blind to the front of the batten, matching the touch-and-close tape. Thread the cords through the screw eyes above them. Thread the cord on the opposite side of the cleat through the other screw eyes. Thread the cord on the same side as the cleat through the outer screw eye. Pull the cords to raise the blind. Knot the cords together level with the cleat. If you wish, thread on an acorn and knot the cords under it, cutting off the excess.

take a seat

Seating takes a lot of wear and tear, and a new piece of furniture is an important financial consideration. A change of address or redecoration does not mean having to discard a favourite chair because it no longer matches your home style. There are masses of ways to revitalise and update chairs that you already have, just by changing their fabric. Mismatched chairs can be harmonised by making them smart new covers.

Loose covers are very practical. Once you have made the pattern, you could mark the seasons by creating simple chair covers for the chilly autumn and winter months from warm, cosy fabrics, then changing to covers made of lightweight, crisp fabrics for spring and summer. Make squashy floor cushions or beanbag chairs for a relaxed, contemporary feel, or spruce up second-hand chairs with new covers or cushions. You may be surprised to find how easy it is to create stunning new seating arrangements at minimal cost.

choosing seating and fabrics

Sofas, chairs and footstools are another investment that it is best to get right first time. There are hundreds of different versions and styles on the market and prices vary greatly too. It is often cheaper to buy second hand and cover older items of furniture with fabric of your own choosing.

Think carefully about the kind of style you want to achieve and stick to that. If cool and contemporary is your choice, then look for furniture that has clean lines and no fussy detailing. Your fabric choice should also match this. If you prefer a more traditional look, then there are lots of things out there that would suit, and faded chintzes can be bought cheaply.

You can pick up interesting pieces of seating in junk shops or house sales, often at bargain prices. They can be surprisingly easy to revamp, whether it's a sagging seat or a complete re-cover.

Second-hand seating
Bargain hunters will enjoy sourcing old, forlorn chairs and stools that just need a bit of care and attention to transform them into something special. House sales, auctions and junk shops offer seating at knockdown prices. Always sit on the item, not only to see if it is comfortable but also to make sure that the arms and legs are rigid and level. A creaking chair may have had woodworm and should be considered with caution. Fine sawdust means live woodworm and the piece should be treated with a proprietary woodworm killer.

If the framework of the chair needs repairing, do so before making patterns for the soft furnishings, as some refurbishments will alter the shape of the furniture. If it will be visible, sand scruffy paintwork and treat rust on metal furniture. Fill any knocks and gouges with wood filler then repaint the chair. Use spray paints on metal chairs. Replace flattened foam seats.

Do not just consider existing chairs and stools for recovering. If they are well made, other pieces of furniture, such as low tables, chests and boxes, can be made into seating. Either glue a piece

A favourite chair can be given new life by replacing the webbing and flattened seat before making a new loose cover. Sand the exposed woodwork and repaint or varnish.

Fabric for seating should be closely woven, hardwearing and crease-resistant.

of foam to the surface and make a slip-on cover for the entire item, or make a slip-on cover for the furniture and a separate fitted box cushion to sit on top. Similarly, adding a fitted cushion to a formal, hard chair will make it more homely and inviting to sit on.

Webbing

A sagging seat can be rectified by replacing the webbing. Purchase a web stretcher if you intend to upholster more than a couple of chairs. Remove the old webbing. Turn over 2.5cm/1in at the end of a length of woven webbing and hammer five tacks through the turned-under end in a 'W' formation to the back of the chair frame at the centre.

Pull the webbing over the front of the frame, and attach it to a web stretcher or pull it over a block of wood wedged against the front of the chair. Draw the webbing tautly downwards. Hammer in three tacks in a 'V' formation. Cut off the excess webbing, leaving 2.5cm/1in extending. Fold over the end and hammer in two tacks. Attach webbing each side of the first strip about 5cm/2in apart; if the chair front is wider than the back, splay the webbing apart. Attach the crosswise webbing in the same way, first weaving it in and out of the first strips.

Starting from scratch

Some styles of contemporary seating that do not need timber structures are very easy to make, often at much less cost than their shop-bought equivalents. Floor cushions and beanbag chairs are constant favourites with children and teenagers, but when

made from elegant fabrics, especially the excellent fake animal hides and furs available nowadays, they become quite sophisticated. Simple cubes of high-density foam covered with fabric look splendid in loft-style homes.

Choosing fabrics

Fabric for seating should be closely woven, hardwearing, crease-resistant and flame-retardant. Do not use knitted and other stretch fabrics, as they will not hold their shape. Avoid heavyweight fabrics as they will be tough to stitch, especially if piping is to be included. It is more economical to use plain or textured fabric, or one with a small print, rather than a fabric with a nap or large one-way design. This will enable pattern pieces to fit the fabric without too much wastage.

Smart trimmings such as piping and braid will streamline soft furnishings and link the furniture to other design elements or colours within a room. Fastenings on loose covers need not only be unobtrusive zip fastenings; make a feature of them by incorporating ties, buttons or even buckles.

floor cushions

Floor cushions are no longer confined to student digs. Huge squashy cushions made of fake fur, leather, suede or denim are seriously cool, and add an informal air to a living room or bedroom. They are particularly good for children and teenagers, who like to loll about on the floor with their friends.

Large, squashy floor cushions are the simplest form of seating to make. They always lend a relaxed and informal feel to their setting and are ideal when additional seating is needed, at a party for example. The choice of fabric will determine their style, but it must be hardwearing. In general, floor cushions suit earthy, ethnic designs or bright, bold patterns rather than formal, traditional fabrics. Chunky trimmings can be added, such as fringing and bobbles, or tassels or pompoms at the corners. A zip fastening along the centre of the back is most suitable for floor cushion covers, as it makes them easy to remove for laundering.

Readymade feather-filled 90cm/1yd square inner pads are available from department stores. If you want to make a cushion that is not a standard size, it is easy to make an inner pad and fill it with your choice of filling. Make inner pads from cotton, lining fabric or featherproof cambric.

Choosing fillings
Polystyrene beads give firm support and are a popular choice for floor cushions. Fill the pad carefully, as spillages are difficult to clear up and you will probably be finding scattered polystyrene beads for months

afterwards. Foam chips have a bumpy feel and deteriorate with time. Use flame-retardant foam chips only.

Feather and down is soft and resilient. Purely feather fillings are more expensive than a mixture of

feather and down. Make an inner pad for a feather-and-down filling from featherproof fabric. Kapok is a traditional cushion filling made from vegetable fibre that will become lumpy over time.

Making a floor cushion

1 Cut two 95cm/37¼in squares of fabric for the inner cushion. Stitch them together with the right sides facing, leaving a gap 70cm/27½in long on one edge for filling. Clip the corners and turn right side out.

2 Pour the filling into the pad, then push it into the corners and tease out the feathers and kapok to distribute them evenly. The amount of filling needed depends upon how firm you would like the cushion to be. Slipstitch the opening closed.

3 Cut one 95cm/37¼in square of fabric for the outer cushion front, and two rectangles 95 x 49cm/37¼ x 19¼in for the outer cushion backs. With right sides facing, tack the backs together along one long edge. Stitch for 10cm/4in at each end of the seam, taking a 1.5cm/⅝in seam allowance. Press the seam open.

4 With the back lying face down, place the zip centrally along the seam, face down. Pin and tack the zip in position.

5 Using a zipper foot on the sewing machine and with the fabric right side up, stitch the zip in place 8mm/⅜in from the tacked seam and across the ends of the zip. Remove the tacking stitches.

6 Stitch the front and back together with the right sides facing. Clip the corners and turn right side out. Push the inner pad into the cushion cover, making sure the corners are in place. Close the zip.

Making tasselled corners

Add an exotic touch to a floor cushion with a tassel at each corner. Use embroidery yarn, knitting wool or even fine cord.

1 Cut a rectangle of card 15.5 x 10cm/6¼ x 4in. Fold in half, parallel with the short edges. Bind the yarn around the card many times, depending upon the thickness of the tassel needed.

2 Fold a long length of yarn in half and thread the ends through the eye of a tapestry needle. Slip the needle behind the strands close to the fold, then insert the needle through the loop of the yarn and pull tightly.

3 Slip the tips of a pair of scissors between the card layers and cut through the strands. Discard the card.

4 Thread the needle with a single length of yarn and bind it tightly around the head of the tassel, gathering the strands together. To secure, insert the needle into the bulk of the tassel to lose the end of the yarn within the tassel. Cut the tassel ends level. Sew a tassel to each corner of a cushion, using the yarn extending at the top.

box cushions

A box cushion is tailored to cover a foam block or a deep, feather-filled, gusseted inner pad, making it very comfortable to sit on. A gusset forms the sides between the top and base. The shape can be emphasised with piping or any other trimming that takes your fancy.

Making a square or rectangular box cushion

1 *Measure the length, width and depth of the cushion. Cut squares or rectangles of fabric for the top and base, adding a 1.5cm/⅝in seam allowance to all edges. Cut a strip of fabric for the front gusset the length of the front by the cushion depth plus 1.5cm/⅝in on all edges. Cut two strips for the side gussets the length of the sides by the cushion depth plus 1.5cm/⅝in on all edges. Cut two strips for the back gusset the length of the back by half the cushion depth plus 1.5cm/⅝in on all edges.*

2 *With right sides facing, tack the backs together along one long edge. Stitch for 3.8cm/1½in at each end of the seam, taking a 1.5cm/⅝in seam allowance. Press the seam open.*

3 *With the back laying face down, place the zip centrally along the seam, face down. Pin and tack the zip in position. Using a zipper foot on the sewing machine and with the fabric right side up, stitch the zip in place 8mm/⅕in from the tacked seam and across the ends of the zip. Remove the tacking stitches.*

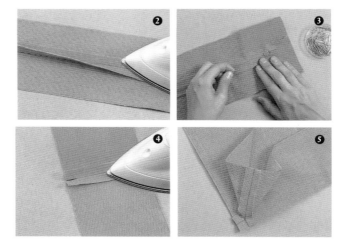

4 *With right sides facing, stitch the front and back gussets between the side gussets at the short ends, taking a 1.5cm/⅝in seam allowance, starting and finishing 1.5cm/⅝in from the long edges. Press the seams open. If you wish to use piping, tack it to the long edges, joining it at the back. Snip the piping seam allowance at the corners.*

5 *With right sides facing and matching the seams to the corners, pin the base to the gusset. Stitch, taking a 1.5cm/⅝in seam allowance and pivoting the seam at the corners. Open the zip and stitch the top to the gusset in the same way. Clip the corners. Press the seams towards the gusset. Turn right side out and insert the cushion. Close the zip.*

Making a circular box cushion

1 *Measure the diameter, circumference and depth of the cushion. Cut two circles of fabric for the top and base, adding 3cm/1¼in to the diameter. Cut a strip of fabric for the front gusset half the circumference of the cushion depth plus 1.5cm/⅝in on all edges. Cut two strips of fabric for the back gusset half the circumference by half the cushion depth plus 1.5cm/⅝in on all the edges.*

2 *Follow step 3 of making a square or rectangular box cushion to insert the zip. With right sides facing, stitch the front and back gussets together, taking a 1.5cm/⅝in seam allowance. Press the seams open. If you wish to insert piping, tack it to the long edges now, joining the ends at the back.*

3 *With right sides facing, stitch the base to the gusset, taking a 1.5cm/⅝in seam allowance. Open the zip and stitch the top to the gusset in the same way. Snip the curves. Press the seams towards the gusset. Turn right side out and insert the cushion. Close the zip.*

Tip
To reduce the bulk in the seams, trim the allowances to different levels. This is especially important if piping has been inserted, as it will make the seam allowance layers very thick and difficult to manage. To stop cushions slipping, sew a 6.3cm/2½in length of sew-on touch-and-close tape to the base of the cushion at the front and back, and apply a corresponding stick-on tape stuck to the seat.

Making irregular-shaped cushions

Some box cushions are shaped, to fit around chair arms for example, and must have a pattern made for them. If you intend to re-cover an existing cushion, take the old cover apart and use it as a pattern, otherwise make a paper pattern.

If a box cushion is narrower at the back than the front, the zip can be extended and the seams can be on the sides of the gusset instead of the back corners. This works well on wedge-shaped cushions. Alternatively, the base can have a seam across its widest part with a zip inserted.

drop-in seats

Many chairs have drop-in seats, which can get tatty if you use them a lot. These kinds of seats are very easy to lift out and cover yourself. You can also buy reasonably priced second-hand chairs to re-cover from scratch, replacing the old upholstery with fabric of your own choosing.

Here is a fast, no-sew way to bring new life to a worn chair by replacing the cover on its seat. Many dining or kitchen chairs or stools have drop-in seats that rest on a recessed ledge. Traditionally, a drop-in seat had a fabric cover over a horsehair stuffing, which was supported by tightly stretched webbing on a wooden frame. Nowadays, mass-produced foam versions are supported by a wooden base. The foam block is easy to work with, but not as comfortable to sit on or as long-lasting as a webbed and horsehair seat.

A calico lining under the outer cover protects the stuffing or foam and means the seat cover can be changed easily for washing or replacing without disturbing the interior of the seat. If you intend to use a thick furnishing fabric to re-cover the seat, check that there is enough clearance for the covered seat to fit the chair. Omitting the calico lining may help the fabric to fit. Use 1.2cm/½in long upholstery tacks or a staple gun to fix the covers.

Tatty drop-in seat covers can be lifted out and re-covered in a favourite fabric and colour – no sewing required!

Re-covering a drop-in seat

1 Lift the seat out of the chair frame. Any backing fabric on the underside will need to be removed. Lever off any tacks or staples with a tack lifter or the blade of a screwdriver. Remove the old seat cover in the same way, but do not discard it.

2 Remove any calico lining. Discard any wadding or top cover to reveal the stuffing or foam. Press the old seat cover and use it as a pattern to cut a seat cover from calico and the outer fabric. If the outer fabric is patterned, experiment by placing the fabric over the seat to judge the best position for its motifs.

3 Cut a piece of wadding 6cm/2½in larger all round to fit the top of the seat and place it in position. Place the calico cover centrally on top and smooth it over the surface. Check that the grain of the fabric is straight. Turn the seat over, holding the layers in place. Pull the calico over the underside of the frame or wood base. Starting on the back edge, secure temporarily in place with a tack hammered in halfway, in the middle of each side.

4 Working outwards from the middle of the back edge, tack or staple the calico to the seat, positioning the tacks or staples about 3.8cm/1½in apart and stopping 3.8cm/1½in each side of the corners. Stretch the calico towards the corners as you work.

5 Fix the front then the side edges in the same way, removing the temporary tack first if the calico is no longer lying taut. Check that the calico is lying taut and smooth on the seat. Pull the calico over one corner and hammer a temporary tack halfway in.

6 Fold the excess fabric under in mitred folds. Run your thumb along the folds to crease them. Open out the folds and cut away excess wadding and calico underneath. Remove the temporary tack and refold the calico. Tack or staple the folds in place. Repeat on all corners. Trim the calico and wadding to just beyond the tacks or staples.

7 Fix the top cover in the same way as the calico, making sure that the second row of tacks does not connect with the first row.

8 To give a professional finish, draw around the seat on black fabric with chalk or a chinagraph pencil. Cut out, adding a 6mm/¼in allowance. Press 1cm/⅜in under on the edges and tack or staple to the underside of the seat, again missing the position of the previous tacks and staples. Replace the seat in the chair recess.

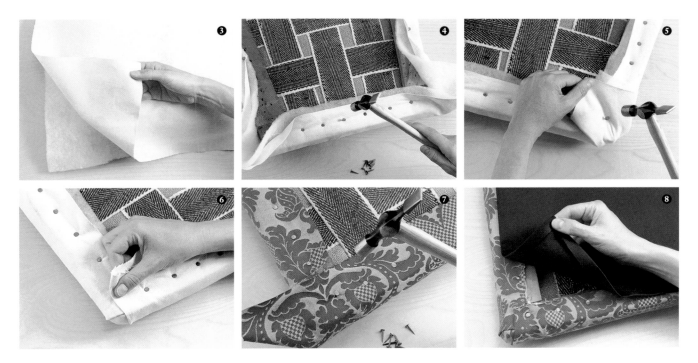

footstools

Smart calico-covered footstools are available from furniture suppliers ready to be covered in a fabric of your choice. Alternatively, you may wish to recover an old, scruffy footstool. Remove any trimmings first. If the existing cover is not falling apart, leave it on and fit the new cover on top.

Slip-on footstool cover
A slip-on cover is an instant makeover for a square, rectangular or circular footstool. The cover is made from a single piece of fabric which can be trimmed with fringing, braid or ribbon.

Because the cover extends below the base of the footstool, this style is not suitable for footstools that have legs that jut or curve outwards. A footstool of this style can be cleverly created from a low coffee table. Stick foam to the top of the table with a foam spray adhesive to make a soft, cushioned top. Place a layer of wadding over the top, fold the fullness under at the corners and staple the wadding to the underside of the table. It is now ready to be covered.

Making a circular slip-on footstool cover

1 *Measure the diameter and circumference of the footstool, then measure the intended drop. Cut a circle of fabric for the top, adding 3cm/1¼in to the diameter. Cut a strip of fabric for the side the length of the circumference plus 3cm/1¼in by the drop plus 4cm/1⅝in. With right sides facing, stitch the ends of the sides together, taking a 1.5cm/⅝in seam allowance. Press the seam open. If you wish to insert piping, then tack it to the upper long edge of the side of the cover now.*

2 *Fold the top and upper edge of the side panel into quarters and mark with pins. With right sides facing, pin the side panel to the top. Stitch, taking 1.5cm/⅝in seam allowance. Snip the curves. Neaten the seam with pinking shears or zigzag stitch. Press the seam towards the side panel. Press under 1cm/⅜in then 1.5cm/⅝in on the lower edge, then slipstitch or machine stitch in place. If you wish, sew a trimming along the lower edge.*

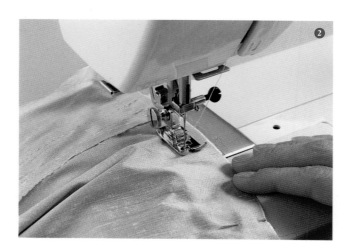

Making a square or rectangular slip-on footstool cover

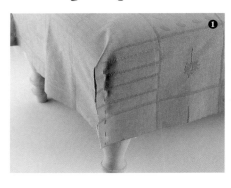 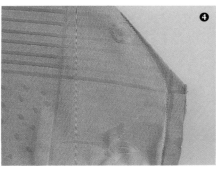 

1 Measure the length and width of the top of the footstool. Measure the drop of the cover, that is how far down the legs you would like the cover to go; it should be at least 2.5cm/1in below the base and can be floor-length.

2 To make a pattern, draw a square or rectangle on paper, the same size as the top of the footstool. Extend each side of the shape for the drop of the cover; these will be the sides of the cover. Add a 1.5cm/⅝in seam allowance to the side edges and a 2.5cm/1in hem to the lower edges.

3 To fit the cover, pin the side edges together with right sides facing, taking a 1.5cm/⅝in seam allowance. Slip the cover over the footstool and check the fit. If it is too tight, make the seams narrower. If the cover is loose, make the seams deeper. Adjust all the seams by the same amount.

4 If the corners of the footstool are quite rounded, pin the top of the seams, following the curves. Stitch the seams as pinned. Neaten the seams with a zigzag stitch. Press the seams open.

5 Press 1cm/⅜in under then 1.5cm/⅝in on the lower edges, and stitch in place. If you wish, sew a trimming along the lower edge.

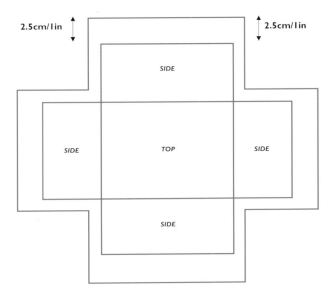

Upholstering a footstool

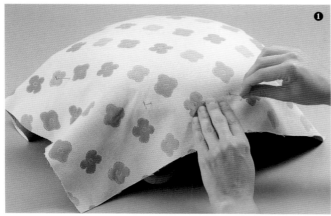

1 Lie the fabric over the footstool, centering any design motifs, and pin the fabric in place with upholstery skewers or T-pins. Smooth the fabric outwards from the centre and over the sides.

2 Check that the fabric is lying smoothly and is not wrinkled or pulling tightly. Lie the stool on its side and staple the lower edge of the fabric onto the frame with a staple gun or hammer in tacks close to the lower edge.

3 Trim away the excess fabric level with the base of the footstool.

4 Use fabric glue to stick braid or fringing over the lower raw edges, overlapping the ends.

beanbag chairs

A squidgy beanbag chair is fun for all the family and surprisingly comfortable and supportive. A fabric handle at the top makes it easy to move around. The beanbag has an inner bag to contain the polystyrene beads so that they are secure. Calico is a good choice for the inner bag, but any cotton or lining fabric will do as an alternative.

Animal hides and fur fabrics

Beanbag chairs made of sumptuous leather and suède and realistic fake animal hides are extremely expensive to buy, yet can be made for a fraction of their cost. Although there are special considerations to remember when stitching real and fake animal hides, these chairs are simple to assemble and should not be problematic.

Because animal skins vary in size, take a paper pattern with you to calculate how many to buy. Cut the skins separately, right side up, so you can avoid any surface flaws or thin areas. Weight the pattern in place and draw around it with tailor's chalk, then cut out. Stitch leather and suède with polyester thread, using a wedge-point needle for both hand and machine stitching. Press with a warm iron on the wrong side. If the iron begins to stick, cover the skin with brown paper.

Leather can be sponged gently with warm water and a little soap or washing-up liquid. Wipe with a damp cloth, then dry with a soft duster. Brush suède with a clothes brush; some suèdes are washable.

Highly realistic imitation leather and suède fabrics are available nowadays and are very easy to work with. Make sure that the pile of imitation suède runs in the same direction on the panels when cutting out. These fabrics often have a knitted back; use a ballpoint needle to stitch with a slight zigzag stitch to allow the seams to stretch when the chair is sat on.

Choose fur fabrics with a short pile, otherwise the chair will lose what little definition it has. Fur fabrics usually come in 150cm/60in widths and are economical to buy. The pile of the fur should run down the length of the panels. Cut through the knitted backing of the fur and not the fur itself, cutting each piece singly to avoid distortion.

Stitch fur fabrics with a ballpoint needle. Trim away the fur in the seam allowances to reduce bulk and pull out any fur caught in the seams with a pin. Press the fabric lightly on the wrong side with a warm iron.

COW PRINT   LEOPARD PRINT   VINYL SNAKESKIN

Making a beanbag chair

1 Refer to the diagrams below to cut patterns from paper for the panel, top and base. Cut six panels, a top and a base from the outer fabric and the inner bag fabric.

2 With right sides together and taking 1.5cm/⅝in seam allowances, stitch the outer bag panels together, starting and finishing 1.5cm/⅝in from the ends of the seams. Snip the corners and press the seams open.

3 Cut a strip of fabric for the handle 22.5 x 10.5cm/9 x 4½in. Fold 1.5cm/⅝in under on the long edges and fold lengthwise in half. Stitch close to the long edges. With right sides uppermost, tack the handle centrally across the top, matching the raw edges.

4 Pin the top to the upper edge of the panels, with right sides facing and matching the seams to the corners. Stitch, taking a 1.5cm/⅝in seam allowance and pivoting the fabric at the corners. Stitch the base to the lower edge in the same way, leaving a gap in one panel to turn through. Snip the corners.

5 Make the inner bag in the same way, omitting the handle. Turn both bags right side out. Slip the inner bag inside the outer bag. Fill the inner bag with 0.14cu m/5 cu ft of polystyrene beads. The best way to do this is to form a funnel from thin card, overlapping the edges and taping them together. Push the narrow end of the funnel into the inner bag and carefully pour in the beads. Slipstitch the openings on both bags securely closed.

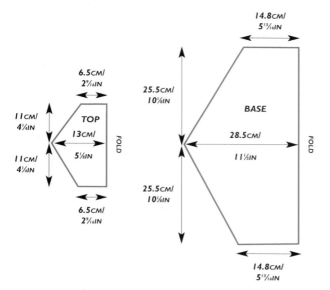

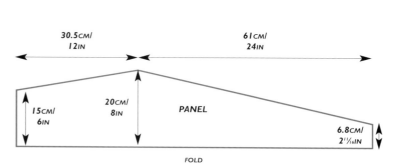

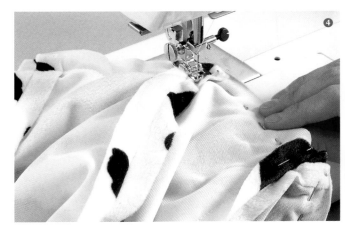

deckchairs

Traditional deckchair canvas is strong and hardwearing and comes in widths of 40–46cm/1ft 4in–1ft 6in in plain colours and distinctive stripes. Other fabrics can be used; they will not last as long as deckchair canvas but they will offer more choice of designs. The fabric must be tough, however, and not likely to stretch.

Preparing the deckchair

Lie the closed chair face down on a flat surface. If the old cover is attached to the top and bottom bars of the chair with tacks, ease them out with a chisel. If the top and bottom bars of the chair have been slotted through a channel of the old cover before the frame was assembled, you will have to cut the cover away. If the cover has channels at each end with a thick wooden dowel slotted through, that is trapped between a pair of wooden bars, simply pull out the dowels to release the cover. Use the old cover as a pattern to cut the new one. If the old cover no longer exists, open the frame, loop a tape measure around the top bar and allow it to drop in a curve before wrapping it over the bottom bar. Allow 1cm/⅜in allowance at each end for a cover attached with tacks. For a cover with channels, add twice the depth of the channels plus 3cm/1⅛in. If you are not using deckchair canvas, measure the width of the top bar. Cut the fabric to that width plus 2cm/¾in hem on each side. Cut out the cover. Sand, paint or varnish the frame if needed.

Choose traditional deckchair canvas in bold stripes, or a more modern fabric and design. Add a matching, removable pillow for ultimate comfort and style.

Using tacks

1 If you are not using deckchair canvas, press 5mm/¼in of fabric under, then a 1.5cm/⅝in hem on the long edges and stitch in place. Press 1cm/⅜in under at each end.

2 Lie the canvas right side down on a flat surface and place the deckchair frame right side down on top. Wrap the top of the canvas around the top bar so that the turned-under edge lies along the underside of the bar. Hammer a tack through the cover into the underside of the bar at the centre. Hammer three tacks, evenly spaced each side of the first tack. Avoid the holes left by the previous tacks as they will not grip the new tacks.

3 Wrap the other end of the fabric around the bottom bar, placing the turned-under edge along the underside of the bar. The bottom bar is sometimes narrower than the top bar. If the canvas is too wide for the bottom bar, turn under the edges by the same amount at each edge so the canvas lies flat. Tack in place as for the top bar.

With channels

1 If not using deckchair canvas, turn under 5mm/¼in then 1.5cm/⅝in on the long edges and stitch in place.

2 Press under 1.5cm/⅝in then the depth of the channel at each end. Stitch close to the inner edge then 5mm/¼in from the inner edge to form a channel.

3 Lie the cover right side down on a flat surface. Place the deckchair frame right side down on top. Pull the ends between the top and lower bars and insert the dowels through the channels.

Removable pillow

A detachable pillow adds extra comfort to a deckchair. It is fixed with touch-and-close tape so that it can be removed for storage.

1 Cut a rectangle of canvas the width of the chair cover by 51cm/1ft 8in. Fold widthwise in half with right sides facing. Taking a 1.5cm/⅝in seam allowance, stitch the short edges and for 2cm/¾in at each end of the long raw edges. Clip the corners and turn the pillow right side out. Press the opening edges to the inside. Fill the pillow with feather and down.

2 Cut a 12.5cm/5in wide strip of canvas the width of the chair cover for the pillow hinge. Turn 1cm/⅜in under then 2.5cm/1in at each end and stitch in place. Press 1cm/⅜in under on one long edge and stitch the sew-on half of touch-and-close tape over the raw edge.

3 Insert the long raw edge into the pillow for 1.5cm/⅝in. Pin in place then stitch close to the pressed edges. Stitch again 6mm/¼in from the first stitching. Apply a corresponding strip of stick-on touch-and-close tape to the back of the bar on the deckchair and press the pillow hinge on top. Flop the pillow over to the front of the chair.

director's chairs

The modest director's chair fits into many room styles. Director's chairs are useful when additional seating is needed, both indoors and in the garden, and they take up little room when folded for storage. The sling-style covers are easy to make, and only a small amount of fabric is needed. Make the covers from durable fabrics.

Director's chairs have a minimalist style that fits many decorative schemes.

Re-covering a director's chair

The back cover of a director's chair can be attached in two ways. The back may be fixed rigidly in place and the cover attached with tacks, or the back may be fixed so that it can be pivoted to different angles and the wooden struts slipped through channels in the cover. Calculate the amount of fabric required by measuring the existing back and seat covers. Add 2.5cm/1in on the long edges for hems. For the seat and a back cover attached with tacks, allow enough fabric to wrap around the wooden struts plus 2cm/¾in. For a back cover with channels, measure the channels on the original covers. Add 1.5cm/⅝in to each channel. The following instructions are for a chair cover that has a back cover with channels and a seat cover with channels with struts inside that are held in place between the wooden edges of the seat frame.

1 Cut out the new back and seat covers, including the allowances. To hem, press under 1cm/¾in then 1.5cm/⅝in on the long edges and stitch in place close to the pressed edges. Use strong thread and a

Making a chair back pocket

A gusseted pocket on the back cover of a director's chair is an extremely useful addition for all sorts of situations: you can slip a book or sunglasses into the pocket when the chair is used in the garden. Attach the pocket to the back of the cover before it is attached to the chair.

1 *Cut a rectangle of fabric 26 x 16.5cm/10¼ x 6⅝in. Press 1cm/⅜in under then 1.5cm/⅝in for the hem on the upper long edge. Stitch in place. Press 1.5cm/⅝in under on the remaining edges. Mark the long edges with a pin 5cm/2in in from the short pressed edges. Bring the pinned marks to the short pressed edges to form pleats. Press in place.*

2 *Position the pocket centrally on the back cover and stitch close to the side edges; do not catch in the pleats. Stitch again 6mm/¼in inside the first stitching. Stitch across the lower edges, securing the pleats in place.*

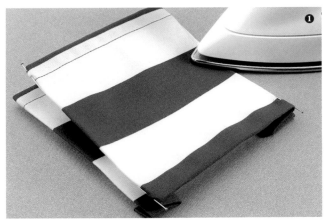

heavy-duty needle. If using deckchair canvas, stitch a single hem as the selvedges will not fray.

2 *Press under 1cm/⅜in on the short raw edges of the covers. Press the channels to the wrong side for the required depth. On the back cover, stitch close to the inner pressed edges. Place each seat strut inside a channel and use a zipper foot to stitch close to the strut.*

3 *Insert the back supports through the back channels and fix the seat securely in position.*

For a director's chair that has the cover attached with tacks, mark the edge of the fabric on the wooden struts of the seat with a pencil. Prise off the tacks and remove the old covers. If the old covers are in a suitable condition, press them flat to use as patterns. Hem the long edges. Press under 1cm/⅜in on the ends of the seat cover. Lie the chair on its side. Wrap the seat cover around one of the wooden struts and match one pressed edge to the pencil line. Hammer a tack into the fabric at the centre, close to the pressed edge. Hammer more tacks on each side of the first tack with the outer tacks close to the hemmed edges. Stretch the cover across the seat and fix the other edge. Press under 1cm/⅜in on the ends of the back cover. Wrap the cover around the back struts with the pressed edges along the inner edges. Working outwards from the centre, hammer tacks close to the pressed edges, having the outer tacks close to the hemmed edges.

armchair cover

Bring new life to an old and tatty armchair with a loose cover. A removable cover is not only an economical alternative to having furniture reupholstered – which can be an enormously expensive undertaking – but it is practical too, as it can be removed as often as you like for laundering.

Make sure that the chair is in reasonably good condition before you start. Piping will define the shape and give a professional finish, and a discreet zip fastening at one side of the back will enable the cover to be removed easily. The cover fits snugly under the chair with a drawstring. Loose covers for sofas are made in exactly the same way as for a chair, but the fabric

for the inner back will need to be joined. A centre seam is unsightly, so have a seam toward the side edges on each side of the inner back and the outer back of the sofa. The zip opening can be in one of these seams on the outer back.

Re-covering an armchair or sofa gives a dramatic new look. Fitting a loose cover also means it can be removed and washed easily.

Making the pattern

Time and care spent preparing the pattern will reward you with a perfect fit. The cover should fit smoothly but not be tight. The pattern must be made from fabric, as paper will not follow the chair's contours. An old sheet will do. If you do not have any old fabric to hand, buy a cheap remnant, such as calico, to use. Of course, if the chair already has a loose cover, simply take it apart and press flat to use as a pattern.

Look at the position of seams and grain lines on the chair as you will match them when making the pattern. So that the pattern-making fabric is not too bulky to handle, roughly cut it into pieces about 20cm/8in longer and wider than the area you are working on. Use T-pins to pin the fabric to the chair, as they are easier to see on the wide expanse of a piece of furniture than dressmaking pins.

1 *Remove any loose cushions. Mark the exact centre of the chair on the front and back with chalk; measure this accurately as the pattern will only be made for one half of the chair.*

2 *Follow the grain line to cut a straight edge along the length of the fabric for the inner back. Pin the straight edge to the chalk line. Smooth the fabric outwards from the pinned edge. If necessary, fold any fullness at the upper corner in neat pleats. Cut the fabric to shape so it lies flat. Allow the fabric to extend 10cm/4in over the seat*

for a tuck-in, and leave a 2.5cm/1in seam allowance on all other edges. Snip the seam allowance around the arm to help the fabric lie smoothly.

3 *Pin the fabric to the seat, matching a straight edge to the chalk line. Extend the fabric up the back and arm, and mark a 10cm/4in allowance at the back edge and taper it along the arm to 2.5cm/1in at the front. Trim to fit, allowing a 2.5cm/1in seam allowance on the front edge.*

4 *Pin the inner arm over one arm of the chair. Extend the fabric onto the seat. As before, mark a 10cm/4in allowance at the back edge and taper along the seat to 2.5cm/1in at the front. Trim to fit, snipping the curves and allowing a 2.5cm/1in seam allowance on the other edges.*

5 *Now pin the fabric to the outer arm, allowing 10cm/4in on the lower edge and 2.5cm/1in on the other edges.*

6 *Pin the fabric to an arm gusset and apron, matching to the chalk line. Trim, allowing 10cm/4in on the lower edges and 2.5cm/1in on the other edges.*

7 *Pin a straight edge to the chalk line on the back of the chair. Smooth the fabric outwards and trim it so it lies flat, allowing 10cm/4in at the lower edge and a 2.5cm/1in seam allowance on other edges.*

8 *Pin fabric to the back gusset, trim to fit, adding a 2.5cm/1in seam allowance on all edges. Snip the curves at the lower edge.*

9 *Make patterns for the shaped cushions. Label the pieces and mark the grain line, any pleats and balance marks. Label the straight centre edges as fold lines. Remove the pieces. Draw a line on the outer back pattern 24cm/9½in from the centre back. Cut along this line (for the zip). Add a 2.5cm/1in seam allowance when cutting out.*

Calculate the fabric needed by laying out the pattern pieces (see page 33).

Making the loose cover

Cut out the fabric pieces and label them on the wrong side with chalk. Pin the seams together on the chair. Clip the seam allowance at the curves. Unpin each section as you are about to stitch it, then try it on the chair again. Most chairs are not completely symmetrical, so it is important to keep trying the cover on and making adjustments to ensure a good fit. After stitching each seam, trim it to 2cm/¾in and neaten with a zigzag stitch or pinking shears.

1 Tack and press any pleats. Tack piping along seam lines on the right side. This chair has piping applied to the back gussets and arm gussets. If tacking by sewing machine, use a zipper or piping foot.

2 Stitch the upper end of the zip seams on the outer back for 20cm/8in, taking

a 2.5cm/1in seam allowance. Press the seams open. Stitch the inner back to the outer back along the upper edges. Press the seam towards the inner back.

3 Stitch the back gussets to the inner and outer back, starting 2.5cm/1in above the lower edge of the back gussets. Press the seams towards the gussets.

4 Stitch each inner arm to an outer arm. Clip the curves and press the seams open. Pin and tack then stitch the arm gusset to the front of the arms, starting 2.5cm/1in above the lower edge of the back gussets. Press the seams towards the gussets.

5 Pin then stitch each inner arm to the inner back and back gusset, starting at the outer back seam line and finishing

10cm/4in above the lower edge of the inner back. Snip the curves and press the seam open. Stitch the outer arms to the outer back.

6 Stitch the apron to the seat along the front edge.

7 Pin the inner back to the back edge of the seat, matching the centres. Stitch the back edge, starting and finishing 2.5cm/1in from the side edges of the inner back.

8 Pin the side edges of the apron to the arm gussets. Continue pinning the side edges of the seat to the lower edge of the inner arms. Stitch in place, starting 2.5cm/1in from the back edges of the inner arms and continuing the seams to the lower edge of the apron. Press the arm gusset and apron seams open.

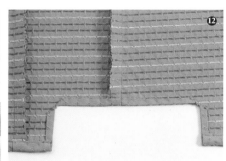

9 *Lie the lower, unstitched edges of the inner back and inner arms flat on the seat. Pin and stitch the lower edges to the seat between the seams to form the tuck-in.*

10 *Clip the corners and trim the back corners and seam allowance to 2cm/¾in. Turn the cover right side out and try it on the chair. Push the tuck-ins down the sides and back of the seat. Pin under the zip opening edges so they meet edge to edge. Remove the cover and insert the zips, having the opening ends 12cm/4¾in above the lower edge.*

11 *Slip the cover on the chair, fastening the zips. Snip the lower edge each side of the feet to 2cm/¾in below the chair base. Cut away the fabric and remove the cover. Stay stitch 2cm/¾in inside the cut corners then snip to the inner corners.*

12 *Turn under a 1cm/⅜in double hem on the stay stitched edges. Press under 1cm/⅜in then 2cm/¾in on the lower edges. Stitch close to the inner edges to form channels.*

13 *Insert a length of cotton tape or cord through the channel. Slip the cover on the chair, pull up the cord and tie the ends in a bow. See pages 94–95 if you need to cover box cushions for the chair.*

squab cushion

A tie-on cushion filled with a thin layer of foam adds some padding to a hard kitchen chair seat. Make a feature of the ties at the back of the cushion by binding them around the chair legs. You could use contrasting coloured ribbons for this if you wanted.

Making a squab cushion

1 To make a pattern, cut a piece of pattern paper or brown parcel paper larger than the seat. Place it on the seat with a weight on top. Fold the edges of the paper over the seat to define the shape. If necessary, snip the paper around the rails so it lies flat.

2 Remove the pattern. Add 1.5cm/⅝in seam allowance on all edges. Use the pattern to cut two cushion covers from fabric. Cut the seam allowance off the pattern. Tape the pattern to 1.2cm/½in thick foam with masking tape. Draw around the pattern with an air-erasable pen. Remove the pattern and cut out the foam.

3 Make up a length of piping for the side and front edges using the cover fabric (see page 46). Pin and tack the piping to the side and front edges on the right side of one cover, starting and finishing 1.5cm/⅝in from the back edges. With right sides facing, stitch the covers together, taking a 1.5cm/⅝in seam allowance and leaving a 27cm/11in opening to turn on the back edge.

4 Layer the seam to reduce the bulk. Snip the curves and corners. Lay the foam cushion on top of the cover within the seam. Reach inside the cover and pin the foam to the top cover. Turn the cover right side out and slipstitch the opening closed. Remove the pins.

5 Cut four 3.5cm/1⅜in wide bias strips 45cm/18in long for the ties. Fold the ties lengthwise in half with the right sides facing. Stitch, taking a 5mm/¼in seam allowance. Use a bodkin to turn the ties right side out. Turn in the ends and slipstitch closed. Place the cushion on the seat and pin the ties each side of the back rails. Sew securely in place then tie around the legs.

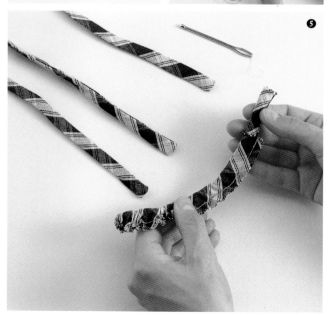

seat cover with skirt

Soften the look of a hard-seated chair with a skirted seat cover edged with a band of rich velvet. The cover is fastened to the chair with large mother-of-pearl buttons. Take a 1.5cm/⅝in seam allowance unless stated otherwise.

Making a seat cover

1 To make the pattern, cut a piece of pattern paper or brown parcel paper larger than the seat. Place it on the seat with a weight on top. Fold the edges of the paper over the seat to define the shape. If necessary, snip the paper around the rails so it lies flat. Measure the side and back edge of one back rail.

2 Remove the pattern from the chair. Add a 1.5cm/⅝in seam allowance on all edges. Use the seat pattern to cut one seat from fabric then use the pattern to make a 6cm/2¼in deep pattern of one back corner, which will make a pattern for a corner facing. Cut two corner facings from the lining fabric.

3 Stitch a 5mm/¼in hem on the long outer edges of the corner facings. With right sides together, stitch each facing to a back corner of the seat along the inner corner edges. Snip to the inner corners. Press the facings to the underside. Tack the raw edges of the fabric together.

4 Cut a strip of fabric for the front skirt that is the length of the front of the seat plus 3cm/1¼in x 16cm/6¼in. Cut two strips of fabric for the side skirts that are the length of the side of the seat plus the side of the back rail measurement plus 3cm/1¼in. With right sides facing, stitch the front skirt between the side skirts along the

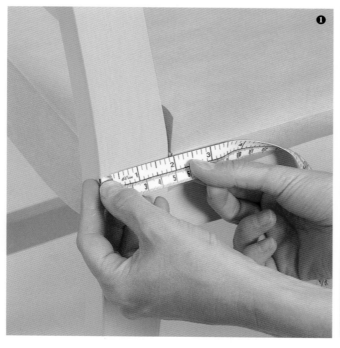

①

②

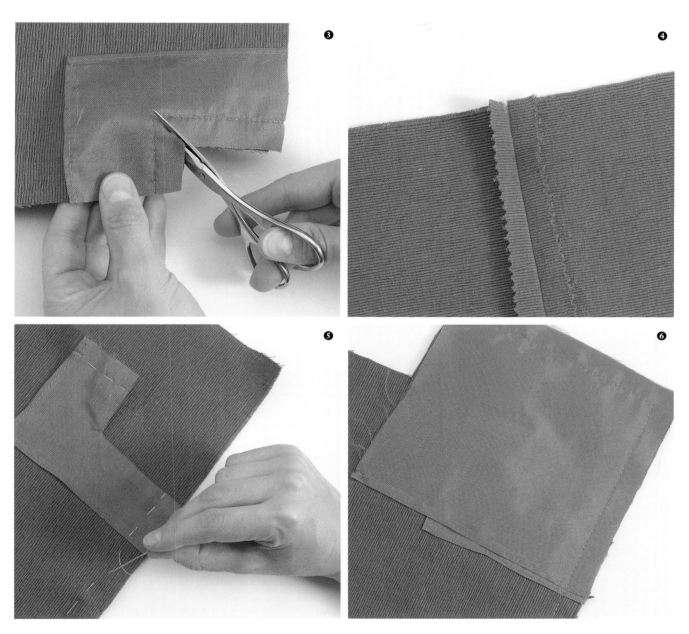

short edges, starting 1.5cm/⅝in below the upper long edges. Neaten the seams with pinking shears or a zigzag stitch. Press the seams open.

5 Matching centres, pin and tack the front and side skirts to the front and side edges of the seat with the right sides facing, pivoting the seam at the front corners and with the ends of the side skirts extending beyond the faced corners.

6 Cut two rectangles of lining 16 x 10cm/6¼ x 4in for side facings and two rectangles of lining 16 x 15cm/6¼ x 6in for the back facings. Stitch a 5mm/¼in hem on one long edge of each facing. With the right sides of the facings and skirt together, pin the side facings to the ends of the side skirts, enclosing the faced corners of the seat. Stitch the ends of the side skirts then the side and front edges of the seat. Neaten the seat seams with pinking shears or a zigzag stitch. Clip the corners, turn right side out and press the seat seam towards the skirt. Press the facings to the underside of the skirt.

7 Cut a strip of fabric for the back skirt that is the length of the
  back of the seat plus 22 x 16cm/8⅝ x 6¼in. Matching centres,
pin and tack the back skirt to the back edge of the seat with the right
sides facing, with the ends of the back skirt extending beyond the
faced corners. Stitch the ends of the back skirt and along the back
edge of the seat. Neaten the seat seam with pinking shears or a
zigzag stitch. Clip the corners, turn right side out, and press the seat
seam towards the skirt. Press the facings to the underside. Tack the
lower edges together.

8 Cut 5.5cm/2¼in wide strips of velvet; join the strips if necessary
  to fit the lower edge of the skirts with 1.5cm/⅝in extending at
each end. Resting the material on a towel so that the velvet is not
flattened, press under 1cm/⅝in on one long edge of the strips. With
the right side of the strips facing the wrong side of the skirts, stitch
the long raw edges of the strips to the skirts, taking a 5mm/¼in seam
allowance, with 1.5cm/⅝in extending beyond each end.

9 Fold the strips to the right side over the lower edge of the skirts.
  Turn in the raw ends and pin the long pressed edges to the skirts.
Stitch close to the ends and long pressed edges. Work a pair of
buttonholes 2cm/¾in in from the ends of the side skirts. Slip the
cover on the chair and mark the position of the buttons under the
buttonholes. Sew the buttons in place.

cube seat

A smart, fabric-covered foam cube is great for spare seating, and can double as a side table. Have a 46cm/1ft 6in square of foam cut to size professionally, and use medium-to-heavyweight fabric; avoid stretchy fabrics, as they will sag and the cover needs to be taut.

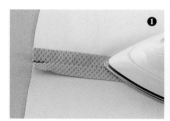

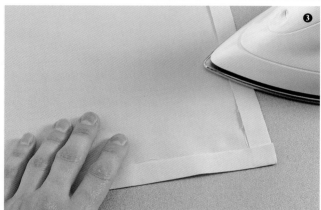

The fabric for covering the base does not have to match the main fabric, as it will not be seen, but it should be hardwearing. A neutral-coloured textured fabric has been used here, in contrast to the graphic straight lines of the cube. Take a 1.5cm/⅝in seam allowance throughout.

Making a cube seat

1 Cut a 49cm/1ft 7¼in square of fabric for the cube top, and four rectangles 50cm/1ft 7⅝in for the side panels. With the right sides facing, stitch the side panels together along the long edges, starting 1.5cm/⅝in below the upper edge. Press the seams open.

2 With the right sides facing, stitch the sides to the base, matching the seams to the corners. Pivot the fabric at the corners, then clip the corners. Press the seam towards the side panels.

3 Cut a 47cm/1ft 6⅜in square of fabric to cover the base. Press 1.5cm/⅝in under on the outer edges.

4 Slip the cover over the foam, positioning the seams at the edges. Pin the raw edges to the base of the foam with upholstery T-pins, folding under the fullness at the corners. Pin the base cover centrally on top. Slipstitch to the base with a double length of thread.

Tip
If you want to use the cube permanently as a side table, place a 46cm/1ft 6in square of hardboard inside to rest on top of the foam, then slip the cover on top.

tailored dining-chair cover

A set of good-quality chairs is an important furniture investment. If you want to ring the changes but avoid spending on new seating, make smart covers for a set of chairs that you have already or for a single chair that has become shabby or needs updating.

Making a tailored dining-chair cover

1 Cut a rectangle of fabric for the inner back that is the height of the inner back plus the depth of the back plus 5cm/2in by the width of the inner back plus twice the depth of the back plus 5cm/2in. Cut a rectangle of fabric for the seat that is the seat depth plus 5cm/2in by the seat width plus 5cm/2in. Matching the centres and with the right sides facing, pin the lower edge of the inner back to the back edge of the seat, taking a 2.5cm/1in seam allowance.

2 With the wrong sides facing outwards, place the inner back and seat on the chair. Fold the corners of the upper edge of the inner back diagonally with the right sides facing. Pin the fabric neatly along the corners of the chair.

3 For the front skirt, cut a square or rectangle of fabric that is the front width plus 5cm/2in by the seat height plus 6.3cm/2½in. With the right sides facing, pin the front skirt to the front edge of the seat.

4 Cut two squares or rectangles of fabric for the side skirts of the cover that are the side width measurement plus 5cm/2in by the seat height plus 6.3cm/2½in. With the right sides facing, pin the side skirts to the side edges of the seat. Snip the seam allowance on the inner back so it lies smoothly around the depth of the back, and pin the side skirts to the inner back. Pin the side edges of the side skirts and front skirt together.

5 For the outer back, cut a rectangle of fabric that is the outer back height plus 6.3cm/2½in by the back width plus 37cm/14½in. Mark the top and lower edge with a pin at the centre and 16cm/6¼in each side of the centre for the pleat.

6 With the right side face up, bring the outer pins to the centre of the fabric to form an inverted pleat. Press the pleat and tack across the upper edge.

❶

❷

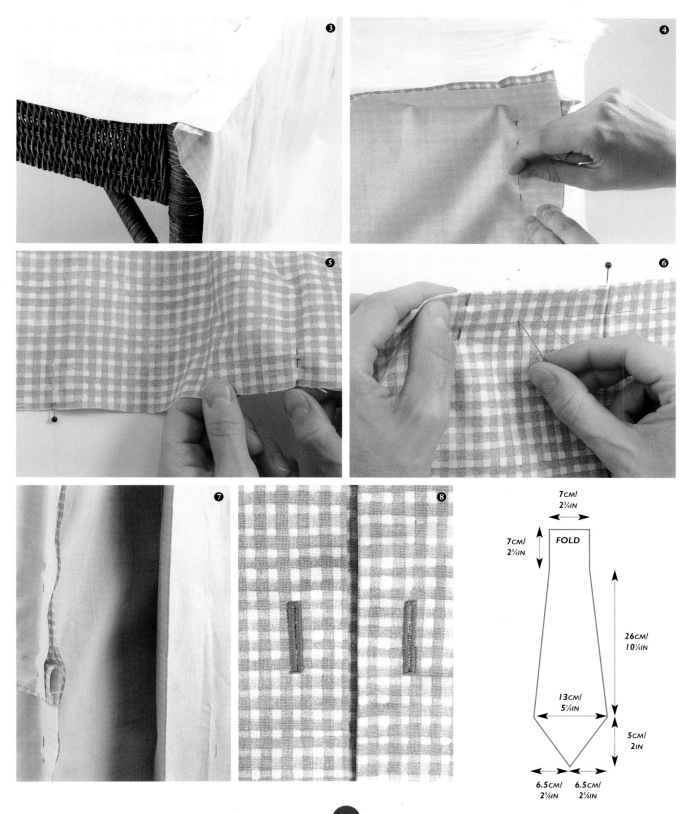

3

4

5

6

7

8

7CM/
2¾IN

FOLD

7CM/
2¾IN

26CM/
10¼IN

13CM/
5¼IN

5CM/
2IN

6.5CM/
2⅝IN

6.5CM/
2⅝IN

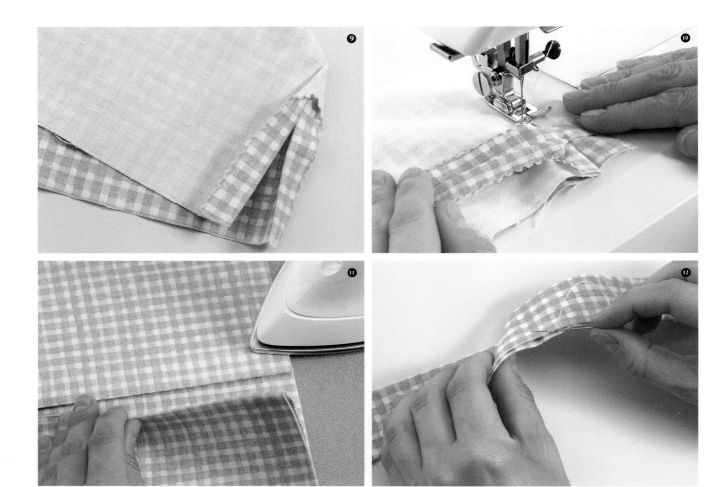

7 With the wrong side facing outwards, pin the outer back to the
inner back and side skirts, repinning the fit where necessary.
Use tailor's chalk carefully to mark all the seam lines where they
are pinned and where the seams intersect.

8 Mark the position on the pleat where you would like the tie
fastening to be. Unpin the outer back and skirts. On the right side
of the back, work a 2.5cm/1in long buttonhole 2cm/³⁄₄in in from
pressed edges of the pleat at the tie position on both edges of the
pleat where they meet.

9 With the right sides facing, stitch the corner seams of the inner
back as far as the outer back intersections. Again with the right
sides facing, pin and stitch the inner back to the seat, starting and
finishing at the side intersections. After stitching each seam, check
the fit and trim the seam allowance to 1.5cm/⁵⁄₈in with pinking shears.
Press the seams open.

10 With the right sides facing, stitch the front skirt between the side
skirts, starting at the seat intersections. Stitch the skirts to the
inner back and seat, pivoting the seam at the front corners of the seat.

11 Pin and stitch the outer back to the inner back and side skirts,
pivoting the seam at the upper corners. Slip the cover onto the
chair and pin up the hem. Remove the cover and trim the hem to
3cm/1¼in. Press 1cm/³⁄₈in under then 2cm/³⁄₄in on the lower edge,
and stitch close to the inner pressed edge. Re-press the pleat at the
lower edge.

12 Refer to the diagram to make a pattern from paper for the tie
(see page 121). Cut the tie from fabric. Fold lengthwise in half
with the right sides facing. Stitch the outer edges, taking a 1cm/³⁄₈in
seam allowance and leaving an opening to turn. Clip the corners and
turn right side out. Press then slipstitch the opening closed. Insert the
tie through the buttonholes and tie together.

top tables

Historically, beautiful table linen has been highly valued and handed down through the generations. Even today, handworked pieces are considered heirlooms and are brought out only for special occasions.

The style of table linen you choose will enhance the presentation of the food. Cosy, romantic dinners for two and full-blown formal dinner parties will both benefit from an ambient setting created by the table dressing. The making of tablecloths and napkins is so simple that time can be lavished upon their decoration.

Alternatively, their simplicity means that when made from easy-care fabrics, they can also be hard-wearing and used daily. On a practical level, a tablecloth and tablemats will help to protect the table from wear and tear and hot plates, or will hide an old, scruffy table. A table runner is a great way of accessorising an attractive table, and also offers some protection to the table, as items can be placed along it.

measuring and choosing fabrics

Fabric for table linen can be purely decorative – think of rich chenille or velvet on a small side table crammed with precious ornaments – or very practical, especially if it is to be used in the kitchen or the garden. Table linen is immensely versatile too, and you can really let your creativity shine through.

Choosing fabrics

Unless the cloth is to be purely decorative, fabric for tablecloths and napkins must be washable and ideally of a wide width, although fabric can be joined if necessary. Sheeting is a practical choice for a large table as it is washable, inexpensive and available in very wide widths. Special occasion table linen can be made from furnishing fabric which comes in wide widths, but bear in mind that it will probably need to be dry-cleaned. Any trimmings should have the same washing instructions as the fabric.

PVC-coated fabrics are great to use for kitchen and garden tablecloths because they are water-resistant, wipe-clean and do not need to be hemmed as the fabric does not fray. Simply cut to size and they are ready to use. Cut a fancy scallop or zigzag edge for a touch of fun. If you want to be able to see the table but feel it needs a covering to soften its lines, make the cloth from a soft, transparent fabric such as voile. Organza is too stiff to drape over the sides of the table, but can be used to make a runner.

Warm, earthy reds are said to stimulate the appetite so they are perfect colours for a cloth to set off a kitchen table.

126

Patchwork works well on table linens and it is less time-consuming than creating patchwork for bed covers and quilts. A patchwork made of handkerchiefs is very effective; one of colourful printed children's hankies, which are inexpensive, would be great for a child's party. Neaten seams with pinking shears or a zigzag stitch, or back the patchwork with a lining. Handkerchiefs are already hemmed, so do not need neatening. Use flat seams throughout and bind the tablecloth edges.

Fabric alone will not totally protect the table from hot plates and serving dishes. Cut a piece of heat-resistant fabric, such as an old blanket or heat-resistant rubberised cotton, which is available at furnishing fabric stores, to the size of the table top and lay it under the cloth.

Measuring up

If you already have a tablecloth the correct size, measure its length and width and add a 2.5cm/1in hem on square and rectangular cloths, and a 2cm/¾in hem on round cloths. Omit the hem allowance if the edges will be bound. If starting from scratch, measure the length and width of the table top, then the required drop. From the top of the table to the seat of a surrounding chair is a good drop for a cloth that will be sat at frequently. A decorative cloth can be floor-length or longer if it is a soft, lightweight fabric that you would like to drape onto the floor.

Decorating table linen

The large, flat expense of a tablecloth is the ideal medium for all sorts of needlework and fabric crafts such as embroidery and appliqué. There is a large range of fabric paints and pens available nowadays that are

hardwearing and washable. Painting fabrics is good fun, and very professional results can be achieved by stencilling and stamping onto fabric. Silk painting is a popular pastime and can be applied to runners or tablecloths for special occasions. Tie-dye takes on a modern slant when applied to silk, and lovely marbled effects can be created.

Before you embark on any embellishments, lay the cloth over the table and consider what will be placed on it. If it is to be used for meals, avoid positioning your design around the edges of the table top, where it will be hidden under plates and cutlery. Similarly, avoid the lower edges of the cloth if chairs are placed around the table and will obscure the design. A table runner or tablecloth for show

Floor-length tablecloths create a dramatic setting for special occasions and white sets off dining ware in a formal style.

only can have delicate decoration, as it will not suffer a lot of wear and will not need to be laundered often. Fine embroidery using metallic threads, cutwork and beading can be lavished on this sort of display. Work the design around items that will be placed on the table. Surround ornaments with an embroidered or beaded circular border on a round table top to isolate them and show them at their best. If displaying a particular collection, add a personal touch by stencilling or embroidering motifs to match the theme of the collectibles.

square and oblong tablecloths

A square or rectangular tablecloth is the easiest of soft-furnishing projects, and is a fast and simple way to co-ordinate a room and disguise an unsightly table: it can also be used for dining purposes. It can be made to any size you need and in any fabric and colourway.

Decide upon the finish that the tablecloth is to have. The simplest method is to hem all the edges. Ribbon, braid or fringing can then be added to the hemmed edges. If you prefer, the cloth can be bound in a contrasting colour. The binding can be narrow and subtle, or deep for a more dramatic effect. A lace edging adds a very pretty touch and is a good way of reusing an antique lace edging if its original tablecloth is very worn or stained. A small square tablecloth looks good on top of a long circular cloth, or alone

on a side table. It should hang at least 10cm/4in down the sides of the table. A tassel sewn to each corner is an exotic finishing touch.

Avoid a centre seam if the fabric needs to be joined: it would be noticeable and could unbalance the crockery. Have the entire width of fabric across the table and a half to full width at each side. Join the widths with flat felled seams, taking a 1.5cm/⅝in seam allowance. Remember to allow extra fabric for matching patterns. If the fabric is just a little narrower than

needed, make a feature of this by having a contrasting band of fabric at each end.

Remember that fabrics that have other purposes can be used for tablecloths. A throw or sumptuous bedcover that no longer suits the bedroom can be cut to size to use as a tablecloth; avoid fluffy fabrics, as the fibres may get into the food. Curtains and saris can also be adapted. Create a stylish and understated tablecloth with a few remnants of co-ordinating dress fabrics joined edge to edge with flat felled seams.

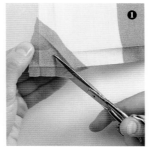

Making a mitred hem

1 Add a 2.5/1in hem to each side of the tablecloth when cutting out. Press 1cm/⅜in under then 1.5cm/⅝in on the edges. Open out the fabric at the corners and cut diagonally across the allowance 6mm/¼in from the corner.

2 Turn the diagonal edge under. Refold the hem. The diagonally folded edges should meet edge to edge. Slipstitch the mitred edges together, then stitch close to the inner edges of the entire hem.

Making a knotted fringed edge

1 Use a loosely woven fabric for this effect. Cut out the tablecloth
very carefully along the grain lines. Use a long needle gently to pull
away the threads along one edge, working on one thread at a time.
Continue until it is at least 7.5cm/3in deep; repeat round the cloth.

2 Divide the strands into sections 1.5cm/⅝in wide and mark the
divisions with pins. Knot each section together just below the cloth.

Making a lace border

Add a 5cm/2in hem to all edges of the tablecloth if using
antique lace, as it is weighty and will need a deep hem for
support. Otherwise, add a 2.5cm/1in hem on all edges.

1 Stitch a mitred hem as described opposite. Press the tablecloth
and lie it out flat. Place the lace edging around it, overlapping
the lace at the corners, if possible matching the lace design at
the overlaps. Tack the lace edge-to-edge to the tablecloth and at
the overlaps. Stitch in place with a shallow zigzag stitch or
slipstitch. Cut away the excess lace where it overlaps.

Making rounded corners

1 The easiest way to bind the edges of a square or rectangular
tablecloth is to round the corners so that the circumference
can be bound in one go, rather than mitring the binding at the
corners. (See pages 144–145 for mitring binding.) Cut out the
tablecloth without adding any allowances to the edges. Place a
plate on one corner and draw around it at the corner with tailor's
chalk or an air-erasable pen. Cut out then bind the edges.

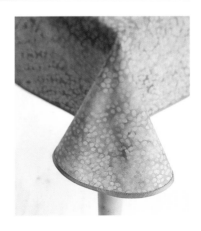

round tablecloths

Round and oval tablecloths are very attractive and emphasise the curved shape of a table. The best ways to finish the edges are to bind them or have a hem faced with bias binding (see page 45 for binding the edge). The cloth can have a turned-under hem, but avoid this if the tablecloth is small and of thick fabric, as it will be too bulky.

Joining widths
The fabric may need to be joined to make a large tablecloth. Cut the fabric the diameter of the tablecloth plus allowances. If using two widths of fabric, cut one width lengthwise in half. Stitch the widths together with the half widths each side of the complete width using flat felled seams, taking a 1.5cm/⅝in seam allowance.

Trim an equal amount from each side edge of the tablecloth to make the entire width the tablecloth diameter plus allowances. Fold into quarters and cut out the circle.

Oval tablecloths
To make a pattern for an oval tablecloth, place a large piece of paper on the table and weight it in the centre.

You may find that you need to join pieces of paper to get the size for a large table. Fold the paper over the edges of the table. Remove the paper and draw along the fold. Add the drop and any allowances to the circumference, then cut out to use as a pattern. The edges of an oval tablecloth can be finished using any of the methods used on a round cloth.

Making a faced hem

Open out the narrow folded edge of a length of 1.2cm/½in wide bias binding. Cut the end diagonally and turn it under. With right sides facing, pin the opened-out edge to the tablecloth, matching the raw edges. Stitch along the crease line, cut the other end of the binding diagonally, and overlap the ends. Press the binding to the underside and slipstitch in place.

Making a plain hem

The raw edges will need to be eased so that they lay flat. Pin up the hem. Tack close to the folded edge – machine tack rather than tack by hand (just set the machine to the longest stitch). Machine tack 6mm/¼in from the raw edge, stitching through the hem only. Gently draw up the last row of stitching so the hem lies flat. Press, then turn the raw edge under along the eased tacking and machine stitch in place. Remove the first row of tacking.

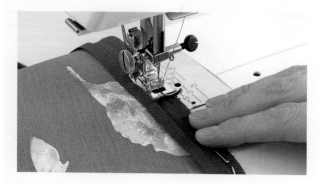

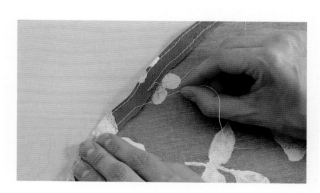

Cutting out a round tablecloth

1 *Measure the diameter of the table and the drop required for the cloth. Add twice the drop to the diameter plus 3.8cm/1½in for a hem. Add a 1.2cm/½in allowance on a faced hem. No allowance is needed on a bound edge. Cut a square of fabric to the cutting measurements and fold it into quarters. Cut a square of paper to the size of the folded fabric to make a pattern.*

2 *Tie a length of fine string to a drawing pin and fix it to one corner of the paper. Tie the other end around a pencil, holding the pencil upright on the next corner. Draw a quarter circle and cut out along the curved line.*

3 *Pin the pattern to the fabric, matching the corner of the pattern to the folded corner of the fabric. Cut out the tablecloth.*

Making a deep border

A deep, luxurious border on a round tablecloth really shows off the curved shape and is a good way of combining contrasting fabrics, maybe to link different colours used in a room.

1 *Measure the diameter and drop of the tablecloth. Cut a square of paper, the sides measuring the radius and drop of the cloth. Follow step 2 of cutting out a round tablecloth to draw a pattern. Decide how deep you would like the border to be, and draw it with the string and pencil compass. Cut out the sections.*

2 *Using the pattern above add a 1.5cm/⅝in seam allowance on the curved edge of the tablecloth and inner edge of the*

border and ends of the border. Add a 6mm/¼in seam allowance on the outer edge of the border. Cut out the pattern, fold the fabric into quarters to cut the tablecloth, and cut four borders.

3 *Join the borders with flat felled seams and press them open. Stitch to the tablecloth, then neaten seams with a zigzag stitch. Make a faced hem on the border.*

garden tablecloths

Hard-wearing, easy-care fabrics are a must for table linen that will frequently be used out of doors. PVC is the obvious practical choice for al fresco eating and a square cut with pinking shears does not fray. A robust washable fabric will work well too, since food, grass and mud stains are always possible in the garden.

Tablecloth weights

Blustery weather can spoil eating outside, as a sudden breeze can make the tablecloth start to lift off! Weighting down the cloth will anchor it in place. Readymade clip-on weights can be attached to the corners and removed for washing, or you could add discreet pockets to the corners on the underside to conceal weights. A practical alternative is to make a tablecloth with patch pockets attached that can hold cutlery and napkins and be weighted to keep it in situ. These can be added to an existing tablecloth.

Tablecloth with corner pockets

❶

❷

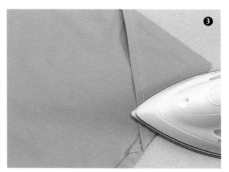
❸

1 Cut out the tablecloth, adding a 2cm/³⁄₄in hem on all edges. Cut two 24cm/9½in squares of fabric. Fold the squares diagonally in half and cut along the folds to give four triangular pockets. Press 1cm/³⁄₈in under then 1.5cm/⁵⁄₈in on the diagonal edges and stitch close to the inner edge. Take care not to stretch the fabric.

2 With the right sides facing and matching the raw edges and corners, stitch each triangle to a corner of the tablecloth, taking a 2cm/³⁄₄in seam allowance. Clip the corners, turn right side out and press.

3 Press 5mm/¼in under then 1.5cm/⁵⁄₈in on the remaining edges of the tablecloth. Stitch close to the inner pressed edges, continuing the stitching along the straight edges of the pockets. Slip pebbles or curtain weights into the pockets to weight them.

Tablecloth with patch pockets

Make a square or rectangular tablecloth (see pages 128–129). Slip the cloth onto the table and decide on the size of the patch pockets. They will be at two opposite ends of the cloth; if the table is rectangular, they should be at the short ends. Bear in mind what you are likely to put in the pockets and allow 2.5cm/1in at the lower edge for the weights. The pockets on this tablecloth are 21cm/8¼in wide and 27cm/10½in deep. Add 1.5 cm/⅝in to the side and lower edges of the pocket and 3cm/1¼in to the upper edge and then cut out.

1 *Press under 1cm/⅜in then 2cm/¾in on the upper edge of the pockets. Stitch close to the inner pressed edge. Press under 1.5cm/⅝in on the side and lower edges.*

2 *Pin the pockets to opposite ends of the cloth 18cm/7in above the lower edge. Stitch close to the side and lower edges then 5mm/¼in inside the first line of stitching.*

3 *Measure the distance between the inner rows of stitching on the side edges of the pocket. Cut a length of curtain chain weight three times the length of the measurement. Fold into thirds and drop to lay along the bottom of the pocket. Catch the chains in place with a few stitches at each end.*

4 *With a zipper or piping foot, stitch across the pockets, 2.5cm/1in above the lower edge, enclosing the weights.*

133

fitted tablecloth

Give a table a smart streamlined look with a fitted cover: this is especially effective on a small display table. Avoid heavyweight fabrics for this project because they will look bulky and inelegant. A piece of glass can be cut to fit the table top and so protect the fabric surface from dust.

Gathered skirt

A gathered skirt is cut in the same way as a pleated skirt, but just gather the upper edge instead of pleating it. If making a cover for a square or rectangular table, snip the skirt where it meets the corners of the cover top so it lies smoothly.

Fitted overcloth

A shallow fitted overcloth can be made to go over an ordinary tablecloth. This looks very effective, especially when made in contrasting firm fabric over a floaty fabric tablecloth. Cut out the cover top as above, then cut the skirt the circumference measurement plus 3.8cm/1½in by the drop plus 4cm/1⅝in. Taking a 1.5cm/⅝in seam allowance, join the ends of the skirt, then stitch the skirt to the cover top. Hem the lower edge.

If you prefer a shaped hem, cut two skirts and join the ends to form two rings. With the right sides facing, stitch together along the lower edges in scallops or zigzags. Trim the seam allowance and turn right side out. Tack the upper edges together and stitch to the cover top.

Fitted cloths particularly suit round tables. Cover with a piece of glass cut to the table top, or a fitted overcloth in a contrasting pattern.

Making a round fitted tablecloth

Although any shape table can have a fitted cloth, they do
particularly seem to suit round or oval tables. This cover has
a pleated skirt, which can be gathered if you prefer. To make
a pattern for the top, turn the table upside down and draw
around it on paper, adding a 1.5cm/⅝in seam allowance to the
circumference. Cut out the pattern. Measure the drop of the
table cover. This can be floor-length, or if the fabric is soft and
lightweight, you may prefer it to bunch up flamboyantly on the
floor – allow extra length for this, but make sure the table is
not placed so the excess fabric could trip anyone up.

1 *Use the pattern to cut the top from fabric. Measure the
circumference of the table top. Cut the skirt twice this measurement
plus 3cm/1¼in by the drop plus 4cm/1⅝in. Join widths of fabric with
flat felled seams if necessary, remembering to add seam allowances if
this is the case. With the right sides facing, stitch the ends together with
a flat felled seam, taking a 1.5cm/⅝in seam allowance.*

2 *Pin the upper edge into 1.2cm/½in deep pleats 2.5cm/1in apart,
all lying in the same direction.*

3 *With the right sides facing, pin the skirt to the top, adjusting
the pleats if needed. Stitch in place, taking a 1.5cm/⅝in
seam allowance.*

4 *Turn right side out and slip the cover over the table. Adjust the top
seam allowance towards the skirt. Check the length and turn up a
double hem, then remove the cover and stitch the hem. Replace the cover
on the table. Although the seam allowance may lie naturally on the table
surface, adjust it toward the skirt so the top of the cover sits smoothly on
the top of the table. Carefully press the top of the pleats if you wish.*

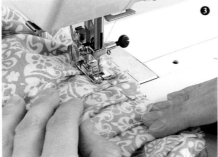

runners

Because they are used mainly for decorative purposes, table runners can give
free rein to your creative ideas. Only a narrow length of fabric is needed, so you
may find remnants of exotic and possibly expensive fabric at a discounted price
that would look fantastic and really brighten up a plain table.

A runner can extend over the edges of a table, or just lie on top if you prefer. Any fabric is suitable, depending upon the effect you wish to achieve, and because runners are small items, they can be changed, maybe to mark the seasons or a festive occasion. The dining room table or sideboard are obvious places to display a runner, but also consider one on a table or chest in a cool, tiled bathroom, which will help to make it homely. A runner would also make a good background to a display of perfume bottles in a bedroom. Damaged or stained antique table linen can be salvaged and the unusable areas cut off and discarded, leaving a length of finely embroidered fabric that just needs hemming or to have a decorative ribbon or lace edging added. A long silk, velvet or chiffon scarf is an instant glamorous table runner.

A decorative runner is a fast way to suggest a theme in a room and to pull a distinctive look together. Hem a strip of rich brocade and add a tassel at each corner to offset an antique piece of furniture; it will also help to protect the surface if ornaments are displayed on top. The same technique can be used on a strip of pale organza, providing a totally different, contemporary look.

Fray a length of rustic hessian and fasten shells to the ends with thick linen thread to give a beachcomber effect. Glue or sew chunky cabouchon jewellery stones at random along the edges of a hemmed length of vibrant silk for some quirky opulence, or sew feathers to a linen runner for display on a kitchen dresser. On a practical level, use a runner to hide a nasty stain or dent on the surface of a table. A layer of curtain interlining or a strip cut from an old blanket, applied to the underside of a runner, offers some protection if hot plates are placed on top.

Table runners add a distinctive splash of style to everyday pieces of furniture. Since they're purely decorative, they offer an ideal opportunity to be as creative as you feel.

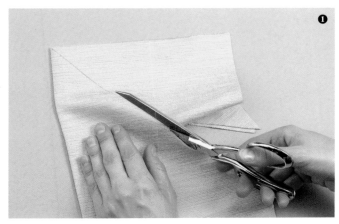

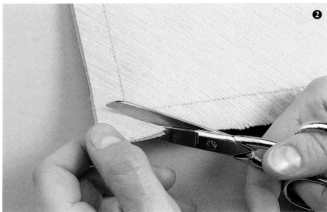

Making a bead-fringed runner

Runners do not have to be rectangular: pointed ends look good when suspended over the ends of a table. A densely beaded fringe makes it extra special.

1 Decide upon the length of the runner. Cut a strip of fabric the length of the runner plus 4cm/1½in by 38cm/1ft 3in. Fold one end lengthwise in half and cut to a point on the fold. Fold the pointed end on top of the opposite end and cut to match. Use the runner as a pattern to cut a matching runner from lightweight lining.

2 With the right sides facing, stitch the runners together, taking a 1.5cm/⅝in seam allowance and leaving a 15cm/6in gap for turning. Clip the corners and turn right side out. Press and slipstitch the opening closed.

3 Pin the tape of a length of bead fringing under the pointed end, turning under the ends of the tape and folding neat mitres at the corners. Oversew the tape to the underside of the runner. Repeat at the other end.

napkins

Napkins are the easiest items of table linen to make. Their small size is ideal for decorative finishes that would be too laborious to apply to anything larger, such as a tablecloth, so you can really let off your creative steam. Make napkins from absorbent easy-care fabrics that wash well and do not fade.

Most napkins are square and range in size from 30.5cm/1ft for teatime napkins to 61cm/2ft for dinner napkins: 40cm/1ft 4in is a size that suits both occasions. The napkin edges can be bound, hemmed, frayed, edged with lace or ribbon, or shaped with a zigzag satin stitch. Work any embroidery in one corner of the napkins before cutting out. Add 2cm/¾in hems for hemmed napkins. To round the corners and make binding the edges simpler, place an upturned glass on a corner and draw around it, cut out the curved shape and repeat on each corner.

Corded hem

1 Cut out the napkin including 3cm/1¼in hems. Press a 1.5cm/⅝in double hem on all edges. Set the sewing machine to a wide, open zigzag stitch. Starting halfway along one side, lie two lengths of contrast-coloured stranded cotton embroidery thread 1.2cm/½in in from the edge. Starting about 7.5cm/3in from the ends of the embroidery threads, zigzag in place with the embroidery threads running along the centre of the pressing foot. Pivot at the corners.

2 Before you reach the start of the stitching, use a large-eyed needle to take the embroidery threads to the underside then continue zigzagging, overlapping the start of the stitching. Knot the embroidery thread ends together and insert the needle into the hem to lose the ends. Cut off the excess threads.

Straight bound edges

1 Cut out the napkin; no seam allowances are needed. Cut two lengths of 2.5cm/1in wide bias binding the same length as the sides of the napkin and two lengths 2.5cm/1in longer than the sides of the napkin. Press the bindings lengthwise in half.

2 Slot one edge of the napkin into a shorter length of binding. Tack in place, sandwiching the napkin between the binding. Repeat on the opposite edge. Stitch close to the inner edges. Apply the longer bindings to the remaining edges in the same way, turning the ends under. Stitch close to the inner edges.

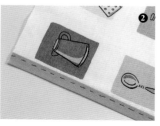

Scalloped edge

1 For a 40cm/1ft 4in square napkin, cut a strip of paper for a template 40 x 3.8cm/1ft 4in x 1½in. Draw a line lengthwise along the centre, and starting 2cm/¾in from one end, use a compass to describe a semicircle with a 2cm/¾in radius. Continue describing semicircles along the centre line to form a row of eight scallops. Cut out the scallops.

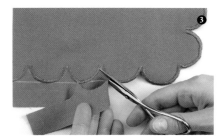

2 Cut a 45cm/1ft 6in square of fabric. Use an air-erasable pen or tailor's chalk to draw a 2.5cm/1in deep margin around the outer edges. Butt the scalloped edge of the template up to the drawn line on one edge, and draw around the scallops with the air-erasable pen or tailor's chalk. Repeat on the other edges.

3 Cut four 45 x 6cm/1ft 6in x 2⅜in strips of stitch-and-tear interfacing, and pin them under the edges of the napkin to reinforce the stitching. Set the sewing machine to a wide, close zigzag stitch and thread the machine with machine embroidery thread. On the right side, work the zigzag stitch along the scalloped lines. Carefully tear away the interfacing. Use a small, sharp pair of scissors to trim away the excess fabric.

Lace edge

Choose a flat lace edging about 2.5cm/1in wide. Neaten the raw edge of the lace with a zigzag stitch. Cut out the napkin with a 1cm/⅜in hem. Stitch a 6mm/¼in deep double hem on all edges. Pin the straight edge of the lace under the hemmed edges, folding under the fullness at the corners in neat mitres. Overlap the ends of the lace at a corner for neatness and cut off the excess lace. Stitch in place.

Frayed edge

Cut the napkin to size from a loosely woven fabric, cutting carefully along the grain lines. Machine zigzag stitch 2.5cm/1in in from the edges. Pull out the threads as far as the stitching on all edges. Remove the threads one at a time to prevent tangling.

table mats

Fabrics for table mats need to be durable and washable, especially if they are to be used daily. Mats made from sturdy, heavyweight fabrics will help protect the table, and a layer of curtain interlining will give added protection from heat and also slightly cushion the crockery.

Because only small amounts of fabric are needed, making a set of table mats is a good way of using up leftover tablecloth fabric. A table mat should be large enough to take a complete place setting: 48 x 35.5cm/1ft 7in x 1ft 2in is a standard size. For just a dinner plate, which is usually 25.5cm/10in diameter, a 35.5 x 30.5cm/1ft 2in mat would be suitable, but measure your own dinner service as the size may be different.

The easiest method of finishing a mat that has a layer of curtain interlining is to bind the edges with bias binding;

there is no need to add a seam allowance. If you prefer to bag out the mat, add 1.5cm/⅝in seam allowances to all edges and carefully trim away the interlining in the seam allowances after stitching, to reduce the bulk. Add a 2.5cm/1in hem to single-layer mats.

To fuse practicality with a decorative touch, make a centre panel for the table mat from a hardwearing fabric, then add a strip of pretty fabric to the side edges – check that all the fabrics have compatible washing instructions. Either hem the outer edges or bag out the mat with a lining. For a quick and

pretty look, hem a rectangle of linen and sew a row of pearl buttons along one side edge; linen can be washed at high temperatures.

Cut shaped mats from PVC for children's mealtimes – a chunky car or chubby teddy is very popular, and the mats just need to be wiped clean after use. Alternatively, make a mat from fabric featuring their favourite cartoon character, and fix a layer of transparent plastic on top with a popper at each corner. The plastic can be wiped clean and removed when the fabric mat needs washing.

Bias-bound quilted table mat

 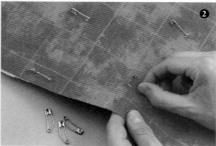 

Ready-quilted fabric is available from fabric departments and can be used for table mats, but it is very easy to quilt fabric yourself, which means that you have a wider choice of fabrics to use. Rounded corners are simple to bind.

1 *To quilt the fabric yourself, cut two rectangles of fabric and one of curtain interlining for the front and back 50 x 38cm/1ft 7¾in x 1ft 2¾in. Sandwich the interlining between the fabric pieces, with the right sides facing outwards.*

2 *Draw a grid of 5cm/2in squares with tailor's chalk on the top fabric. Use curved basting pins to pin the layers smoothly together.*

3 *Starting at the centre, stitch along the vertical drawn lines, stitching down one line,*

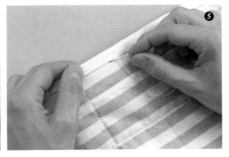

5 Clip the corners to reduce the bulk in the seam allowance. Turn the binding to the underside of the mat. Pin and slipstitch the binding in place.

up the next and so on. Turn the mat and stitch the horizontal lines in the same way. Cut the mat to 48 x 35cm/1ft 7in x 1ft 2in. To round the corners, place a glass upside down on one corner and draw around it with an air-erasable pen. Repeat on the other corners.

4 Open out the narrow edge of 2.5cm/1in wide bias binding. Turn under one end diagonally and pin the binding to the outer mat edge with the right sides facing, taking a 6mm/¼in seam allowance. Overlap the binding ends, stitching along the foldline of the binding.

dressing table

The classic kidney-shaped dressing table looks right in either a traditional or a retro-style bedroom, depending upon the fabric used. Original dressing tables can be made-over or bought plain and ready to be upholstered. They are usually made of chipboard and generally have a curtain rail under the table top.

Making a dressing table cover

Remove any original covering if you are re-covering an existing dressing table. Check the condition of the rail and replace it if necessary. This top has a deep pleated frill over a gathered skirt, which has a front opening. Take a 1.5cm/⅝in seam allowance throughout.

1 *Make a pattern for the table top by turning it upside down and drawing around it on paper, adding the seam allowance. Use the pattern to cut the top from fabric, centering any pattern design if necessary. Cut one top from lining. (Inexpensive lightweight cotton fabric would be suitable for the lining if you want to economise on the main fabric.)*

2 *Measure the circumference of the table top. Cut 27cm/10½in wide strips of fabric for the top frill; the strips will be joined end to end and the finished length should be twice the top circumference. Add seam allowances for joining the strips. Join the strips end to end with flat felled seams to form a ring. Press under 1cm/⅜in then 1.5cm/⅝in on one long edge. Stitch close to the inner pressed edge.*

3 *Pin the upper raw edge of the fabric into 1.2cm/½in deep pleats 2.5cm/1in apart, all laying in the same direction. With the right sides facing, pin the frill to the top. Adjust the pleats if needed, and stitch in place.*

4 *With right sides facing, pin and stitch the lining to the fabric top, sandwiching the frill: leave a 25cm/10in gap to turn through. Trim the seam allowance and snip the curves. Turn right side out and slipstitch the opening closed.*

5 *Measure the drop of the skirt from the top of the rail to the floor. Cut widths of fabric for the skirt that are the drop of the skirt plus 5cm/2in, the widths will be joined to make a continuous length which should be twice the top circumference plus a 2.5cm/1in hem at each end. Add 1.5cm/⅝in seam allowances for joining the widths. Join the widths with flat felled seams.*

6 *Press under 1cm/⅜in then 1.5cm/⅝in on the ends and lower edge of the skirt. Slipstitch or machine stitch close to the inner pressed edges. (See page 57 for how to make mitred corners.)*

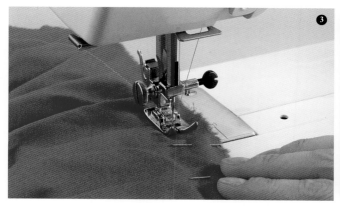

7 Press the upper edge to the wrong side for 2.5cm/1in. Pin standard curtain tape along the upper edge, enclosing the raw edges. Turn under the ends of the tape and stitch close to the edges, taking care not to catch in the cords.

8 Pull up the cords to gather the fabric to fit around the table. Knot the free ends of the cords and adjust the gathers evenly. Slip curtain hooks through the slots in the tape, placing one at each end and at 7.5cm/3in intervals.

9 Hook the skirt onto the rail, positioning the opening edges at the front. Slip the fabric top onto the top of the table. Cut the seam allowance off the paper pattern for the top and take it to a glazier to use as a template to cut a piece of glass to fit the table top. Make sure that you have the edges bevelled. Place the glass carefully on top of the dressing table.

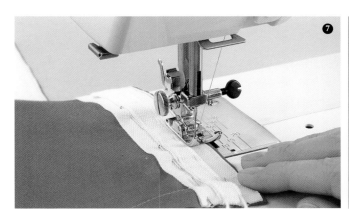

bound-edge napkin

Make a set of napkins with crisp mitred borders to smarten the dinner table. The borders work well in a contrasting colour, and could pick up the colour scheme of your china or tablecloth. This napkin is 40cm/1ft 4in square, but you could make a larger one.

Making a bound edge napkin

1 *Cut a 40cm/1ft 4in square of fabric for the napkin, and two 80cm/2ft 8in long, 7.5cm/3in wide straight strips of fabric in a contrasting colour for the binding. Join the lengths, taking a 6mm/¼in seam allowance to make a continuous length. Press the seam open. Press the binding lengthwise in half with the wrong sides facing. Open out the binding and press the edges to meet at the centre.*

2 *Open out the binding at one end and press 6mm/¼in under. With the right sides facing and starting approximately 5cm/2in from one end, stitch the binding to one edge of the napkin, taking a 2cm/¾in seam allowance stitching along the fold line, finishing 2cm/¾in from the adjacent edge.*

3 *Pivot the binding to lie along the adjacent edge, folding the binding at a 45-degree angle from the corner. Mark the end of the previous stitching with a pin and stitch from this mark, finishing 2cm/¾in from the next adjacent edge. Continue all the way around the napkin.*

4 *Press the binding outwards from the napkin and turn it to the underside along the centre fold line, then pin in place. Press along the mitres with your finger. Slipstitch the pressed edges along the seams.*

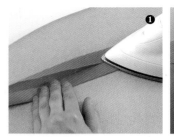

tasselled table runner

Create an air of sophistication at a dinner with an elegant silk table runner edged in sparkling organza. A long silver tassel sewn to each point emphasises the metallic threads in the organza and hangs elegantly off each end of the table.

Making a tasselled table runner

The runner is 1.2m/3ft 11¼in long. Take a 1cm/⅜in seam allowance throughout.

1 Cut a strip of dupion silk 108cm x 27cm/3ft 6½ x 10⅝in for the runner, and cut two strips of organza for the side borders 95 x 14cm/3ft 1⅜in x 5½in. Refer to the diagrams below to cut the ends to points. Use the diagram to cut four end borders from organza.

2 Mark the dots onto the end borders with an air-erasable pen 1cm/⅜in inside the corners. With right sides facing, stitch the end borders together in pairs along the notched ends between the dots. Trim the seam allowance to 6mm/¼in. Clip the corners and press the seams open. Finger-press the seams at the points that are difficult to reach with the tip of the iron.

3 With the right sides facing, stitch the end borders between the side borders, inside the dots. Clip the corners and press the seams open. Trim the seam allowance to 6mm/¼in. Press the border in half with the wrong sides facing, matching the seams and raw edges. Machine-tack the raw edges together.

4 With the right sides facing, pin the border to the runner, matching the seams to the corners. Stitch in place, pivoting the stitching at the dots. Neaten the seam with a zigzag stitch or pinking shears, and press the seam towards the runner. Sew a tassel to the pointed tips of the runner.

Tip

To avoid a noticeable ridge around the edge of the silk caused by pressing, after you have pressed the seam towards the runner, run the tip of the iron around the edge of the runner under the seam allowance.

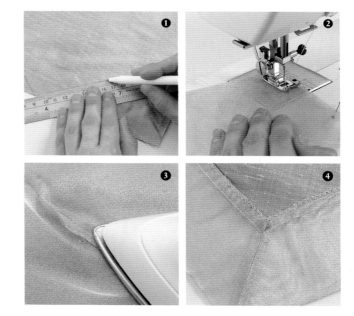

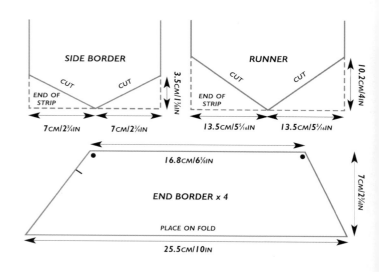

SIDE BORDER
CUT   CUT
END OF STRIP
3.5CM/1⅜IN
7CM/2¾IN   7CM/2¾IN

RUNNER
CUT   CUT
END OF STRIP
10.2CM/4IN
13.5CM/5⅜IN   13.5CM/5⅜IN

16.8CM/6⅝IN
END BORDER x 4
7CM/2¾IN
PLACE ON FOLD
25.5CM/10IN

fitted table cover

Put a shabby coffee table to new use by making a neat fitted cover – the deep pleats at the front make the interior accessible for storing books and other items. The top is edged with co-ordinating piping, either your own or readymade. Use fabrics that hold their shape.

Making a fitted table cover

Measure the width and depth of the table top, and measure the drop of the table. Use a flat felled seam if you need to join fabric for the skirt. Take 1.5cm/⅝in seam allowances throughout.

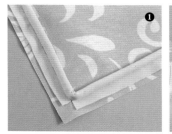

1 *Cut a square or rectangle of fabric for the top that is the table width plus 3cm/1¼in by the depth plus 3cm/1¼in. Pin and tack piping to the outer edge on the right side, snipping the seam allowance of the piping at the corners. Join the piping on the back edge (see page 46).*

2 *For the back and sides skirt, cut a rectangle of fabric twice the table depth plus the width, plus 21cm/8¼in by the drop plus 6cm/2⅜in. Cut a rectangle or square for the front skirt the table width plus 21cm/8¼in by the drop plus 6cm/2⅜in. To hem, press 2cm/¾in under then 2.5cm/1in on one long lower edge of the skirts. Stitch close to the inner pressed edges.*

3 *Stitch the front skirt to the back and sides skirt with French seams to form a continuous length. With the right side face up, mark both edges of the front skirt with a pin 9cm/3½in from one seam. Fold and press the front at the pin mark to lie flat on the side skirt. Tack across the upper edge and repeat on the other end of the front skirt.*

4 *With the right sides facing, pin and tack the skirt to the top, matching the pleats to the front corners. Snip the skirts at the corners. Stitch in place using a zipper foot, pivoting the stitching at the corners. Clip the corners and neaten the seam with a zigzag stitch or pinking shears. Press the table cover, adjusting the top seam towards the skirt. Turn right side out and slip the cover over the table.*

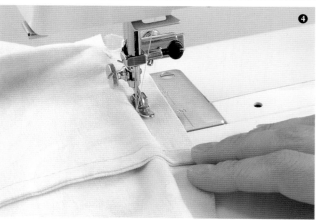

FEATURE PROJECT 4

cutlery roll

Keep cutlery safely together in a padded cutlery roll. This simple roll is very practical and can be made to match a picnic hamper or tablecloth for use in the garden, or to keep in a beach bag for holidays. This is a great project for using up remnants of fabric.

Making a cutlery roll

A lightweight pale blue cotton chambray is used to line the cutlery roll, and the edges are bound with a deeper blue denim. The front of the cutlery roll is made from a woven ikat fabric in toning colours, and the fabrics have the same laundering instructions, which must be taken into consideration when combining different fabrics.

1 Cut one rectangle of fabric for the cutlery roll from the main fabric, lining and 113g/4oz wadding 30 x 26cm/1ft x 10 ¼in. Round off the corners by drawing around an upturned glass, and cut along the curved lines. Cut the pocket from the main fabric 30 x 13cm/12 x 5¼in.

2 Press 6mm/¼in under then 1cm/⅜in on one long edge of the pocket. Stitch close to the inner pressed edge. With the right sides face up, pin the pocket to the lower edge of the lining, matching the raw edges. Cut the pocket corners in a curve to match the lining.

3 To form the individual pockets, use an air-erasable pen or tailor's chalk to divide the pocket into quarters parallel with the short edges. Stitch along the divisions. Stitch back and forth a few times at the neatened edge of the pocket to reinforce. Sandwich the wadding between the main fabric front and the lining, with the right sides facing outwards. Tack the outer edges together.

4 From denim, cut two 5cm/2in wide bias strips, one 25.5cm/10in long for the strap and one 7.5cm/3in long for the D-ring holder. Fold lengthwise in half with the right sides facing and stitch the long edges, taking a 6mm/¼in seam allowance. Press the seam open. Turn right side out with a bodkin and press. Turn in one end of the strap and slipstitch it closed. With the right sides uppermost, tack the raw end to the centre of one short side of the front. Slip two 2cm/¾in D-rings onto the D-ring holder. Pin the raw ends together and tack on top of the strap.

5 Cut a 3.8cm/1½in wide bias strip of denim 110cm/1ft 9in long, joining strips if necessary. Use a bias binding maker to turn the raw edges under (see page 45). Open out one long edge and pin it to the outer edges of the cutlery roll, turning an end under to start and cutting off the excess. Stitch along the foldline. Turn the binding to the inside and slipstitch in place.

storage solutions

There cannot be many people lucky enough not to have a problem with storage. Lack of space, too many items and a tendency to hoard are all familiar problems. This chapter suggests ingenious ways of making the most of neglected space around the home, and of creating stylish containers that can store all sorts of items and you will be proud to display.

Have a ruthless clear out before embarking on any of the storage projects, as only then can you see exactly what is needed and where it should be kept. Items not constantly needed, such as spare bedding and seasonal clothing, can be kept in fabric bags in less accessible areas, such as in the loft or under the bed. Items that are used regularly can have smart covers to keep off the dust, or can be kept in a matching set of attractive bags.

drawstring bags

Drawstring bags are fantastically useful, and if you make yourself a set in pretty toning colours, you'll wonder how you managed without them. They can be used in the bedroom to hold make-up and jewellery and in the bathroom for cotton wool balls and cotton buds. They are essential for keeping children's rooms tidy too!

Do not be deterred by the thought of drawstring bags! Although the concept is the same, they do not have to look like the dreary bags you kept your games shoes in at school. They are very easy to make and can be custom-made to any size for storing all sorts of things: a row of matching bags hung on a peg rail can be of practical use in the kitchen, a child's room or bathroom.

Line the bags in waterproof fabric, and they can be used as a washbag or beach bag. Jazz the bags up with trimmings such as fringing or bead edging, and they may even encourage an untidy teenager to tidy his or her belongings away. Mini-sized bags made of velvet or silk can hold jewellery, and large bags made from ticking could hold laundry. Choose light-to-mediumweight fabrics.

Trimming your bag

If you wish to embellish the bag, decorate the rectangles before making up. Create an understated Swedish-style bag from gingham, using the chequered fabric as a guide for embroidering a cross-stitch heart or monogram on one rectangle.

Children can decorate their own bags. Cut the rectangles from calico, then supervise the children to create their own masterpieces on the fabric using fabric markers, which are like large felt-tipped pens. Follow the manufacturer's instructions to fix the drawings, then make up the bags.

To make a washbag, cut two rectangles of fabric 39 x 25.5cm/1ft 3½in x 10in and two of waterproof fabric 28 x 25.5cm/11¼ x 10in for the lining. Tack the lining to the wrong side of the fabric pieces matching the side and lower edges, then make up as described above.

Drawstring bags keep clutter out of sight. Choose a pretty floral pattern (right) or embellish a rich velvet bag with sumptuous fringing (left).

Making a drawstring bag

This medium-sized drawstring bag is very versatile and is a good size for storing footwear or clothing. Take a 1.5cm/⅝in seam allowance throughout, and simply change the dimensions of the rectangles to make a bag that will match your exact requirements.

1 Cut two rectangles of fabric 63 x 38cm/2ft ¾in x 1ft 3in. With the right sides facing, stitch the bags together along the long side edges and lower short edge, starting and finishing 14cm/5½in below the upper edges. Clip the corners.

2 Press the seam open, and press the side edges above the seam open. Neaten the seam with pinking shears. Press 1.5cm/⅝in under then 6.5cm/2⅝in on the upper edges for the drawstring channels. Pin in place.

3 Stitch 6mm/¼in above the lower pressed edge then 3cm/1¼in below the upper pressed edge to form the drawstring channels. Turn the bag right side out.

4 Sew the end of an 80cm/2ft 7½in length of cord to a bodkin and thread through the channel from the left-hand side of the front channel and out of the right-hand side of the back channel. Repeat with another length of cord through the right-hand side of the front channel, emerging through the left-hand side of the back channel. Knot the cord ends together and adjust them so the knots are hidden in the channels.

lined baskets

Baskets come in all shapes and sizes, and a complementary lining adds a nice touch as well as giving protection to the contents. Linings can be attached to the baskets with ties threaded through the weave of the basket or tied around the handles. A lined basket is useful in lots of situations.

Lining a square or rectangular basket

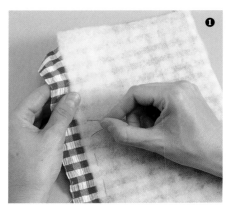

Choose light-to-mediumweight fabrics, and use a straight-sided basket for the best results. This lining for a picnic basket is padded to give some protection to breakables. The tie fastenings can be in a contrasting colour if you wish.

1 Measure the height of the inside of the basket, then measure the length of the sides at the top of the basket, again on the inside. Cut a strip of fabric for the side panel that is the length of the four sides plus 3cm/1¼in by the height measurement plus 5cm/2in. Cut a strip of 56g/2oz wadding that is the length of the four sides plus 3cm/1¼in by the height measurement plus 1.5cm/⅝in. Tack the wadding to the side panel 2.5cm/1in below the upper edge.

2 Cut one square or rectangle of fabric and 56g/2oz wadding for the base that is the length of one side plus 3cm/1¼in by the length of an adjacent side plus 3cm/1¼in. Tack the fabric and wadding base together along the outer edges.

3 With the right sides facing, stitch the short edges of the side panel together, taking a 1.5cm/⅝in seam allowance. Trim away the wadding in the seam allowance. Press the seam open, taking care not to squash the wadding flat. Press 1cm/⅜in under then 2.5cm/1in on the upper edge. Stitch close to the inner pressed edge.

4 With the right sides facing, pin the side panel to the base, taking a 1.5cm/⅝in seam allowance and snipping the panel at the corners so the fabric lies flat. Stitch in place, pivoting the seam at the corners. Trim away the wadding in the seam allowance, and neatly clip the corners.

5 Cut eight bias strips of fabric for ties 46 x 3.8cm/1ft 6in x 1½in. Fold lengthwise in half with the right sides facing and stitch the long edges, taking a 6mm/¼in seam allowance. Turn right side out with a bodkin. Turn in the ends and press flat. Slipstitch the ends closed.

6 Slip the lining into the basket and mark the position of the ties, such as one at each side of the corners. Remove the lining and match the centre of each tie to the stitching line of the hem on the wrong side of the lining at the positions marked. Stitch back and forth a few times across the centre of the tie to attach it securely.

Lining round and oval baskets

Make a paper pattern of the base by placing the paper inside the basket and tracing the base edges. Remove, and add a 1.5cm/⅝in seam allowance to the circumference. Use the pattern to cut a base from fabric. On the inside, measure the circumference around the top of the basket and the height.

Cut a strip of fabric for the side panel that is the circumference measurement plus 3cm/1¼in by the height measurement plus 5cm/2in. Join the ends, taking a 1.5cm/⅝in seam allowance. Stitch a 3.8cm/1½in hem at the upper edge. Gather the lower edge and stitch to the base. Attach four ties to the upper edge, either equidistant apart or at the handles.

spare duvet bolster bag

Spare duvets never seem to have a home of their own, and often get packed away at the top of the airing cupboard, where they can get musty. Sew a simple bolster bag to keep your spare bedding neat, tidy and clean. It can be displayed and hung up on a rail, put away in a cupboard or stowed neatly under the spare-room bed.

Extra bedding for overnight guests takes up a lot of space, considering that it is probably not used regularly. If you have little storage space, storing bedding in an attractive container allows it to become part of the furniture, not hidden away, thereby freeing valuable storage space for other items. A large bolster bag holds a spare duvet and can be used as a generous squashy cushion – fold the duvet in half, roll it up and push it into the bolster. A drawstring top gives easy access.

The bolster design is very versatile, and there are endless variations to suit all occasions. Make it in luxurious fabric with a gold cord fastening to use in a lounge, or in soft, faded floral print with ribbon drawstrings to match a feminine bedroom, where it could store holiday clothes or spare linens. It could alternatively be used as a laundry bag in the bathroom: make the bag from towelling, and instead of stitching a channel, fix metal eyelets to the upper edge to thread with cord. Made from a vibrant fabric, it could hold lots of toys, and made shallower, it becomes a handy beach bag for towels and lotions.

Keep spare duvets dust-free in an easy-to-make bolster bag – this will make sure they are fresh for your next visitor.

158

Making a bolster bag

Make the bolster bag from light-to-mediumweight fabric, bearing in mind that lightweight fabrics are easier to draw up than thick fabrics. Take 1.5cm/⅝in seam allowances throughout.

1 *Cut two rectangles of fabric for the bolster 127.5cm x 66cm/ 4ft 2in x 2ft 2in. Pin the bolsters together along the long edges with the right sides facing, forming a tube. Stitch the side seams, leaving a 2.5cm/1in gap 5.6cm/2¼in below the upper edge for the drawstring channel.*

2 *Press the seams open and neaten them with pinking shears or a zigzag stitch. Press 2cm/¾in under then 3.8cm/1½in on the upper edge for the drawstring channel, and pin in place. Stitch close to the upper edge then 2.5cm below the upper edge to form the channel.*

3 *To make a pattern for the base, use a pair of compasses to describe a 43cm/1ft 5in diameter circle on paper. Cut out the circle to use as a pattern to cut one base from fabric. Fold the base into quarters and snip into the circumference at the folds. Fold the lower edge of the bag in half and snip the fabric at the folds.*

4 *With the right sides facing, pin and stitch the base to the bolster, matching the snipped notches and the notches to the seams. Neaten the seam with pinking shears or a zigzag stitch. Turn right side out.*

5 *Using a bodkin, thread a 170cm/5ft 8in length of cord through the channel, entering and emerging through the same hole. Knot the ends together, then fray the cord below the knot. Thread another length of cord through the other hole in the same way.*

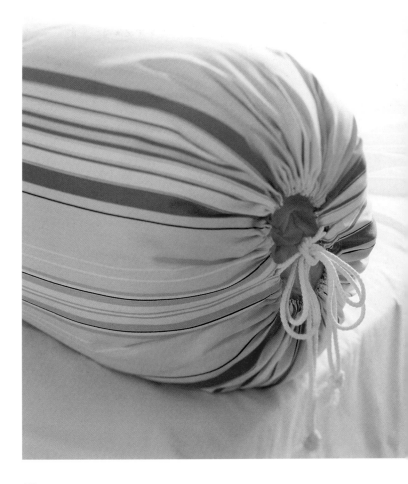

Tip

If you wish to trim the bag with ribbon, stitch one bolster seam first. Stitch ribbons or braid in bands across the piece, then stitch the other seam.

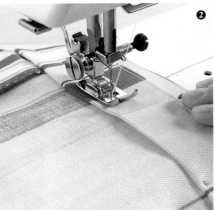

clothes covers

Clothes covers protect clothing from snagging on other items and keep them clean. Covers made in closely woven natural fabrics keep dust out but allow the clothes to breathe. Plastic-coated fabrics are ideal for covers used for travelling as they will protect against bad weather, but do not store clothes in them for long periods.

Making a plain clothes cover

This simple cover will hold a full-length outfit. A hanging loop at the lower edge can be slipped over the clothes hanger hook for carrying. Use a 110cm/3ft 7in zip that has been cut from a continuous length.

1 *Refer to the diagram on page 161 to make a pattern for a cover on paper. Cut out the pattern and use it to cut two fronts and one back to the fold from fabric.*

2 *With right sides facing, tack the centre front seam, taking a 1.5cm/⅝in seam allowance. Stitch the seam for 2cm/¾in at the upper end and 18cm/7in at the lower end then press open.*

3 *With the front lying face down and starting at the base of the zip, place a 110cm/3ft 7in zip face down centrally along the tacked seam. Pin and tack the zip in position. A zip cut from a continuous length will be unfinished at the top so open the top of the zip a little and pin the top teeth under the seam allowances so the zipper does not slip off before stitching.*

4 *Using a zipper foot on the sewing machine and with the front right side up, stitch the zip in place 8mm/⅜in from the tacked seam and across the base end of the zip. Continue the stitching to the upper edge of the fronts. Remove the tacking stitches.*

5 *Cut a strip of fabric 17 x 6cm/6¾ x 2¼in for the hanging loop. Press 1cm/⅜in under along the long edges. Press the strip lengthwise in half and stitch close to both pressed edges. Pin and tack the ends 3cm/1¼in each side of the centre front seam at the lower edge on the right side.*

6 *Open the zip. Pin and stitch the front and back together with right sides facing, taking a 1cm/⅜in seam allowance. Clip the corners and snip the curves, then turn right side out and press. Topstitch 1cm/⅜in from the outer edges.*

Tip

If you would prefer a shorter basic length plain cover, make the pattern to the suit cover length and omit the hanging loop.

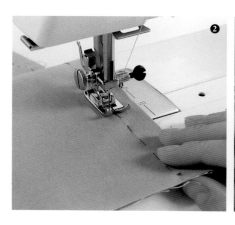
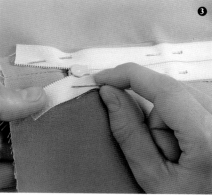
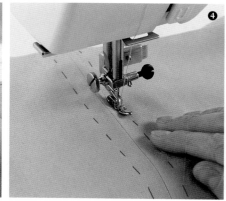

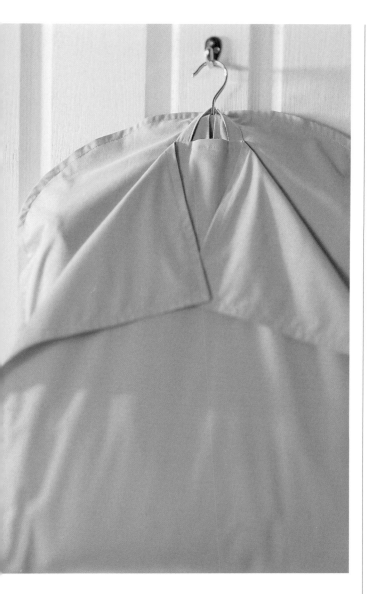

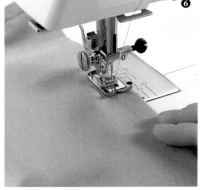

Making a gussetted suit cover

This clothes cover has a generous gusset, making it deep enough to hold a suit or a few lightweight garments. Use a 96cm/3ft 2in zip that has been cut from a continuous length.

1 *Refer to the diagram to make a pattern for a cover on paper. Cut out the pattern and use it to cut two fronts and one back to the fold from fabric. With the right sides facing, tack the centre front seam, taking a 1.5cm/⅝in seam allowance. Stitch the seam for 3.8cm/1½in at each end and press the seam open.*

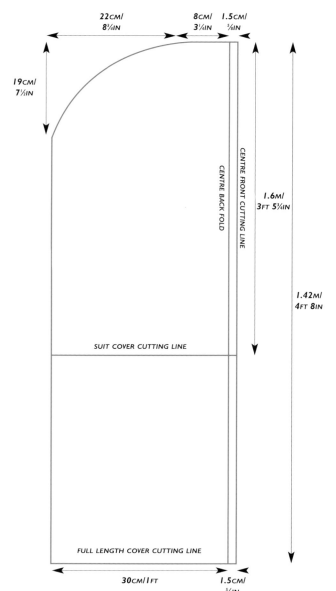

22CM/ 8¾IN   8CM/ 3¼IN   1.5CM/ ⅝IN

19CM/ 7½IN

CENTRE BACK FOLD

CENTRE FRONT CUTTING LINE

1.6M/ 3FT 5¾IN

1.42M/ 4FT 8IN

SUIT COVER CUTTING LINE

FULL LENGTH COVER CUTTING LINE

30CM/1FT   1.5CM/ ⅝IN

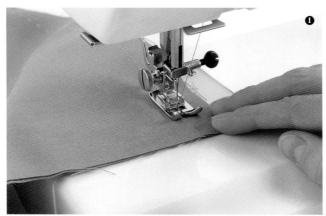

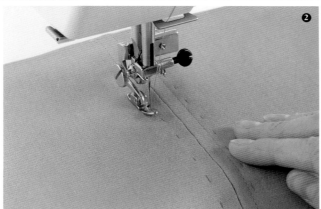

2 With the front lying face down, place a 96cm/3ft 2in zip centrally face down along the tacked seam. Pin and tack the zip in position, pinning the top teeth under the seam allowances so the zipper does not slip off before stitching. Using a zipper foot on the sewing machine and with the front right side up, stitch the zip in place 8mm/⁵⁄₁₆in from the tacked seam and across the ends of the zip. Remove the tacking stitches.

3 Measure the outer edge of one half of the front, 1cm/⅜in in from the raw outer edges. Cut two 8cm/3¼in wide strips of fabric for the gusset that are the front measurement plus 2.5cm/1in. With the right sides facing, stitch one end of the gussets together to make one long length, taking a 1cm/⅜in seam allowance. Neaten the seam with pinking shears and press open. Press 6mm/¼in under then 1cm/⅜in on the raw ends, and stitch close to the inner pressed edges.

4 Pin and stitch the gusset to the front with the right sides facing, with the ends of the gusset meeting end to end at the top of the centre front seam, taking a 1cm/⅜in seam allowance. Snip the gusset at the corners so the fabric lies smoothly. Stitch a few times over the top of the centre front seam to reinforce it.

5 Open the zip, then pin and stitch the gusset to the back in the same way. Clip the corners and neaten the seams with a zigzag stitch or pinking shears. Turn right side out.

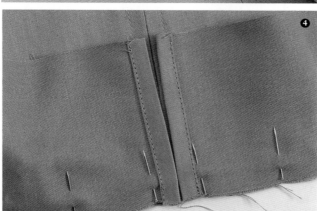

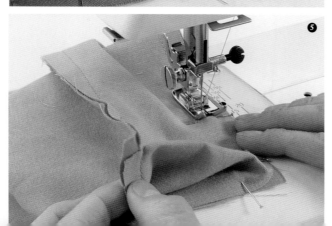

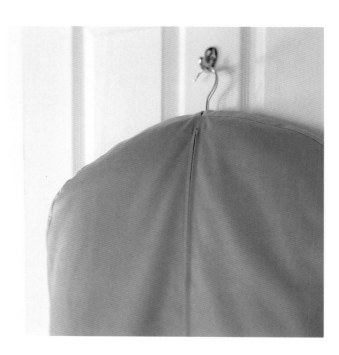

underbed case

The empty space under the bed is often neglected as a storage area, yet it is ideal for storing spare bed-linen and out-of-season clothing. The items need to be concealed inside containers to protect them from dust: a slim fabric case with a deep gusset can hold many items. You will need two 1m/3ft 3in zips.

Making an underbed case

 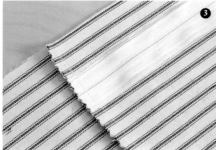 

1 Cut a strip of fabric for the base gusset 197cm x 14.5cm/6ft 6in x 5¾in and strip of fabric for the lid gusset 197cm x 5.5cm/6ft 6in x 2¼in. Press 1.5cm/⅝in under on one long edge of both pieces, and mark the centres of the pressed edges with a pin.

2 Pin two 1m/3ft 3in zips under the pressed edges, with the top ends 1cm/⅜in each side of the centre pins, positioning the pressed edges against the zipper teeth. Zips cut from a continuous length will be unfinished at the top, so open the tops a little and pin the top teeth under the pressed edges so that they do not slip off before stitching. Using a zipper foot, stitch close to each side of the zip.

3 Cut a strip of fabric for the back gusset 107 x 17.5cm/ 3ft 6¼in x 7in. With the right sides facing, stitch the ends of the zippered gussets to the ends of the back gusset, taking a 1cm/⅜in seam allowance, and starting and finishing the seams 1cm/⅜in from the long edges. Neaten the seams with pinking shears or a zigzag stitch. Press toward the back gusset.

4 Partly unzip the zips to turn right side out. Cut two rectangles of fabric 107 x 47cm/3ft 6¼in x 1ft 6½in for the lid and base. Open out the back seam at the top of the lid gusset. With the right sides

facing, pin the back gusset to one long edge of the lid, then continue pinning the lid gusset to the lid. Snip the gusset at the front corners of the lid so the fabric lies smoothly. Stitch in place, taking a 1cm/⅜in seam allowance, and pivoting the seam at the corners. Stitch the base gusset to the base in the same way. Neaten the seams with pinking shears or a zigzag stitch. Turn right side out.

shoe caddy

There is not always enough space to store shoes at the bottom of a wardrobe and a shoe caddy is a practical solution. It can be hung on a wall or the inside of the wardrobe door. Make the caddy from a hardwearing fabric such as canvas, heavyweight calico or mediumweight denim.

Making a shoe caddy

This caddy has pockets for twelve pairs of shoes. Metal eyelets are fixed to the upper corners so that the caddy can hang on hooks off the floor.

1 Cut three pocket strips from fabric 130 x 27cm/4ft 3in x 10⅝in. Press 1cm/⅜in then 1.5cm/⅝in to the wrong side on the upper raw edges and stitch close to the inner pressed edges. Refer to the diagram (see page 248) to fold the pleats along the solid lines to meet the broken lines. Pin and tack then press the pleats.

2 Press 1.5cm/⅝in to the wrong side on the lower raw edge and tack in place.

3 Cut a rectangle of fabric 1m x 58cm/39 x 1ft 10¾in for the caddy. With right sides uppermost, lay the strips across the front, matching the short raw edges to the long edges of the caddy. Pin the lower strip 2cm/¾in above the lower edge. Pin the middle and top strips leaving a 6cm/2⅜in gap between all the pocket strips.

4 Tack the side and lower pressed edges of all the strips. Topstitch close to the lower pressed edges of the pocket strips then 5mm/¼in above the first stitching.

5 To form separate pockets, stitch between the broken lines of the pleats. Stitch back and forth a few times at the top of the stitching to reinforce the seam.

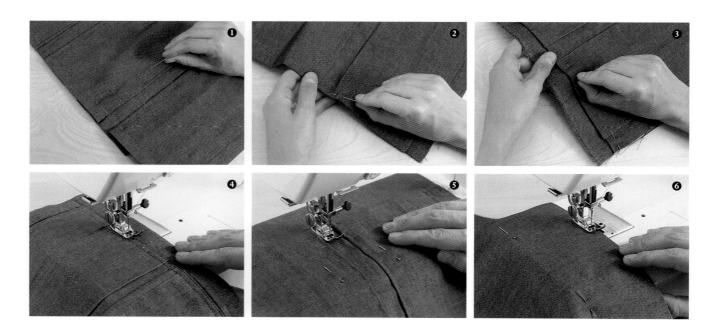

6 Cut a strip of fabric 58 x 11cm/1ft 10¾in x 4¼in for a facing. Press under 1.5cm/⅝in on the long lower edge. With right sides facing, stitch the facing to the upper edge taking a 1.5cm/⅝in seam allowance. Press the facing to the wrong side and topstitch close to the upper edge then 5mm/¼in below the first stitching.

7 Stitch close to the lower edge of the facing then 4cm/1⅝in above the lower pressed edge to form a casing. Slip a 51cm/1ft 8in long length of 2.5cm/1in wide and 4mm/³⁄₁₆in thick stripwood into the casing.

8 To bind the side and lower edge of the caddy, cut two straight 6cm/2½in wide strips of fabric 1m/39in long for the side edges and one strip 61cm/2ft long for the lower edge. Press under 1cm/⅜in on the long edges of the bindings then press lengthwise in half with the wrong sides facing.

9 Slip one long edge of the caddy inside a side binding with the lower edges level. Turn under the end of the binding at the upper edge and tack together through all the layers. Repeat on the other side edge. Stitch close to the inner pressed edge of the bindings.

10 Slip the lower edge of the caddy inside the lower binding with the binding extending at each end. Turn under the ends and tack through all the layers. Stitch close to the inner pressed edge of the binding. Remove the tacking. Lay the batten centrally in the casing. Fix an eyelet 2.5cm/1in inside each top corner to hang on hooks.

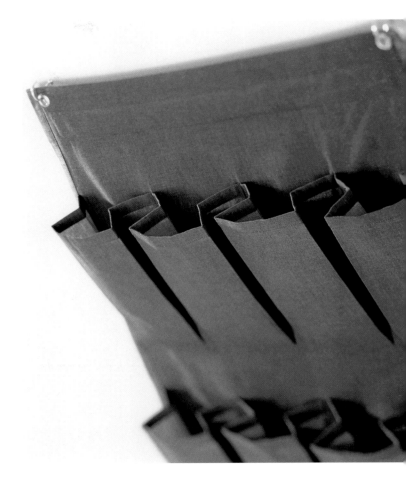

Tip
The caddy can also be made from waterproof fabric to store toiletries in the bathroom or for gardening equipment in the garden shed. Adapt the size of the pockets to custom-make it for its contents.

shelving hideaways

Most of us have areas in the home that would benefit from being kept hidden – an alcove of dishevelled books or a bathroom shelving unit of mismatched toiletries that need to be concealed from view. A blind is great for hiding all sorts of clutter because you can just draw it up for access.

Swedish blinds are not just for windows. Attached to shelving they are ideal for hiding clutter and can be made to fit the decorative scheme of a room.

Making a shelving cover

Make this smart cover to hang in front of an open cupboard, alcove or shelving unit. The cover is hung from a wooden batten fixed to the upper edge, and a row of eyelets along the side edges is slipped onto hooks so the cover can be held open at different levels. The cover has a contrast lining, so it is reversible to ring the changes and can be hooked open to reveal the underside.

1 *Fix a 1.2cm/½in thick, 2.5cm/1in wide wooden batten to the upper edge of the open area. It should extend at least 2.5cm/1in on each side of the open area. Staple the stiff section of sew-on touch-and-close tape to the batten. Measure the length of the batten and the drop of the cover from the top of the batten. For the cover, cut one rectangle or square of the main fabric and one of contrast fabric that is the length of the batten plus 3cm/1¼in by the drop plus 3cm/1¼in.*

2 *With the right sides facing, stitch the covers together, taking a 1.5cm/⅝in seam allowance and leaving a gap to turn on the upper edge. Clip the corners, turn right side out and press.*

3 *Tack and stitch the corresponding length of touch-and-close tape to the upper edge of the cover.*

4 *Following the manufacturer's instructions, fix a 1.5cm/⅝in diameter metal eyelet 2cm/¾in within the lower corners. Use an air-erasable pen to mark eyelet positions 2cm/¾in within the side edges approximately 23cm/9in apart. Fix the eyelets in place. Press the cover onto the batten. Fix cup hooks to the wall or wood surround under each eyelet.*

screens

Not surprisingly, screens are enjoying a renewed popularity. They add a regal touch to a room and can hide clutter or divide a room, concealing gym equipment or a home office. Plain wooden or MDF screens, available ready to be painted or covered in your choice of fabric, come with different shaped tops.

Old screens can be found at secondhand shops and if they are scruffy and battered, covering them with a smart fabric will make them look brand new and disguise imperfections. Alternatively, a carpenter could make one to your specifications.

Most fabrics are suitable. Sheer fabrics need to be mounted on a plain, closely woven fabric and treated as one thickness if covering a solid screen. If you wish to use a luxurious but expensive fabric, use it on the side of the screen that faces into a room, with a cheaper co-ordinating fabric on the other side. Extra fabric will be needed to match printed patterns across the screen.

A screen with frames instead of solid panels can have tension wires strung across and sheer fabric panels suspended between them. Alternatively, lightweight fabric panels can be attached to the top and bottom frame with touch-and-close tape.

Covering a solid screen

If you are re-covering an old screen, remove any old fabric covering and trimmings. Lever out tin tacks: if any are impossible to remove, hammer them into the screen so they do not snag you or the fabric. Separate the screen panels by unscrewing the hinges.

Give careful thought to the positioning of printed fabrics. If the screen is to be stood with one panel more prominent than the others, place the main pattern on the prominent panel. Lay the screen panels side by side flat on the floor and lay the fabric on top. Tuck the edges under the panels. Try different arrangements to see what looks best: centring the design is the obvious choice, but try placing it off-centre as an alternative. This screen is slightly padded with wadding on one side; pad both sides if you prefer.

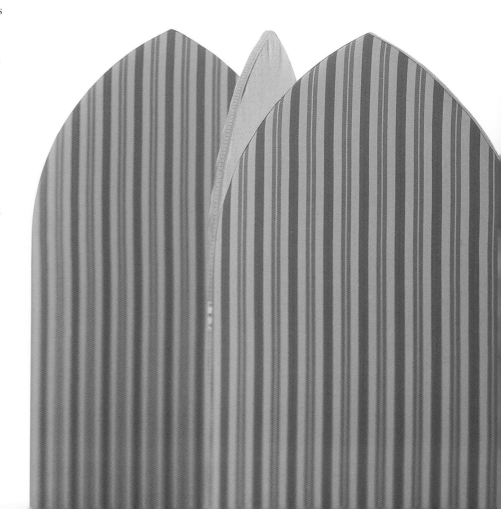

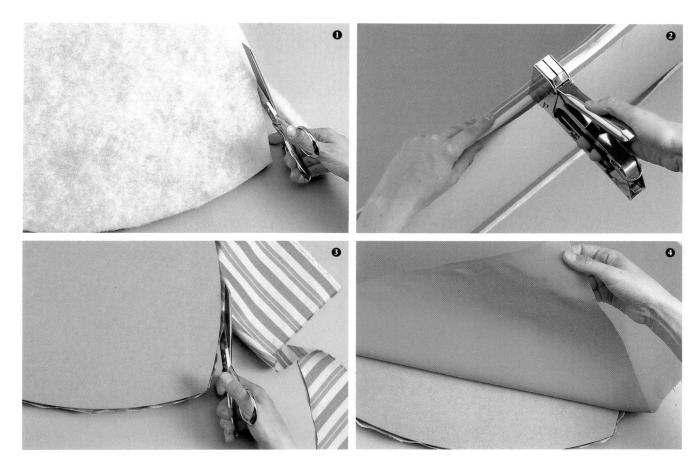

Covering a solid screen

1 Cut 56g/2oz wadding 2.5cm/1in larger on all edges than each
screen panel. Use a spray adhesive especially recommended for
upholstery to stick the wadding to the screen panels. Cut away the
excess wadding.

2 Cut the fabric for each panel front, adding 3cm/1¼in to all edges.
Press the fabric and lay the first piece centrally on the panel. Pin
to the wadding with T-pins. Fold the fabric smoothly over the side
edges and use a staple gun to fix the fabric in place, working
outwards from the centre.

3 Smooth the fabric along the length of the panel and over the
upper and lower edges, folding under the fullness neatly at the
corners. Staple in place then trim away the excess fabric just inside
the edges of the screen.

4 Turn the panel over and cover the other side in the same way,
positioning the staples between the first row. Trim away the excess
fabric as before.

5 Starting on the lower edge, use fabric glue to stick braid that is the
width of the panel on the edges. Cover the remaining panels. Join
the panels with hinges.

tented wardrobes

Freestanding wooden units with hanging rails are very cheap and are great for storage purposes. The only drawback is that they are usually unattractive to look at and everything in them is on display. Make a streamlined fabric cover to hide the unit's contents which rolls up and fastens with buttons to give access inside the unit.

Making a tented wardrobe

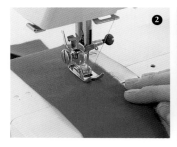   

Take a 1.5cm/⅝in seam allowance throughout.

1 Measure the width, depth and height of the unit. For the door, cut two rectangles of fabric the height of the unit minus 4cm/1½in by the width of the unit. With right sides facing, stitch together along the side and lower edges. Clip the corners and turn right side out. Press and pin the upper raw edges together.

2 Cut two strips of fabric 45 x 12cm/1ft 6in x 4¾in for the straps. With right sides facing, fold the straps lengthwise in half and stitch down the long edges and across one end. Clip the corners, turn right side out and press.

3 Work a buttonhole to fit your buttons 1.5cm/⅝in from the finished ends. Pin and tack each strap to the upper raw edge of the underside of the door 7cm/2¾in in from the side edges.

4 Cut two strips of fabric for the pediment that are the unit width plus 3cm/1¼in by 10cm/4in. With right sides facing, pin the upper edge of the door centrally to a long edge of one pediment.

5 For the front borders, cut two 17cm/6¾in wide strips of fabric that are the height of the unit minus 2cm/¾in. Press the borders lengthwise in half with the wrong sides facing. Pin and tack the long raw edges together.

6 Matching the raw edges, pin the short upper edges of the borders to the pediment, overlapping the edges of the door. With right sides facing, tack the remaining pediment on top, sandwiching the door, straps and borders. Stitch the upper edge. Turn the pediment right side out and press. Tack the raw edges of the pediments together. Topstitch the pediment close to the seam then 5mm/¼in from the first stitching.

7 Cut a rectangle of fabric for the sides and back, which is the height of the unit plus 5cm/2in, by the width and twice the depth plus 3cm/1¼in. Join fabric widths if necessary with a flat felled seam. With right sides facing, stitch the front borders and ends of the pediment to

the height edges, starting 1.5cm/⅝in below the upper edge. Press the seam open and neaten the edges with a zigzag stitch.

8 Cut a square or rectangle for the roof that measures the width plus 3cm/1¼in by the depth plus 3cm/1¼in. With right sides facing, pin the roof to the upper edge of the unit cover, matching the pediment to the width edges. Stitch, pivoting the fabric at the corners.

9 Turn right side out and slip the cover over the unit. Pin up a double hem. Remove the cover and sew a touch-and-fasten disc to the lower edge inside the front borders. Glue corresponding discs to the lower edge of the unit. Roll up the door. Sew buttons to the pediment.

FEATURE PROJECT 1

clothing envelopes

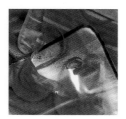

These indispensable clothing envelopes are ideal for storing summer beachwear when it is not in use in the winter, and underwear all year round. You don't have to stick to the dimensions shown here – make them as big as you need them to be.

Neat plastic-fronted envelopes will keep their contents safe, free of dust and easy to see at a glance. A popper fastening seals the envelope and provides easy access when travelling, or for storing underwear or T-shirts and sweaters at home. Choose plain or woven striped or checked fabric, as both sides of the fabric will be seen. The edges are bound with readymade bias binding.

Making a clothing envelope

1 Cut a 41cm/1ft 4¼in square of fabric for the back, and a 41 x 30.5cm/1ft 4¼in x 1ft rectangle of transparent plastic for the front. Place an upturned glass on a corner of the back and draw around it to make a curve. Cut out and repeat on each corner of the back. Pin the front to the back, matching the lower and side edges. Cut the lower front corners to match.

2 Open out one edge of 2.5cm/1in wide bias binding. Turn one end under to start and pin to the outer edges, overlapping the ends. Stitch along the fold line taking a 1cm/⅜in seam allowance on the envelope.

3 Turn the binding to the back, enclosing the raw edges. Tack in place, then topstitch close to the pressed edges of the binding.

4 Following the manufacturer's instructions, attach a popper centrally to the flap. Slip a few items of clothing inside to judge the position of the corresponding popper. Remove the clothes and attach the popper to the front.

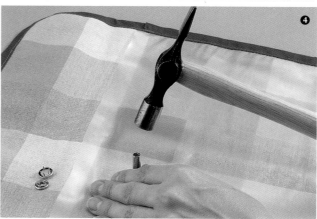

toaster and food-mixer covers

Co-ordinate your kitchen appliances with a set of matching covers made from light-to-mediumweight fabrics. Here, linen-look fabrics in contemporary designs have a contrasting striped fabric for the lining and binding.

Because toasters and food mixers vary in size, you will need to make your own paper pattern. Measure the height and depth of the machine and add 3cm/1¼in to the measurements. Draw a square or rectangle on paper to these measurements for the end panel. Round off the top corners by drawing around an upturned glass. Cut out the pattern and check it against the end of the toaster or mixer; it should be at least 1cm/⅜in larger on all sides. Draw the grain line parallel with the side edges.

For the front and back panels, use a tape measure to measure around the sides and top of the end panel pattern, from one corner of the base edge to the other corner of the base edge. Measure the length of the toaster and add 3cm/1¼in to this measurement.

Making the covers

1 Use the pattern to cut two end panels from fabric, lining and 56g/2oz wadding. Cut one rectangle each of fabric, lining and wadding to the front and back panel measurements. Sandwich the wadding between the fabric and lining, with the right sides facing outwards. Tack the layers together along the outer edges.

2 Set the sewing machine to a slightly longer stitch length than usual. Starting at the centre of the upper edges, stitch along the length of the panels in random wavy lines about 7cm/2¾in apart. Draw guidelines with an air-erasable pen first if you prefer.

3 With the wrong sides facing, pin and tack each end piece to the long edges of the front and back panel, taking a 1cm/⅜in seam allowance.

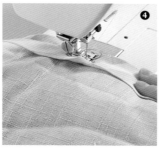

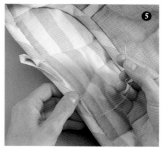

4 Cut two 8cm/3¼in wide bias strips of contrast fabric the length of the front and back panel, to bind the end seams. Press lengthwise in half. The binding is applied double: pin each binding to the tacked seam with the right sides and front and back panel facing. Stitch, taking a 1cm/⅜in seam allowance. Turn the pressed edges over the raw edges and slipstitch along the seam on the end panels.

5 Cut an 8cm/3¼in wide bias strip of contrast fabric the length of the lower edge plus 2.5cm/1in. Press the binding lengthwise in half. Turn under one edge to start, then pin the binding to the lower edge with the right sides facing. Stitch, taking a 1cm/⅜in seam allowance. Turn the pressed edges over the raw edges and slipstitch along the seam inside the cover.

child's wall tidy

Encourage children to tidy up with a jolly wall tidy for storing small toys and stationery. There are four generously pleated pockets and three patch pockets for smaller items. It is stiffened with a wooden batten at the top and hangs from hooks on coloured ribbons.

Choose durable fabrics: a plain, dark blue cotton fabric was used here. The pockets can be made from leftover fabrics from other furnishings in the bedroom. Only small amounts of fabric are needed for the pockets, so it may not be too costly to buy just 30cm/1ft of a special feature fabric.

Making a wall tidy

Take a 1.5cm/⅝in seam allowance throughout.

1 From plain fabric, cut two rectangles for the wall tidy 88 x 58cm/3ft 35in x 2ft 10⅝in. Cut four 2.5cm/1in wide ribbons 25.5cm/10in long. Tack the ribbons in pairs to the short upper edge of one wall tidy on the right side, 8cm/3¼in in from the long side edges. With the right sides facing, stitch the wall tidies together, leaving a 20cm/8in gap 2.5cm/1in below the upper edge on one long side edge. Clip the corners, turn through and press.

2 Cut four rectangles 34 x 25.5cm/1ft 1½in x 10¼in from three different fabrics for the pleated pockets. Centre any design motifs. Press 1cm/⅜in then 2cm/¾in to the wrong side on the upper raw edges. Stitch close to the inner pressed edges. Press 1.5cm/⅝in under on the side edges.

3 Follow the diagram and fold the pleats along the solid lines to meet the broken lines (see page 248). Pin and press the pleats. Press 1.5cm/⅝in to the wrong side on the lower edge.

4 Cut three rectangles 19.5 x 15cm/7¾ x 6in from three different fabrics for the patch pockets. Centre any design motifs. Press 1cm/⅜in then 2cm/¾in to the wrong side on the upper raw edges. Stitch close to the inner pressed edges. Press 1.5cm/⅝in under on the side and lower edges.

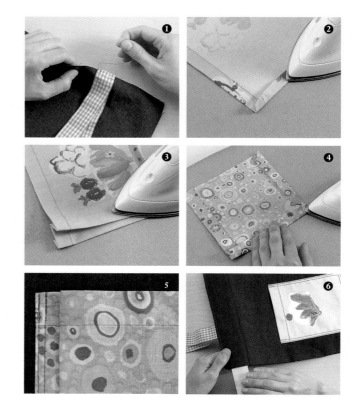

5 Arrange the pockets on the tidy, 4cm/1½in within the side and lower edges and 13cm/5¼in below the upper edge. Topstitch close to the side and lower edges then 6mm/¼in inside the first stitching. Stitch back and forth a few times at the hemmed edge of the pockets as reinforcement.

6 Stitch across the wall tidy 6mm/¼in then 4.5cm/1¾in below the upper edge to form a channel. Insert a 3cm/1¼in wide wooden batten 54cm/1ft 9¼in long into the channel. Slipstitch the opening closed.

hanging shelves

A set of sturdy fabric hanging shelves is great for storing T-shirts and knitwear. The shelves are applied to a wardrobe rail with a hanging strap that fastens with touch-and-close tape. The shelves are reinforced with corrugated card and are very lightweight.

Choose a hardwearing, closely woven fabric such as calico, denim or canvas. A colourful striped canvas has been used for these hanging shelves – position the stripes centrally when cutting the fabric pieces.

Making a set of hanging shelves

1 Refer to the diagram on page 180 to cut a rectangle of fabric for the support (the sides) 98 x 88cm/3ft 2¾in x 2ft 10¾in. Press 1cm/⅜in under then 1.5cm/⅝in on the short edges. Stitch close to the inner pressed edges.

2 Cut three shelves from fabric 62 x 31cm/2ft ½in x 1ft ¼in. With the wrong sides facing, press the shelves widthwise in half and topstitch 6mm/¼in from the pressed edges; these will be the front edges. Pin the opposite raw edges together; these will be at the back of the shelves.

3 Draw the solid lines on the wrong side of the support using tailor's chalk. With the underside of the shelves facing the support, pin the back edge of the shelves along the lines, matching the centres.

4 Tack the shelves in place. Cut five 27cm/10¾in squares of corrugated card. Slip one square centrally inside the middle shelf. Pin the raw edges together to enclose the card.

5 Fold the support around each side of the middle shelf, matching the raw edges to the drawn lines. Pin and tack the side edges of the shelves to the support. Insert a square of card into the remaining shelves, and pin and tack them to the support in the same way.

6 Fold the support along the lines at the back of the shelves, enclosing the raw shelf edges. Pin and stitch the back edge taking a 6mm/¼in seam allowance, and starting and finishing 6mm/¼in from the side edges of the shelves. Fold the support along the lines at the sides of the shelves, enclosing the raw shelf edges. Pin and stitch the side edges, taking a 6mm/¼in seam allowance, starting at the back seam and continuing to the front hemmed edges.

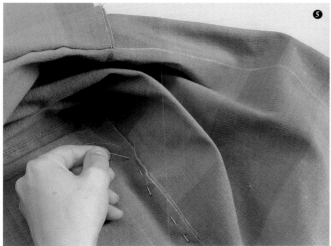

7 Cut a rectangle of fabric for the hanging strap 29 x 20cm/
11½ x 8in. Press 6mm/¼in under then 1cm/⅜in on the short
edges. Stitch close to the inner edges. Press 1cm/⅜in under on one
long edge. Pin and stitch one section of sew-on touch-and-close tape
on top. Press 1cm/⅜in to the right side on the other long edge. Pin
and stitch the other section of touch-and-close tape on top.

8 Cut two rectangles from fabric 64.2 x 33cm/2ft 1¼in x 1ft 1in for
the roof and base. Mark widthwise across the centre of the roof
with pins. Pin the hanging strap centrally to one half of the roof, with
the right sides facing and the long edges of the strap parallel to the
centre line. Stitch the strap to the roof 1.2cm/½in each side of the
centre of the strap. Remove the pins.

9 With the right sides facing, fold the roof and base widthwise in half. Stitch the short edges, taking a 1cm/³⁄₈in seam allowance. Clip the corners, turn right side out and press. Topstitch 6cm/¼in from the pressed edges; these will be the front edges. Slip a card square inside. Secure the roof layers together with three metal paper fasteners along the centre of the strap. With the top of the roof facing the right side of the back of the support, stitch the roof centrally to the upper edge, taking a 1cm/³⁄₈in seam allowance. Stitch the base to the lower edge in the same way. Clip the seam allowance at the end of the seam on the roof and base diagonally.

10 Press 1cm/³⁄₈in under on the raw edges of the support. Fold the roof and base over the seams. Stitch the back edge 8mm/⁵⁄₁₆in from the seam, starting and finishing 8mm/⁵⁄₁₆in inside the side edges. Pin the pressed edges and sides of the roof together. Stitch close to the outer edges. Stitch 6mm/¼in inside the edges, starting 8mm/⁵⁄₁₆in from the back edge. Repeat for the base.

Tip

For strength, use double or treble wall corrugated card at least 6mm/¼in thick. Secure the hanging strap with large metal fasteners and washers.

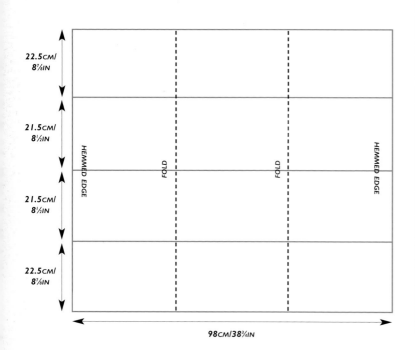

22.5CM/ 8⅞IN

21.5CM/ 8½IN

HEMMED EDGE   FOLD   FOLD   HEMMED EDGE

21.5CM/ 8½IN

22.5CM/ 8⅞IN

98CM/38¾IN

and so to bed

Although the scale is large compared to other soft furnishings, the basic techniques involved in making bedding are simple. Designer-style bedding is terribly expensive to buy but can be created easily using fine fabrics. A hand-worked detail on a sheet edging or pillowcase gives an instant touch of individuality. Making your own bed-linen also means that you can use the exact choice or colour of fabric to suit the bedroom, as readymade ranges are rather limited.

Flamboyant interior design styles, such as bed canopies and coronas, look fantastic but can be intimidating to create yourself. They only need a bit of daring on your part, as they are easy to construct and can completely change the look of a room. Once you start experimenting, you will gain the confidence to try out bolder styles – in fact, you may not know when to stop!

choosing bed fabrics

Most furnishing fabrics are not suitable for bed-linen that will be against the skin because they are too coarse or textured, but they can be used for bedspreads and valances. Materials used for sheeting and pillowcases should be soft to the touch and easily washable, as they will be laundered on a regular basis.

Pure cotton can be bought in wide widths for bedding; it is prone to creasing, but some cottons have an 'easy-care' finish. Percale is a closely woven cotton fabric with a fine, smooth surface that makes it a popular choice for sheets and pillowcases. Cotton polyester is hard-wearing and does not crease as much as pure cotton; it is also less expensive, but does not have the softness or absorbency of pure cotton. Egyptian cotton is the best-quality cotton, being soft and hard-wearing.

Flannelette is a lightweight version of wool flannel, made of cotton or man-made fibres; it is soft and slightly fluffy, so is good for use in cold weather. Flannelette is often highly inflammable. Linen is the luxury choice. It is long-lasting and feels luxurious but is expensive, creases badly and therefore needs a lot of ironing.

Measuring up

The sizes opposite are a guide for standard sizes. It is best to measure up for bed-linen yourself, as manufacturers' sizes do vary. Make up the bed with sheets, pillows, duvet or

Sheets, pillowcases, duvet covers and cushions can all be made in a choice of fabrics to suit the decorative scheme of a room.

Bedding sizes

Mattresses are usually about 17.5cm/7in deep.

Small single

MATTRESS	75 x 190cm	2ft 6in x 6ft
FLAT SHEET	165 x 250cm	5ft 6in x 8ft 3in
DUVET	120 x 195cm	4ft x 6ft 5in

Standard single

MATTRESS	90 x 200cm	3ft x 6ft 3in
FLAT SHEET	180 x 260cm	5ft 10in x 8ft 6in
DUVET	135 x 200cm	4ft 5in x 6ft 7in

Standard double

MATTRESS	135 x 200cm	4ft 6in x 6ft 3in
FLAT SHEET	230 x 260cm	7ft 6in x 8ft 6in
DUVET	200 x 200cm	6ft 7in x 6ft 7in

King size

MATTRESS	150 x 210cm	5ft x 6ft 6in
FLAT SHEET	275 x 275cm	9ft x 9ft
DUVET	220 x 220cm	7ft 3in x 7ft 3in

Standard pillow	74 x 46cm	2ft 5in x 19in
Square pillow	66 x 66cm	2ft 2in x 2ft 2in

The beauty of making your own bedding is that it gives the opportunity to add a touch of individuality. You can buy pre-patterned fabric or add a pattern yourself with decorative patches.

blankets if measuring for a bedspread or coverlet. If a flexible measure does not reach the full distance to be measured, mark the place the tape ends with a pin and start again from the pin.

When measuring the bed base for a valance, a metre/yard stick can be poked between the mattress and base about 5cm/2in in from the edge. Measure from the outermost edges, for example, if there is piping around the edge of the base. Do not worry about noting any rounded corners on the base, as the valance will curve naturally around these edges. Measure pillows and duvets with a cloth tape from seam to seam.

sheets

Sheets are very simple to make and you can save an awful lot of money if you do decide to make your own. Readymade sheets are certainly expensive for what they are. You can also individualise your bed-linen if you make it yourself – you can add personal touches such as blocks of embroidery or trimmings.

Bed sheets are quick and easy to make. It may seem a waste of time to make sheets yourself, as they are generally widely available, but it is easier to incorporate your own design features before construction. A fabric-painted motif or embroidered border gives a lovely finishing touch, and just a simple length of ribbon or a strip of contrast fabric applied along the top edge can tie into a bedroom's colour scheme.

Choose a smooth, easy-care fabric. Sheeting fabric is recommended as it is very wide – usually 228cm/90½in – and is available in pure cotton and cotton/polyester mixes, which crease less than pure cotton. Flat sheets should be at least 73.5cm/2ft 4in wider than the bed and 86cm/2ft 9in longer, to allow for tucking in. Add 12cm/4¾in to the length of the sheet and 5cm/2in to the width for hems.

Always check that the fabric grain is straight before cutting out. Cut out the sheet with the selvedge parallel with the long side edges. Use a flat felled seam to join fabric to make a king-size sheet.

Fitted sheet

Fitted sheets are used for bottom sheets only and fit the mattress smoothly and snugly. The corners are elasticated to give a tight fit so they cannot become untucked and they don't wrinkle up uncomfortably if you happen to have a restless night.

A fitted sheet measures the length of the mattress plus twice the depth plus 21cm/8½in for tucking in and the hem, by the width of the mattress plus twice the depth plus 21cm/8½in for tucking in and the hem.

Making a flat sheet

1 Press 1cm/⅜in then 1.5cm/⅝in to the wrong side on the side edges. Stitch close to the inner pressed edges.

2 Press 1cm/⅜in to the wrong side on the top and bottom edges. Open out the corners then press under diagonally. Press 5cm/2in to the wrong side. Stitch close to the inner pressed edges.

Making a fitted sheet

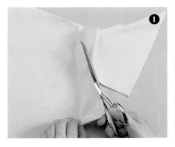   

1 With wrong sides facing, fold the sheet diagonally from one corner, matching the straight edges. Mark a point that is the depth plus 10cm/4in along the raw edges from one corner. Stitch from the mark at right angles to the diagonal fold. Trim the seam allowance to 6mm/¼in.

2 Turn to the wrong side and stitch again 1cm/⅜in from the seam. Repeat at each corner.

3 Fold under 6cm/¼in then 2cm/¾in on the outer edges. Stitch in place close to the inner edge, leaving a 2cm/¾in gap 17.5cm/7in each side of the seam.

4 Insert a 20cm/8in length of 1cm/⅜in wide length of elastic through one gap and out of the other with a bodkin. Pin then stitch the elastic securely across the ends. Stitch the gap closed. Repeat on the other corners.

Corded trim

It is simple to create the elegant rows of fine cording found on the top edge of some sheets. Press 1cm/⅜in then 5cm/2in to the wrong side at the upper edge of the sheet. Lay a length of perle cotton embroidery yarn along the right side 4.5cm/1¼in from the fold. Use a cording foot to zigzag over the yarn. Repeat 3.8cm/1½in from the fold. You could omit the cord and use a twin needle on the sewing machine, or work two rows of close zigzag stitch using a machine embroidery thread. Turn the lower edge and side edges under, and hem.

pillowcases

Pillowcases lend themselves to many decorative features, and you can really go to town if you are handy with your needle. Decorate the edges of pillowcases with ribbons or lace, or work a design in fine embroidery silk. You can also experiment with fabric paints and pens, which can be used over the whole of the pillow.

A housewife pillowcase has a flap to hold the pillow in place and supports the head whilst sleeping. A pillow sham is a pillow cover for a decorative pillow or for back support. Pillow shams that are to be propped upright often have decorative borders: scalloped or flat, or frills extending beyond three edges. The fourth, lower edge conceals the fastening. Pillow shams are made in the same way as cushions but do not have zip fastenings.

The size of a pillowcase provides an ideal opportunity for decoration. Apply the decoration to the front before it is made up. Position any motifs about 5cm/2in in from the flap and up from the lower edge so it does not get lost over the curve of the pillow. Avoid placing any decoration other than fabric painting on the centre of the pillowcase, as it could irritate the sleeper. A little lavender oil sprinkled on the pillow will aid peaceful sleep.

Delicate decorative touches can be applied to the edges of pillows and the whole of cushions.

Making a housewife pillowcase

1 To make a standard-size housewife pillowcase, cut a front 96.5 x 51cm/3ft 2in x 1ft 8¼in and a back 80.5 x 51.6cm/2ft 7⅝in x 1ft 8¼in. Press 1cm/⅜in under then 4cm/1⅝in on one short edge of the front and back. Stitch close to the inner pressed edges.

2 With right sides facing, pin the front and back together along the remaining short edges. Fold the other end of the front over to form a flap, then pin the layers together.

3 Stitch the raw edges together, taking a 1.5cm/⅝in seam allowance. Clip the corners. Neaten the seam with a zigzag stitch or pinking shears. Turn right side out, turning the flap inside.

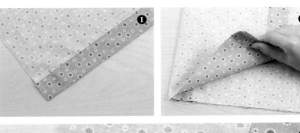

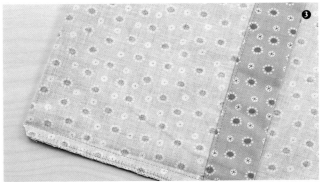

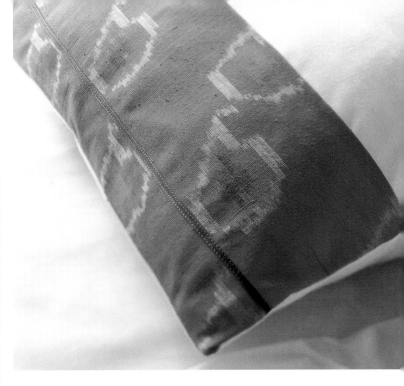

Making a decorative flap housewife pillowcase

This version of a housewife pillowcase has a flap that closes over the front of the pillowcase; this can be of a contrasting colour or fabric to the pillowcase, or decorated with all sorts of techniques or fastened with buttons and buttonholes. The buttonholes are worked on the flap.

1 Cut a front and back 77 x 51cm/2ft 6¼in x 1ft 8¼in. Cut a flap 22.5 x 51cm/9 x 1ft 8¼in. Press 1cm/⅜in under then 1.5cm/⅝in on one short edge of the front, and stitch close to the inner pressed edges. Press the flap in half with right sides facing, parallel with the long edges. If you wish to decorate the flap, open it out flat and apply the decoration to one half only.

2 With right sides facing, tack the raw edges of the flap to one end of the back.

3 With right sides facing, pin the front on top, with the hemmed edge over the flap. Stitch the outer edges, taking a 1.5cm/⅝in seam allowance. Clip the corners. Neaten with a zigzag stitch or pinking shears. Turn right side out, turning the flap over the front.

pillow shams and cushions

Pillow shams are used to lean on when you sit up in bed – cushions are generally more decorative but can also be used for the same purpose. Don't be mean with cushions, pile them up generously and let them spill over the bed to create an inviting atmosphere. Use luxurious fabrics for that feel-good factor.

A pile of squashy pillows and cushions on a bed looks very cosy and welcoming. Pillows and cushions are easy to make and offer lots of opportunities for trying out different needlecraft techniques. If you wish to add trimmings, such as fringing or beading to the outer edges, apply these to three sides only – pillow shams are traditionally meant to sit upright to support the back, so any trimming on the lower edge would be squashed and hidden from view.

The traditional craft of patchwork has long been associated with making beautiful heirloom quilts for the bedroom. They are time-consuming and labour-intensive to create, but a work of art when completed. Making a patchwork pillow sham is a much simpler process, as well as being a great introduction to the technique. Patchwork is a super way to use up small pieces of fabric and those that have sentimental value. Choose fabrics of similar weight: lightweight interfacing can be applied to the back of very fine or unstable fabrics to give them more body. Tack lightweight sew-in interfacing to the back of a piece of lace, worn fabric from a favourite dress you want to incorporate for sentimental reasons, or a delicate piece of an antique textile.

Making a patchwork pillow sham

The finished size of the pillow sham is 30cm/1ft square.
Take 1cm/⅜in seam allowances throughout. The patchwork
is machine stitched using silk fabrics in co-ordinating colours.
The seams are outlined with rows of shiny sequins.

1 *Cut sixteen 9.5cm/3¾in squares from four co-ordinating fabrics.
Arrange the squares in different sequences of four rows of four
squares to see what looks best. With the right sides facing, stitch the
four squares together in four rows. Press the seams of the first row
in the same direction, the seams of the next row in the opposite
direction, and so on.*

2 *With the right sides facing, stitch the first two rows together,
matching the seams. Join the remaining rows to form a square
for the front of the sham. Press the seams downwards.*

3 *Cut two rectangles of fabric for the back 21.5 x 32cm/8½ x
12¾in. Press a 1cm/⅜in deep double hem under on one long
edge of each piece, and stitch in place.*

4 *With the right sides facing, pin the backs to the front, matching
the raw edges and overlapping the hems at the centre. Stitch the
outer edges. Clip the corners and turn right side out. Handsew a string
of iridescent sequins along each seam, then slip a 30cm/12in cushion
pad inside.*

fancy pillowcase

Develop your craft skills with some fancy decorative touches on pillowcases. A design that is painted, stamped or stencilled with fabric paint can be machine washed and is very long-lasting. Choose matching colours to your colour scheme or go for a bold or subtle contrast.

Keep any hand-worked decoration to the opening or upper edges of the pillowcase, where they will be away from the face. Do not decorate the lower edge as it will be obscured. Appliqué is very effective on bed-linen. Apply simple shapes in contrasting fabrics, making sure the fabrics have the same washing instructions. Add a touch of embroidery for emphasis. You could embroider a garland on a pillow sham, for example, then pick out single flowers to embroider on the edges of pillowcases and you could scatter them on a duvet cover or quilt.

Gingham looks particularly fresh in a bedroom – choose larger checks for a duvet cover and smaller ones for pillows and sheets, or mix and match them on the same item. A housewife pillowcase with the main case in larger check and the flap in a smaller check would look very pretty – and you could even work a set of curtains to match. Your bedroom is the most personal space in your home, so this means that you can choose to decorate it however you like – and you don't necessarily have to invite visitors in if you don't want to! Shades of blue are restful in a bedroom – and lilacs and purples – so if you have a stressful working life, go for these calming colours and you'll be guaranteed a good night's sleep.

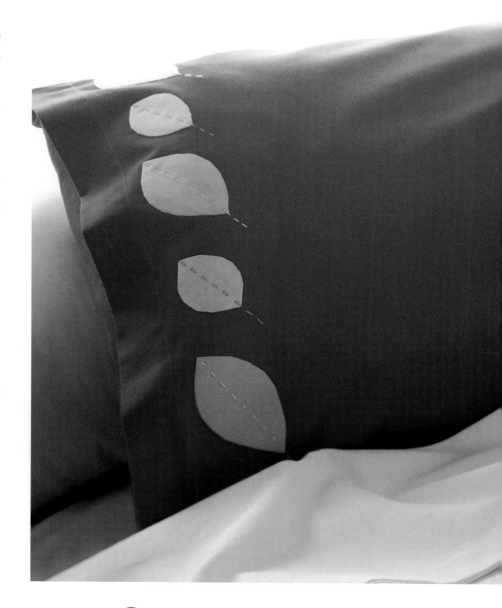

Making a hand appliqué pillowcase

1 From deep red fabric, cut one rectangle for the front of the pillowcase 96.5 x 51cm/3ft 2in x 1ft 8¼in and one rectangle for the back 80.5 x 51cm/2ft 7⅝in x 1ft 8¼in. Cut a selection of leaves from mediumweight iron-on interfacing. Press the leaves to the wrong side of two shades of light brown fabric to fuse them together.

2 Trim the fabric, leaving an 8mm/⁵⁄₁₆in allowance around the interfacing. Press the tips of the fabric over the leaves. Snip the curves of the fabric and turn the allowance to the back of the leaves. Tack in place.

3 Arrange the leaves 10cm/4in in from one short edge of the pillowcase and 4cm/1½in within both long edges of the front on the right side. Pin in place, then slipstitch the outer edges securely to the front.

4 Using three strands of stranded cotton embroidery thread, work a running stitch along the centre of the leaves, extending onto the front for a few stitches to suggest stems. Unpick the tacking and press. Refer to the instructions on page 189 to make a housewife pillowcase, positioning the appliqué at the flap end.

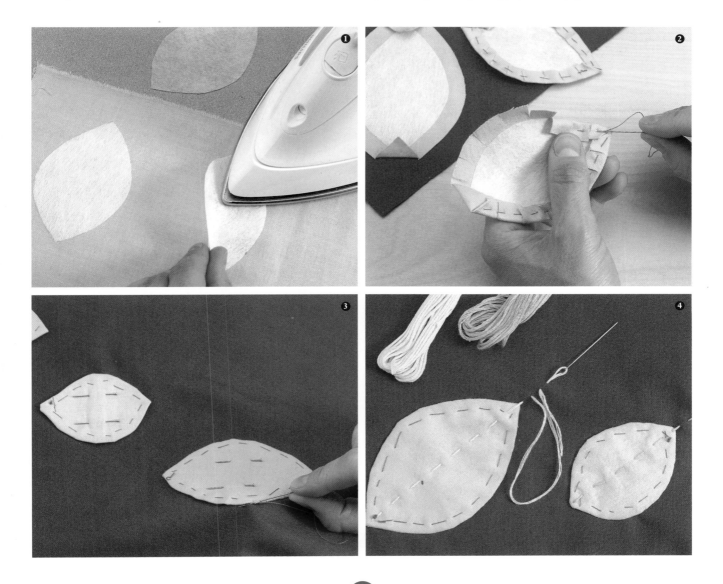

duvet covers

Duvets are popular the world over – probably because they make bedmaking easy – and covers are so simple to make. Sheeting fabric is recommended for making duvet covers because it comes in wide widths in easy-care fabrics, but if you want something different, any smooth, washable fabric will do.

Most duvet covers have an opening at the bottom edge and can be fastened in many ways: a press-fastener tape is the most usual and discreet method, or you could make a feature of the fastening by using buttons and buttonholes or fabric ties.

Unless you use sheeting, the fabric will probably need to be joined to achieve the required width of a duvet cover. Avoid a centre seam, but try to have a full width of fabric along the centre of the length of the bed and an equal amount of fabric at each side. The central panel on the top layer could be of a contrasting fabric to those at each side and a feature can be made of the seams by adding ribbon or lace along them. If you do use more than one fabric and add trimmings, make sure that the wash-care instructions are compatible. Add 1.5cm/⅝in seam allowances for joining the widths, and join the fabrics with flat felled seams.

For versatility, make the front and back of the duvet cover in contrasting colours so you can ring the changes by just turning over the cover.

As long as it is soft to the touch and easily washable, fabric for duvet covers can be used to make pillowcases and curtains, to tie in with the decorative scheme of a room.

Making a duvet cover

  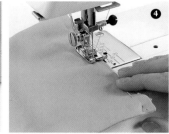 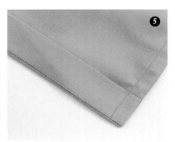

1 Measure the duvet, adding 3cm/1¼in to the width and
7.5cm/3in to the length. Cut out a back and front to these
measurements. Press 1cm/⅜in then 2.5cm/1in to the wrong side
on the lower end of the front and back. Stitch close to the inner
pressed edges.

2 Cut a length of press-fastener tape 40cm/1ft 4in shorter than the
width of the duvet, and separate the tape sections. Pin one half of
the tape centrally to the right side of each hem. Check that the press
fasteners correspond on both tapes and turn under the ends. Stitch
close to the long edges of the tapes, using a zipper foot if the press
studs are large and butting against a standard presser foot.

3 With the right sides facing, match the front and back together
along the opening edges and fasten the poppers. Pin then stitch
across the ends of the tapes, then stitch to the side edges just above
the hem.

4 With the wrong sides facing, stitch the front and back together
along the raw edges, taking a 6cm/¼in seam allowance.
Snip the corners.

5 Turn the duvet through to the wrong side and stitch again 1cm/
⅜in from the seam. Snip the corners. Turn the duvet right side out.

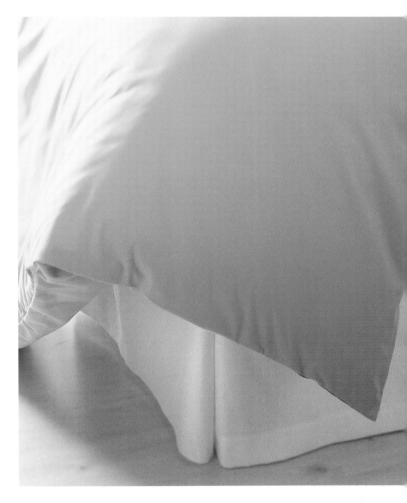

Tip

If you wish to fasten the duvet cover with buttons and
buttonholes or fabric ties instead of press-fastener tape, make
the cover as described above, this time omitting the tape. To
make a buttoned cover, work a row of buttonholes along one
hemmed edge about 17.8cm/7in apart. Sew buttons at
corresponding positions on the opposite edge. To fasten a
duvet cover with ties, mark one hemmed edge with pins about
17.8cm/7in apart. Make two narrow ties 23cm/9in long for
each pin mark. Neaten the ends of the ties and stitch them
securely at the pinned marks.

bed valances

A bed valance hides the base of a bed. It is particularly necessary when a duvet is used and there is no bedspread to hide an unsightly base and legs. If the base is not at floor level, a valance will also obscure anything stored under the bed and give it some protection from dust. (Another name for a bed valance is a dust ruffle.)

The valance can be plain with a box pleat at each corner, gathered, or pleated all round. You can make the valance of the same fabric as the duvet, so it blends in seamlessly, or you can go for a contrast to it. A valance with pleats will benefit from a good-quality fabric that will hold the pleats well for a tailored look.

The valance has a base the same size as the bed base; this will be hidden from view, so it can be made of any inexpensive fabric – sheeting is a good choice for the valance base because it is available in wide widths and is therefore more economical. A border of the valance fabric is applied on top of the edges of the valance base for a neat appearance.

Measuring up

For the valance base, measure the length and width of the bed base, then measure from the top of the bed base to the floor for the drop of the skirt. The average drop is 30.5–35.5cm/ 1ft–1ft 2in. The skirt does not continue around the head of the bed. To make it more economical, cut the skirts across the width of the fabric, add seam allowances and join with flat felled seams. This is particularly important if the fabric is too narrow to cut from a continuous length.

Making a plain valance with corner pleats

A plain valance needs a box pleat at the corners of the foot of the bed for ease and to allow access under the bed. The skirt is assembled from five pieces, one for each side, one for the foot end and two pleat inserts.

1 Cut out the valance base, adding 6cm/2⅜in to the length and 3cm/1¼in to the width for allowances. Join the fabric with a flat felled seam if necessary. To hem the base, press 2cm/¾in under then 2.5cm/1in on one short edge. Stitch close to the inner pressed edges. This will be the head end.

2 Cut two side skirts the length of the bed base plus 13.5cm/5⅜in by the drop plus 6cm/2⅜in, and one end skirt the width of the bed base plus 18cm/7¼in by the drop plus 6cm/2⅜in. Cut two pleat inserts 18cm/7in by the drop plus 6cm/2⅜in.

3 To hem, press 2cm/¾in under then 2.5cm/1in on one long lower edge of the skirts, lower edge of the pleat inserts, and one end of each side skirt. Stitch close to the inner pressed edges.

4 Using flat felled seams and taking a 1.5cm/⅝in seam allowance, stitch a pleat insert between the side and end skirts to form a continuous length.

5 With the right sides uppermost, bring the side and end skirts to meet at the centre of the pleat inserts to form the box pleats. Tack across the upper edges and press the pleats.

6 With wrong sides facing, tack the skirt to the raw edges of the valance base, matching the side skirts to the long edges and the end skirt to the foot end. Match the centre of the pleats to the corners, snipping the seam allowance so it lies smoothly.

7 For the borders, cut two strips of fabric the length of the bed base plus 3 x 13cm/1¼ x 5¼in and one strip of fabric the width of the bed base less 17 x 13cm/6¾in x 5¼in.

8 With the right sides together and taking a 1.5cm/⅝in seam allowance, stitch the ends of the short border between one long

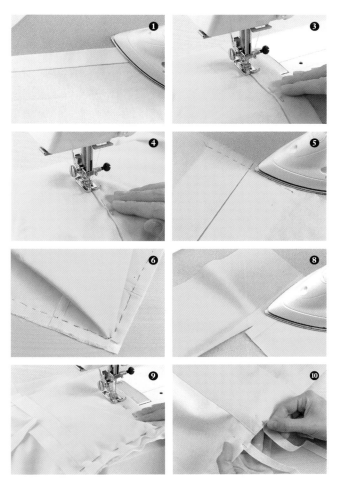

edge of the long border, starting 1.5cm/⅝in from the inner edges. Press the seams open.

9 With the right sides facing and taking a 1.5cm/⅝in seam allowance, tack the borders to the base, enclosing the skirt. Stitch through all the layers. Clip the corners and turn right side out.

10 Press the border to the right side of the base. Press 1.5cm/⅝in under on the raw edges, and stitch close to the pressed ends. Cut four 30.5cm/1ft lengths of seam tape. Pin and then sew them in pairs to the head end of the valance base to tie around the headboard supports.

bed valances

Making a gathered valance

Make a gathered valance to add a gentle, feminine touch to
a bedroom. Avoid heavyweight fabrics, as soft, lightweight
fabrics work best for gathers. The skirt should be three times
the length of the bed plus one and a half times its width. Cut
strips across the width of the fabric to make up the entire
length of the skirt plus 9cm/3½in that are the drop of the
skirt, plus 6cm/2⅜in in depth.

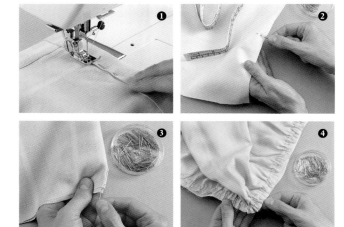

1 *To prepare the valance base, see step 1 of making a plain
valance with corner pleats on page 197. Join the skirts end to
end with flat felled seams. To hem the skirt, press 2cm/¾in under
then 2.5cm/1in on one long, lower edge and the ends. Stitch close to
the inner pressed edges.*

2 *On such a large expanse of fabric, balance marks will be needed
for placing the gathers evenly. Add both sides and the foot end of
the valance base and divide the measurement into sixths, then mark
the valance base with pins, dividing the raw edges into six equal sections.*

3 *Fold the skirt in half, matching the ends and upper raw edges.
Mark the fold with a pin at the raw edge. Divide the skirt into
three equal sections between the ends and fold, marking the divisions
with pins on both layers of fabric.*

4 *To gather the raw edges of the skirt, set the sewing machine to
the longest stitch length and stitch two rows 6mm/¼in apart,
7mm/5⁄16in from the raw edges. With the wrong sides facing, pin the
skirt to the valance base, matching the pins and skirt ends to the
head end of the base. Adjust the gathers evenly, but allow slightly more
gathers around each corner. To complete, follow from step 6 of making
a plain valance with corner pleats on page 197.*

Making a pleated valance with piping

A valance that is pleated all round uses more fabric than the other methods, but you will be rewarded with a smart, tailored finish to the bed. Choose crisp fabric that will hold the pleats well. Piping around the valance base will add definition.

Add together the width of the bed base and twice the length. The length of the skirt should be three times this measurement. Add 8cm/3½in to this amount for hems. Cut strips across the width of the fabric to make up the entire length of the skirt that are the drop of the skirt plus 6cm/2⅜in in depth. Add 3cm/1¼in to each piece cut for skirt seams.

1 To prepare the valance base, see step 1 of making a plain valance with corner pleats on page 197. Join the skirts with flat felled seams to make one long length. To hem the skirt, press 2cm/¾in under then 2.5cm/1in on one long edge and the ends. Stitch close to the inner pressed edges.

2 Mark the centre of the skirt with a pin at the raw edge. Working outwards from this point, fold and pin the skirt into even-sized box pleats, aiming to work the pleats so there will be an inverted pleat at the corners of the base. Tack the pleats in place.

3 With the wrong sides facing, pin the skirt to the valance base, matching the raw edges and the skirt ends to the head end. Check the fit. If adjustments need to be made to the size of the pleats, make the end pleats smaller or larger, as they will be less noticeable at the head end of the bed. Snip the skirt seam allowance at the corners so the fabric lies smoothly. Tack the skirt in position.

4 See the technique on page 46 to make a length of piping from the valance fabric, or use ready-made piping twice the length of the bed base plus its width and 5cm/2in. With the right sides facing, pin and tack the piping to the raw edges of the skirt, taking a 1.5cm/⅝in seam allowance.

5 Snip the seam allowance of the piping at the corners so it lies flat. To make the border, follow steps 7–8 of making a plain valance with corner pleats on page 197.

6 With the right sides facing and taking a 1.5cm/⅝in seam allowance, tack the borders. Working on the right side of the base, stitch through all the layers, using a piping foot. Clip the corners and turn right side out. To finish, follow step 10 on page 197.

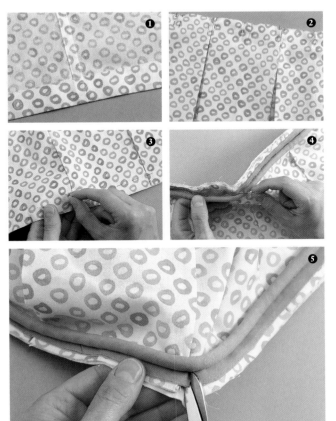
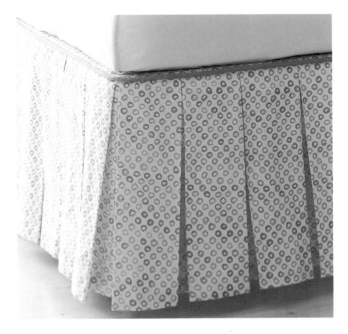

eiderdowns and quilts

Eiderdowns, quilts, comforters and coverlets are all terms for sumptuous padded bed coverings. They add warmth to a bed in addition to looking inviting. Wadding is sandwiched between two layers of fabric which can then be quilted or left unadorned, or the layers can be joined with buttons or knotted threads.

Lightweight furnishing fabrics such as glazed cottons are ideal for making eiderdowns and quilts. If you have chosen an expensive fabric, it is economical to use a cheaper fabric such as curtain lining for the lining. Quilting can be worked in straight lines in bands or a grid, at random or along the outlines of printed designs. Quilting a striped or chequered fabric is easy, as you simply follow the lines of the stripes or checks. Ready-quilted fabric is available, although in a limited choice of fabrics and colours. Alternatively, create a family heirloom by making a patchwork for the top layer and quilt it by hand or machine.

Measuring up

Make up the bed with its blankets or duvet, but not the pillows. Measure the width and length of the bed. Decide how far you would like the cover to overhang the sides, double the overhang measurements and add them to the width. Decide how far you would like the cover to overhang the foot of the bed – this may be the same as for the sides, or less if there is a footboard. Add the foot overhang measurement to the length. Do not add seam allowances, as the edges will be bound. If the cover is to be quilted, add 10cm/4in to the width and length to allow for slippage.

Joining widths

If the fabric needs to be joined to achieve the required width, have a full width of fabric along the centre of the length of the bed and an equal amount of fabric at each side. Remember to allow extra fabric for matching patterns. Add 1.5cm/⅝in seam allowances for joining the widths. Join the widths with flat seams and press the seams open.

Quilts add a sumptuous and inviting look to beds. A simple, two-coloured chequered pattern is easiest to quilt but random patterns or printed designs can also be used.

Making a quilt

3 Lay the lining wrong side up on a flat surface and stick it in place with masking tape. Lay the wadding then the top fabric on top, right side up, 5cm/2in in from the taped edges. Use curved basting pins to pin or tack the layers together, smoothing the fabric from the centre.

4 Set the sewing machine to the longest stitch length, and use a walking foot or dual feed foot if your machine has one. Using quilting thread and, working outwards from the centre, stitch along the drawn lines. Stitch all the diagonal rows in the same direction, then stitch those running across them. Use both hands to smooth the fabric as it passes under the sewing machine. Check the size and cut the quilt smaller if necessary, trimming an equal amount from both the opposite edges rather than just the one edge.

5 The quilt is easier to bind if it has rounded edges. Place an upturned dinner plate on one corner, draw around it with tailor's chalk or an air-erasable pen and cut out. Use this corner as a template to trim the other corners. Bind the outer edges with 2.5cm/1in wide bias binding, following the technique on page 45 and again using a walking foot or dual feed foot if you have one on your machine.

Tip
Because the quilt is large and bulky, roll up the right-hand side to allow it to pass comfortably under the arm of the sewing machine.

1 Cut two quilts from fabric and one from 56g/2oz polyester wadding, cutting the wadding and lining about 5cm/2in larger on all sides than the top fabric. Join the fabric widths if necessary with flat seams. You will probably need to join the wadding widths by butting the edges together and oversewing them with a large herringbone stitch.

2 Lay the top fabric right side up. Start at the centre and draw quilting lines using tailor's chalk and a ruler. This has a diagonal grid, and the lines are 8cm/3¼in apart.

bedspreads

As a bedspread covers such a large expanse, it will be a major focal point of the bedroom. Bedspreads are a great way of either creating a dramatic effect with a bright splash of colour in an otherwise subtle room, or of calming down a colour scheme by making the bedspread in gentle, soothing tones.

From a practical point of view, a bedspread will add warmth and hide dreary blankets. It will also hide the bed base and anything stored under it, making a bed valance unnecessary.

A throw-over bedspread is very simple to make as it is just a rectangle of fabric that is large enough to reach the floor at the sides and foot of the bed. It can be a single layer of fabric or it can be lined. A contrasting coloured lining makes the bedspread reversible, which is very versatile. On a single layer bedspread, add a 2.5cm/1in hem to all edges or, alternatively, bind the edges, in which case no allowances are needed. Lined bedspreads can also have bound edges, or add a 1.5cm/⅝in seam allowance to all edges if you prefer to bag it out. Most fabrics are suitable, but avoid any that are stiff because the bedspread will not drape nicely over the bed. If lining the bedspread, make sure the fabrics have compatible wash-care instructions.

Joining widths

The large size of a bedspread means that fabric will probably need to be joined to achieve the required width. As on curtains and tablecloths, a central join will look ugly, so try to have a full width of fabric along the centre of the length of the bed and an equal amount of fabric at each side. Making the central panel from a contrasting fabric to those at each side can be very effective. Add 1.5cm/⅝in seam allowances for joining the widths. Use flat felled seams on single layer bedspreads and flat seams on lined bedspreads. The corners at the foot end will need to be rounded off on a floor-length bedspread otherwise they will bunch up on the floor and could be tripped over.

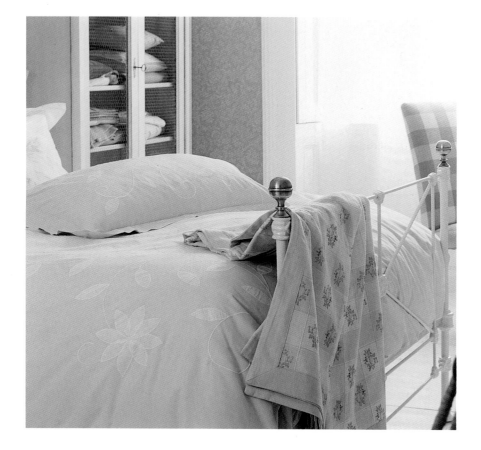

A bedspread can add a decorative touch to an otherwise plain room as well as keeping dust off duvets and pillowcases.

Making a throw-over bedspread with bound edges

To measure for a throw-over bedspread, make up the bed in your usual way, complete with pillows and duvet or blankets. With a tape measure, measure the width from the floor at one side of the bed, up over the bed and to the floor at the other side. Measure the length from the floor at the foot of the bed, up and along the length of the bed, over the pillows to the headboard. If you require a tuck-in under the pillows, add 40cm/1ft 4in to the length. Add a 2.5cm/1in hem to the head end.

1 *Cut out the bedspread. Join the widths if necessary, matching patterns. Press under 1cm/³⁄₈in then 1.5cm/⁵⁄₈in on the head end. Stitch close to the inner pressed edge. Fold the bedspread lengthwise in half with the right sides facing. Measure the height of the made-up bed. On paper, use a compass or improvise with string and a drawing pin (see page 131) to describe a quarter circle with a radius that is the bed height measurement. Cut out the quarter circle pattern and pin it to the foot end corners. Cut around the curves.*

2 *Remove the pattern and open the bedspread out flat. Open out a length of fold-over braid and turn under one end. Starting at the hemmed edge, slot the raw edge of the bedspread into the braid. Tack in place, through all the layers, enclosing the raw edges. Turn under the extending end to finish. Stitch close to the inner edges of the braid through all the layers then carefully remove all the tacking.*

headboards

Fabric-covered headboards give a neat finishing touch to a bed, and are comfortable to rest against if they are padded. A wooden headboard can be transformed by having a layer of foam glued to the front which is then covered with fabric. Readymade headboards can be covered with your choice of fabric.

Alternatively, make a slip-over cover which fastens around the existing headboard with ties at the sides and can be removed for laundering. A row of laced eyelets could be used instead.

Straight-sided and convex-edged headboards are easier to upholster than those with concave curves because the excess fullness of fabric that occurs at corners and convex edges can be neatly folded under. The fabric on concave edges needs to be snipped to lie smoothly, which will allow the headboard to show through. If the headboard is shallow in depth, braid can be glued on to cover the snipped fabric.

A deep headboard with concave edges will need a different approach, and a fitted cover can look very good. Draw around the headboard on paper. Measure the outer edges, omitting the lower edge. Add a 2.5cm/1in hem on the lower edge and a 1.5cm/⅝in seam allowance on the other edges, and cut out. Use as a pattern to cut two headboard covers. Cut a gusset from fabric the depth of the headboard plus 3cm/1¼in by the outer edge measurement plus 5cm/2in. Stitch a 2.5cm/1in hem on each end of the gusset and the lower edges of the headboard covers. Stitch the gusset between the outer raw edges of the covers. Snip the curves, turn through and slip the cover over the headboard. Fasten the lower edges with tape ties.

Upholstering a headboard

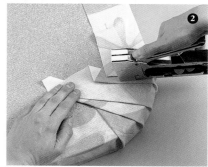

Measure the height, width and depth of the headboard. Cut fabric that is the height plus twice the depth plus 5.6cm/2¼in by the width plus twice the depth plus 5.6cm/2¼in.

1 *Lay the headboard face up and place the fabric on top, centring any design motifs. Pin the fabric in place with T-pins.*

2 *Turn the headboard over and fold the fabric to the underside. Working outwards from the centre on the upper edge and sides, use a staple gun to staple the fabric to the back of the headboard. Neatly fold under any fullness at the curves and corners and staple in place. Staple the fabric to the back of the headboard at the lower edge. If necessary, snip the fabric to lie smoothly around the supports.*

Making a slip-over headboard cover

1 Measure the height, depth and width of the headboard. Cut one rectangle of fabric, 56g/2oz wadding and lining that is twice the height plus the depth plus 3.8cm/1½in by the width plus the depth plus 3.8cm/1½in. Cut eight 46cm/1ft 6in lengths of 3.8cm/1½in wide ribbon for the side ties. Tack each ribbon to the side edges 13cm/5¼in and 56.6cm/1ft 10¼in from the lower and upper edges. Cut the extending ends in chevrons.

2 Cut four 35.5cm/1ft 2in lengths of 1.2cm/½in wide seam tape. Pin and tack to the upper and lower edges 21.5cm/8⅝in in from the side edges. Pin the fabric right side up on the wadding, smoothing the fabric outwards from the centre.

3 With the right sides facing, stitch the lining on top, taking a 1.5cm/⅝in of seam allowance and leaving a 40.5cm/1ft 4in gap in the lower edge to turn through. Trim away the wadding in the seam allowance and clip the corners. Turn right side out and press. Slipstitch the opening closed.

4 Slip the cover over the headboard and tie the ribbons together. Tie the tapes together under the headboard. (The ribbons can be omitted if preferred.)

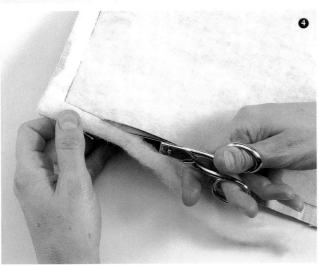

bed canopies

A canopy of fabric over the bed will give the bedroom a very individual look and set a distinctive style. The canopy can be at the head end or above the entire bed. Choose muslin or voile for a delicate touch. Even if you choose bright colours the look will still be soft and filmy. Thicker fabric will soften the hard support edges.

To create an instant canopy to be draped either side of the bed, fix a cup hook into a ceiling joist, about 30.5cm/1ft out from the head end of the bed. Thread two tab-headed sheer curtains onto a 61cm/2ft long curtain pole, alternating the tabs from the two curtains. Fix a finial onto each end and suspend from the hook with a fine chain. Drape the curtains down each side of the bed.

The style of the canopy that you choose can instantly transform a bedroom. You can create a minimalist look, using pale-coloured gingham or smart, thin stripes, with a narrow border to the fabric. An exotic, ethnic room can be instantly conjured up using rich fabrics – choose deep reds and pinks, and ultramarine and jade green as a contrast – and you can really dress it up with chunky silk tassels and deep thick fringing. Alternatively you can opt for a more romantic 'cottage' look, using faded flowered chintz and sprigged cotton, accessorised with plenty of vintage lace and large luxurious bows. The choice is yours!

Canopies can give beds a dramatic, regal effect, the centrepiece of any bedroom. Choose thick, voluptuous fabric that hangs in deep folds or sheer muslin or voile for a more delicate look.

Making a bed canopy

This canopy, made from voile, is suspended on two curtain poles threaded through channels above the head end of the bed. A deep swathe of the canopy will hang at the head end against the wall and a narrower pelmet at the front of the canopy. The finials on the poles have been chosen to match the vibrant colour of the fabric.

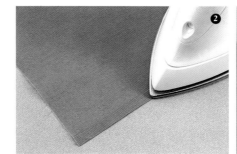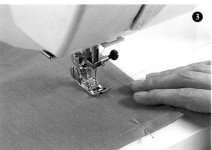

1 *Use a tape measure to measure the circumference of the curtain poles. Add 1.2cm/½in to the measurement for the channel measurement. Refer to the diagram (see page 249) to cut the canopy from lightweight fabric to your chosen width, such as the width of the bed; add 4cm/1½in to the width for hems.*

2 *Press and stitch a 1cm/⅜in deep double hem on all edges. Mark the position of the channels on the long edges with pins.*

3 *With right sides facing, bring the pins at one set of marks together on each long edge. Stitch between the marks to form the channel. Repeat with the other marks to make the other channel.*

4 *Insert a curtain pole through both the top channels, check the length, allowing for finials at each end, and cut the pole shorter if necessary. Fix on the finials and hang the canopy on the wall.*

corona

Coronas make an attractive addition to any bedroom and they will create a cosy atmosphere around your bed. They can be simple to put up – to create a gauzy corona quickly, fix a mosquito net above the bed. Use fabric glue to stick silk flower heads or silk leaves at random to the fabric.

Bed curtains were traditionally used for functional purposes only – to maintain privacy and to keep out draughts. In the 19th century, heavily curtained four-poster beds were thought to be unhealthy and the half-tester became the popular alternative. The half-tester is a rectangular canopy at the head end of the bed only and will keep out draughts while adding a traditional and aristocratic feel to a bedroom. A corona has a curved board with curtains attached which are draped to either side of the bed; it has a softer look than a half-tester and lends itself to both traditional and contemporary styles.

The corona curtains are attached with hooks to screw eyes fixed to the underside of a corona board. The board can have a pelmet attached and curtains with a standard heading underneath or no pelmet and curtains with a pencil pleat heading. The curtains can continue behind the head end of the bed, in which case, it would be best to line them, maybe in a co-ordinating plain fabric.

As a modern adaptation of bed curtains around a four-poster, coronas add a regal, aristocratic look to any bedroom. Choose strong patterns or simple, sheer fabrics in plain colours to create your throne!

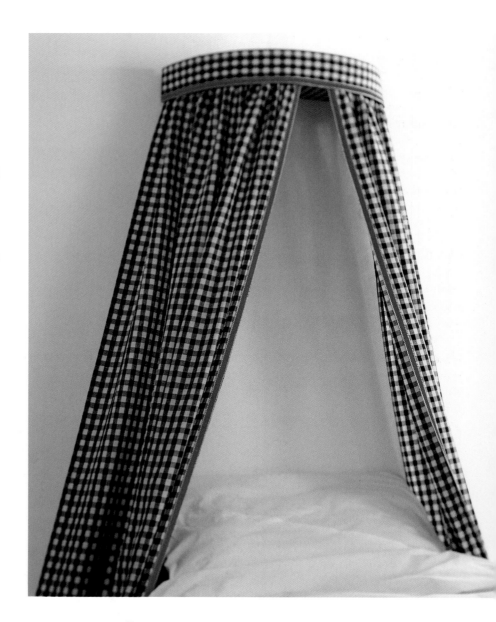

Making a corona

This corona has a matching pelmet with unlined curtains edged in braid.

1 Cut a 60cm/2ft diameter semicircle of 1.5cm/⅝in thick plywood for the corona board. Cut a 68cm/2ft 4in diameter semicircle of fabric. Place the corona centrally on the wrong side of the fabric. Working outwards from the centre, lift the edges of the fabric over the corona board and staple in place with a staple gun, folding under the fullness at the corners.

2 Staple a length of touch-and-close tape to the curved edge with a staple gun. Screw an L-shaped bracket to the top of the corona board on the straight edge, 10cm/4in in from the ends.

3 On the underside of the corona board, make an even number of holes with an awl 1cm/⅜in in from each corner, then approximately 4cm/1½in apart 1cm/⅜in within the curved edge. Fix a screw eye into each hole, with the eyes parallel to the curved edge. Attach the corona board centrally above the bed. If the windows in the bedroom have a pelmet, match the height of the corona board with that of the pelmet shelf if possible.

4 Measure the length of the curve of the semicircle. Cut a 10 cm/4in wide strip of self-adhesive pelmet interfacing the length of the curve. Cut 2 strips of fabric for the pelmet, adding a 1.5cm/⅝in allowance on each edge. Peel the paper backing off one side and stick centrally to one strip of fabric.

5 Cut diagonally across the fabric 5mm/¼in from the corners of the pelmet. Peel away the pelmet backing paper from the edges and press the corners then the straight edges of the fabric to the back of the pelmet.

6 For the lining, pin the corresponding half of the touch-and-close tape 2.5cm/1in below the upper long edge of the remaining strip of fabric, 1.5cm/⅝in in from the short edges. Stitch in place close to the edges of the tape. Press under 1.5cm/⅝in on the edges of the fabric.

7 Peel off the backing paper completely. Press the lining smoothly on top. Slipstitch together along the outer edges. Handsew or glue a decorative trim along the lower edge of the pelmet. Press the pelmet to the corona, matching the touch-and-close tapes.

8 Use a tape measure to measure the intended drop of the curtains from the underside of the corona to the floor. Refer to the unlined curtain instructions on page 57 to make a pair of curtains, each the length of the pelmet in width. Stitch a decorative trim along the inner edges if you wish. Use standard curtain tape for the curtain heading.

9 Slip curtain hooks through the tape and slot the hooks through the eyelets on the underside of the corona. Fix a curtain boss or holdback either side of the bed to keep the curtains in place.

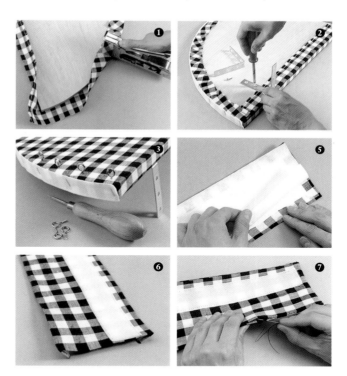

cot bumpers

Creating items for a baby is always rewarding, and a cot bumper is a practical and beautiful gift. The bumper is tied to the inside of the cot, protecting the youngster from knocks, and keeping out draughts. As babies are fascinated by bright colours and patterns, back this bumper with a muted colour for reversing at night time.

Making cot bumpers

Choose washable fabrics such as cotton or polyester or polyester/cotton mixes. Sheeting is ideal because its wide widths make it economical to use.

This bumper extends halfway along each side of the cot and across the head end. Measure the drop from the top rail to the base of the mattress, and measure the width and length of the cot. The bumper is spot-quilted, which is a simple technique to master and looks great when it's finished.

1 *Cut one rectangle of printed fabric the length of one side and the width of the cot by the drop measurement. Join the fabric if necessary, remembering to match patterns. Cut 170g/6oz wadding and plain fabric 5cm/2in larger on all sides. If necessary, join the wadding by butting the short edges together and oversewing with a large herringbone stitch.*

2 *Prepare the bumper for quilting by laying the plain fabric rectangle wrong side up on the flat surface and taping it in place with masking tape. Lay the wadding smoothly on top. Place the printed rectangle on top, 5cm/2in within the taped edges. Secure the layers together with curved basting pins or rows of tacking.*

3 *Within 5cm/2in of the outer edges, use an air-erasable pen to mark a grid of dots on the top layer about 20cm/8in apart. To spot-quilt, thread a crewel needle with a double length of single twist thread. Here, a variegated coton à broder embroidery yarn was used. Make a small stitch at one dot through to the back of the lining and back through to the right side, leaving a tail of about 6.3cm/2½in of thread.*

4 *Make another stitch back through the same holes and tie the thread ends together with a double knot on top of the fabric. Trim the thread ends to 2cm/¾in.*

5 *Trim the the outer edges level with the top fabric. Round the upper corners by drawing around a saucer with tailor's chalk or an air-erasable pen. Cut out the curves.*

6 *Tuck the lining out of the way around the upper and side edges. Pin then use a zipper or piping foot to stitch a length of piping along the side and upper edges, taking a 1.5cm/⅝in seam allowance and taking care not to catch in the lining. Carefully trim away the wadding in the seam allowance. Snip the corners of the piping in the seam allowance so it lays flat.*

  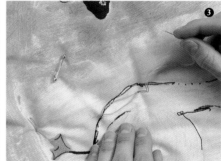

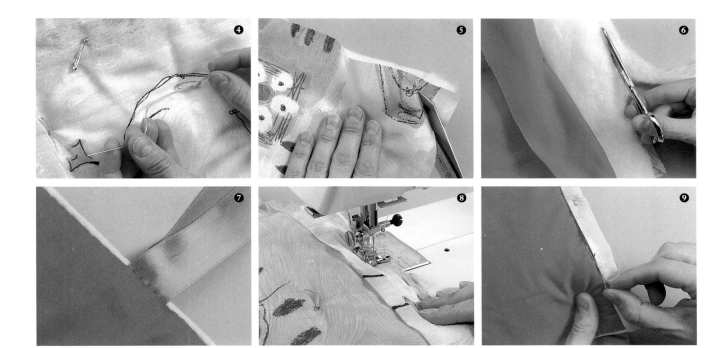

7 Cut four 81.5cm/2ft 8in lengths of
2.5cm/1in wide ribbon. Place the
bumper in position in the cot. Fold the
ribbons in half and pin to the bumper at the
best positions for tying to the rails. Remove
the bumper. Stitch the ribbons securely to
the bumper, cutting the ends in chevrons.
Turn the upper and side edges of the lining
under. Pin and slipstitch to the bumper.

8 Tack the lower edges together. Cut a
5cm/2in wide straight strip of fabric the
length of the lower edge plus 5cm/2in for a
binding. Press 1cm/³⁄₈in under along one long
edge. With the right sides facing, stitch the
long raw edge of the binding to the lower
edge, taking a 1cm/³⁄₈in seam allowance and
with 2.5cm/1in extending at each end.

9 Turn the binding to the underside.
Turn the ends under and slipstitch
the ends together and the pressed edge
along the seam.

paisley border sheet

Appliqué applied by the sewing machine gives a very professional finish. This sheet is edged with a colourful border of paisley shapes, highlighted with simple hand embroidery. The border can also be applied to a readymade sheet.

Making a paisley border sheet

The measurements given here are for making a single sheet. To make a double sheet, cut the sheet 235 x 259cm/7ft 8in x 8ft 7½in and the border 233 x 21cm/7ft 7¼in x 8⅛in.

1 *Cut a rectangle of white sheeting 249 x 170cm/8ft 2in x 5ft 7in. Press 1cm/⅜in then 1.5cm/⅝in to the wrong side on the long side edges. Stitch close to the inner pressed edge. Press 1cm/⅜in then 5cm/2in to the wrong side on the short lower edge. Stitch close to the inner pressed edge.*

2 *Cut a strip of turquoise sheeting for the border 168 x 21cm/5ft 6¼in x 8⅛in. Press the border lengthwise in half with the wrong sides facing. Open the border out flat again and press under 1cm/⅜in on one long edge.*

3 *Make a paper template of the paisley pattern and draw around it seven times on the paper backing side of bonding web. Apply the paisley motifs to two striped fabrics and cut them out. Working outwards from the centre, refer to the bonding web technique on page 47 to apply the motifs in alternate directions and colourways to the unpressed half of the border 10.5cm/4⅛in apart and 2.5cm/1in in from the long raw edge.*

4 *Set the sewing machine to a close zigzag stitch 3mm/⅛in wide. Stitch along the edges of the motifs to conceal the raw edges. Pull the end threads to the back of the border and knot together.*

5 *Thread a crewel needle with six strands of stranded cotton embroidery thread. Embroider three stars on each paisley with six straight stitches radiating outwards from the dots. Press the paisleys face down on a towel so the embroidery is not flattened.*

6 *Fold the ends of the border along the foldline with right sides facing. Stitch the ends, taking a 1.5cm/⅝in seam allowance. Clip the corners and turn right side out. With right sides facing, stitch the border to the upper edge of the sheet, matching the raw edges and taking a 1.5cm/⅝in seam allowance. Clip the corners. Press the seam towards the border.*

7 *Re-press the border in half along the centre foldline. Pin the pressed edge of the back of the border along the seam, enclosing the seam allowance. On the right side, topstitch close to the seam.*

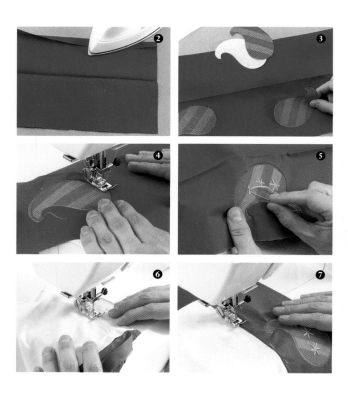

header title block

FEATURE PROJECT 2

oxford pillowcase

Shiny satin ribbon outlines this pillowcase to emphasise the generous flange edge that is characteristic of an Oxford pillowcase. Choose a smooth, closely woven easy-care fabric to make the pillowcase.

Making an Oxford pillowcase

1 Cut one front 88 x 62cm/34½in x 24½in, one back 82 x 62cm/32¼in x 24½in and one flap 62 x 35.5cm/24½in x 1ft 2in. Press 1cm/⅜in under then 4cm/1⅝in on one short edge of the back and one long edge of the flap. Stitch close to the inner pressed edges.

2 With the right sides facing, pin the back and flap to the front, matching the raw edges and overlapping the hemmed edge of the flap over the hemmed edge of the back. Stitch close to the outer edges, taking a 1cm/⅜in seam allowance. Clip the corners, turn right side out and press.

3 Use an air-erasable pen or tailor's chalk and a ruler to draw a border 6cm/2½in inside the outer edges to form the flange. Starting 1cm/⅜in beyond one drawn corner and placing the inner edge of the ribbon on the stitching line, stitch 7mm/⁵⁄₁₆in wide satin ribbon along the drawn line to 7mm/⁵⁄₁₆in beyond the next corner. Fold the ribbon at the end of the stitching with the right sides facing.

4 Fold the ribbon diagonally at the corner and pin it along the adjacent drawn line. Tack the mitre in place at the corner.

5 Fold the ribbon diagonally under at the first corner. Cut off the excess ribbon under the folded corner. Tack in place, then stitch the outer edges of the ribbon.

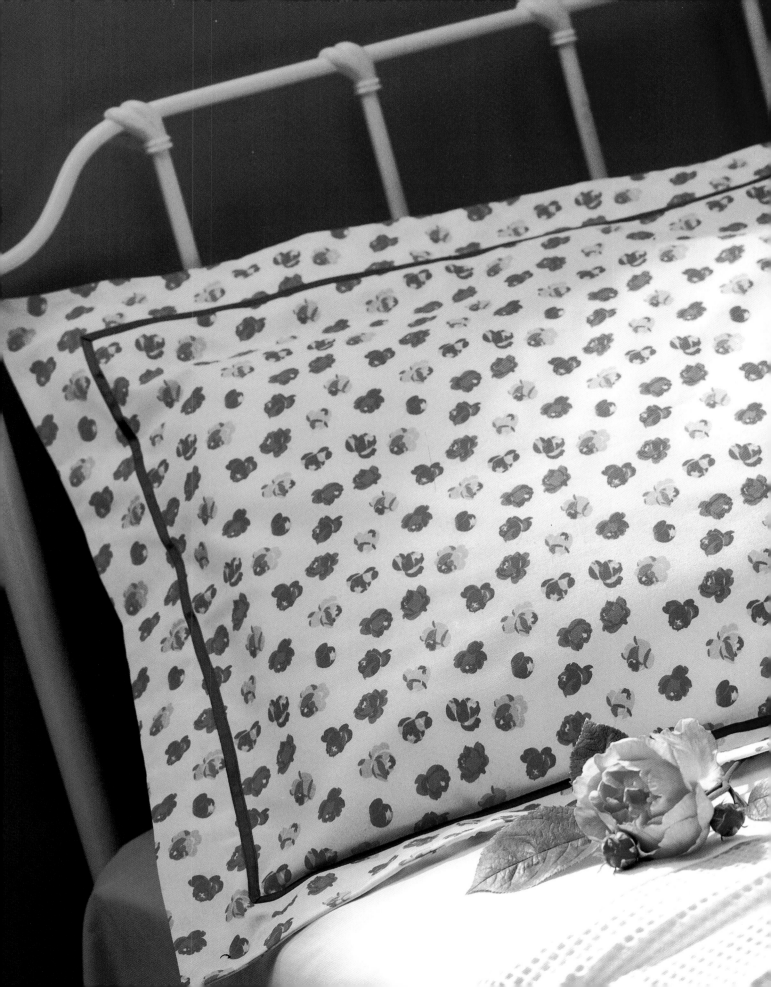

FEATURE PROJECT 3

duvet cover with ties

Make a feature of the fastening on a duvet cover with a row of pretty ties across the top of the cover. A generous flap is made from classic checked gingham with matching ties. Gingham is cheap to buy, and most of the duvet cover is made from inexpensive sheeting.

Making a single duvet cover with ties

1 Cut a front 1.93m x 143cm/6ft 4in x 4ft 8¼in and a back 203 x 143cm/6ft 8in x 4ft 8¼in from plain sheeting fabric. Press 1.5cm/¾in under then 5cm/2in on one short edge of the front. Stitch close to the inner pressed edge.

2 Cut ten 11cm/4⅜in wide strips of gingham for the ties 27cm/10⅝in long. Fold lengthwise in half with the right sides facing, and cut diagonally across one end. Stitch the outer edges, taking a 1cm/⅜in seam allowance, leaving a 7.5cm/3in gap to turn through. Clip the corners, turn right side out and press. Slipstitch the openings closed.

3 Cut a strip of gingham fabric 143 x 54cm/4ft 8¼in x 21¼in for the flap. Press the flap lengthwise in half with the wrong sides facing. Pin the raw edges together. Mark the centre with a row of pins parallel with the short edges. Pin one tie to the centre line with the tie extending over the fold the the straight end 5cm/2in from the fold.

4 Tack the remaining ties to the flap 20.5cm/8¼in apart. Stitch in place close to the edges and across the tie at the straight end, forming a 3.8cm/1½in square. Stitch a cross formation within the square.

5 With the wrong sides facing, pin the front to the back, matching the short lower and long side raw edges. Pin the flap on top. The seams are stitched with a French seam. Stitch the outer edges, taking a 6mm/¼in seam allowance. Clip the corners. Turn wrong side out and stitch again, taking a 1cm/⅜in seam allowance. Turn right side out. Pin the remaining ties to the front 12cm/4¾in from the lower edge of the flap.

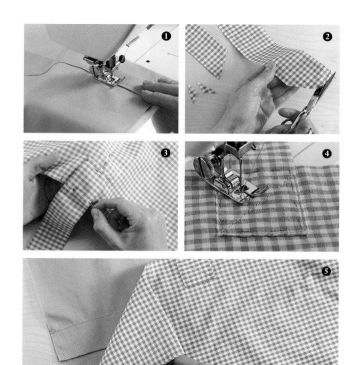

Making a double duvet cover with ties

Cut a front 193 x 203cm/6ft 4in x 6ft 8in and a back 203 x 143cm/6ft 8in x 4ft 8¼in. Cut a strip of fabric 203 x 54cm/6ft 8in x 1ft 9¼in for the flap and cut fourteen ties. Make a double duvet cover in the same way as a single one.

scalloped quilt

This pretty, scallop-edged quilt is reversible, with a classic Toile de Jouy fabric on one side and a muted plain fabric on the other. The quilt measures 192 x 144cm/6ft 4in x 4ft 9in, and can thus be made from 150cm/60in wide fabric.

Making a scalloped quilt

If using a narrower width fabric, join the widths with flat seams, with the full width along the centre and an equal amount at each side. Remember to allow extra fabric to match patterns. Join the widths before drawing the scallops.

1 Cut a 12cm/4¾in diameter circle of thin card for a template for the scallops. Divide the circle into quarters with a pen. Lie the plain fabric out flat, wrong side face up. With tailor's chalk, draw a 192 x 144cm/6ft 4in x 4ft 9in rectangle on the plain fabric. Draw a 6cm/2⅜in deep margin inside the rectangle. Place the circle template on one corner, matching the quarter lines to the inner corner of the margin. Draw around three-quarters of the circle on the margin. Repeat on each corner. Move the template along the inner edges of the margin and draw a row of semicircles edge to edge for the scallops.

2 Cut 4m/13ft of 90cm/36in wide 56g/2oz wadding widthwise in half. Butt the long edges together and join with a herringbone stitch. Place the printed fabric on top with the right side face up, smoothing the layers outwards from the centre.

3 With the right sides facing, place the plain fabric wrong side up on the printed fabric. Smooth the layers outwards from the centre and tack or pin together with curved basting pins. Stitch along the scallops, leaving a 50cm/1ft 8in gap to turn.

4 On the right side of the printed fabric, mark the position of the unstitched scallops with tailor's chalk. Stitch along the drawn lines to secure the wadding to the fabric, taking care not to catch in the plain fabric.

5 Carefully trim away the wadding in the seam allowance close to the stitching. Trim the seam allowance to 6mm/¼in. Snip the curves and corners. Turn right side out and gently press the edges of the scallops so the wadding is not squashed flat. Turn the raw edges to the inside and slipstitch together.

6 Tack the layers together or pin with curved basting pins. Lie the quilt out flat, printed side face up. Use a long ruler and tailor's chalk to draw straight lines along the length between the inner corners of the scallops. Starting on a centre line, stitch along the lines with the sewing machine set to a long stitch length.

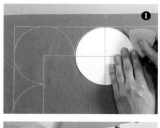

finishing touches

It is the final decorative touches that can really make a soft furnishing project special. A touch of ribbon or braid is quick to apply and is a great way to introduce a new colour or to play down an overpowering pattern.

Similarly, a small handcrafted accessory, such as a photo frame or lampshade, will make a room complete and can solve the problem of hunting in shops for a certain item in an exact colour that probably doesn't actually exist. A handcrafted present is great to give as a gift, as it will have a very special personal touch and show that thought and care has gone into the choice.

braids and trimmings

Trimmings can really finish off a soft furnishings project beautifully. Take your time to choose the braid or trimming that really matches your fabric and the style of your room. Many trimmings are handmade and expensive in their own right, so choose with care and you won't made a costly mistake.

Many decorative braids and tapes are handmade using traditional methods. This naturally makes them expensive, but only a small amount is usually needed to add that special finishing touch. A trimming should not overpower the item, but enhance it. Many fabric manufacturers produce a range of cords, braids, fringing and gimp in matching colours to offset their fabrics.

You can add to cheap trimmings to make them fuller and more substantial. If you cannot find the exact colour of a tassel, for instance, you can make your own (see page 93) or add a few yarns to hang amongst the top layer of threads. Make an exotic tassel from fine silk or organza ribbon. A row of beads or jewellery stones sewn around the edge of a tassel adds a touch of sparkle.

Exotic ribbons can transform the look of your cushions and tablecloths.

Trimming projects

A cushion can be livened up with an insertion into its seams. Cut strips of imitation suède or leather and cut a fringe along one side or trim with pinking shears. Sew readymade ribbon roses about 5cm/2in apart along a length of ribbon and attach them to bedroom furnishings for a feminine touch.

Collect fallen feathers, or buy them from craft suppliers, and glue them to a lampshade. To make a feather-trimmed fastening, dab all-purpose household glue on the ends of a length of leather thonging, and poke each end into beads with large holes. Dab glue on the ends of the feathers and poke them into the other side of the beads for a Santa Fe-style curtain tieback. Colourful

Ribbons can set off a curtain rail and make a real feature of a window. Choose wire-edged ribbons to hold their shape when tied in bows.

marabou feathers can be sewn to the curtain heading – this is particularly effective on sheer curtains.

Surprisingly, silk flowers and leaves have many soft furnishing applications: they can be taken apart and sewn to cushion covers, curtains, tiebacks and tablecloths. Sew a bead or sequin in the flower centres. Silk leaves trapped beneath a layer of organza on a cushion front look very pretty.

Using trimming effectively

Sew beads, jewellery stones and sequins at random to a curtain – they will sparkle when the light catches them. Buttons can be used decoratively in the same way: glistening mother-of-pearl buttons sewn in grid formation to the front of a cushion or along the edge of a throw provide an instant designer look. A string of tiny pearls or sequins can be used as an edging on curtains, cushions and throws. Lampshades can be lavished with all sorts of items: attach gemstones or tiny pebbles to the shade by 'sewing'

them on with fine wire. A row of shells hung from curtain clips adds a beach-comber theme to a bathroom.

If you have seen a beautiful trimming but cannot think of a soft-furnishing use for it, consider other applications. A tassel fastened to a cupboard key gives it a sense of importance. Similarly, fasten a length of pretty gimp around the neck of a vase, or wind fringing around a lamp base.

Ribbons come in masses of colours, materials and finishes. Wire-edged ribbons hold their shape well when formed into bows. Organza ribbons can be used quite lavishly without being overpowering. Lace edging instantly softens soft furnishings and gives a romantic, feminine look. To make a match for an antique lace setting, dye white cotton lace by placing it in a cup of tea (without milk) for a few minutes, or longer for a darker shade.

bows and rosettes

Trimmings that have been personally handcrafted always look extra special, and there are many opportunities to use them to show off a soft furnishing feature. Bows can be added to pelmets and tiebacks for a romantic look, and rosettes attached to the corners of cushions and throws give them a sense of importance.

Making a rosette

1 Cut a strip of fabric 45 x 8.5cm/1ft 6in x 3½in. Pin and tack a 45cm/1ft 6in length of 1.2cm/½in wide ribbon along one long edge on the wrong side, overlapping the fabric by 5mm/¼in. Stitch close to the long inner edge of the ribbon.

2 Press the ribbon to the right side. Stitch close to the new inner edge of the ribbon. Pin a length of ribbon along the opposite long edge on the right side, overlapping the fabric by 5mm/¼in. Stitch close to the inner edge of the ribbon. Press the ribbon to the wrong side. Stitch close to the ribbon's new inner edge.

3 Stitch the short ends together with a French seam taking 1cm/⅜in seam allowance, forming a ring. Set the sewing machine to its longest stitch length. Run a gathering stitch 2.5cm/1in from the outer edge of the second ribbon.

4 Pull up the gathers tightly, folding the second ribbon to the outside along the gathering. Secure with hand stitches. Fan open the rosette.

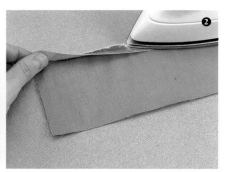
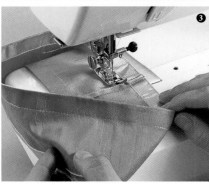
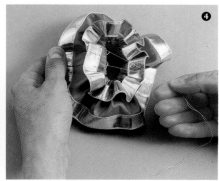

Making a bow

1 Cut a strip of fabric 43.5 x 17.8cm/1ft 5in x 7in for the bow.
Fold in half with the right sides together and stitch the long edges,
taking a 1cm/⅜in seam allowance. Press the seam open. Turn right
side out, position the seam along the centre, and press. Mark
the centre with a row of pins on the seamed side of the bow.

2 With the seamed side inside, lap each end over the centre by
1.5cm/⅝in. Tack across the centre through all the layers.

3 Cut a strip of fabric 12.5 x 5.6cm/4¾ x 2¼in for the 'knot'.
Press 1.5cm/⅝in under on one long edge, then press the knot
lengthwise in half.

4 Fold across the centre of the bow in concertina pleats about
8mm/⁵⁄₁₆in deep. Bind the pleats with thread to secure them.
Starting on the back of the bow, wrap the knot strip tightly around
the bow centre. Turn under the end and sew to the back of the bow.

5 Refer to the diagram to cut the tails (see page 248). Press
1cm/⅜in under at the narrow ends. Fold and pin lengthwise in
half, with the right sides facing. Stitch the raw edges, taking a 1cm/⅜in
seam allowance. Clip the corners and turn right side out.

6 Pin the upper edges of the tails into thirds to make a pleat, then
oversew the edges. Pin the tails to the bow back and sew in place.

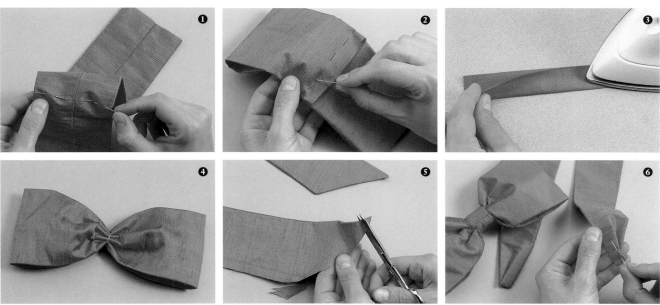

embellished cushions

You can really go to town with decorative techniques on cushions. Ready-made cushions can be further enhanced by sewing on buttons, adding a beaded fringe or stamping, stencilling and hand-painting the surface. Handweaving a cushion from strips of luxurious ribbon is also very effective.

Remove the cushion pad and slip a piece of plastic, such as a carrier bag, inside when stamping or painting to stop paint seeping through to the back of the cushion. Relief-paint pens are great fun to use – paint is squeezed from a tube through a nozzle leaving a fine line that stands proud of the fabric. When the paint has dried, simply follow the manufacturer's instructions to fix the paint. Relief-paint pens come in lots of bright colours, and also in exciting pearlised and glitter effects. (Children particularly love using these.) Sew ready-made embroidered or sequinned motifs to cushions for instant glamour. Ribbons can be applied to ready-made cushions too. Sew a scattering of ribbon roses to a cushion front or gather along the centre of a length of ribbon and handsew it in swirling patterns.

More intricate ribbon designs will need to be worked on a cushion before it is made up. In this project, woven ribbons are applied to iron-on interfacing to form a panel or complete cushion front. They are extremely effective when a mix of printed and plain ribbons are used. Once you have mastered the basic weaving technique, experiment with other effects by mixing different textured ribbons in differing widths.

Making a woven ribbon cushion

To make a 30cm/1ft square woven ribbon cushion, you will need 3m/3½yd of two 3.9cm/1½in wide ribbons. Here, a printed ribbon is woven with a plain metallic ribbon. The cushion is made from metallic fabric to continue the effect.

1 Cut a 33cm/1ft 1¼in square of mediumweight iron-on interfacing and fabric for the front. Place the interfacing on an ironing board with the adhesive side face up. Cut eight 35cm/1ft 1¾in lengths of 3.9cm/1½in wide printed ribbon for the 'warp' ribbons. Working outwards from the centre, lay the ribbons across the interfacing, pinning them in place along the top edge only.

2 Cut eight 35cm/1ft 1¾in lengths of 3.9cm/1½in wide plain ribbon for the 'weft' ribbons. Weave the first weft ribbon in and out of the warp ribbons, passing it over one warp ribbon and under the next until you reach the opposite side.

3 Weave the second weft ribbon under the first warp ribbon, over the next and so on. Continue with the remaining ribbons, forming a chequered pattern. Adjust the ribbons so they lay evenly. Press with a hot iron to fuse the ribbons to the interfacing. Remove the pins and cut off the excess.

4 Tack the interfacing to the fabric front with right sides uppermost. Cut two rectangles of fabric for the back 19 x 33cm/7½in x 1ft 1¼in. Press under a 1cm/⅜in deep double hem on one long edge of each piece and stitch in place.

5 With right sides facing, pin the backs to the front, matching the raw edges and overlapping the hems at the centre. Stitch the outer edges. Clip the corners and turn right side out. Slip a 30cm/1ft cushion pad inside.

loose lampshade cover

A softly pleated lampshade can be made from a remnant of lightweight furnishing fabric that has been used elsewhere in the room, or from a remnant of silk in a dramatic colour. You can trim it with marabou feathers (as here) for a fun look or pompoms for a more retro style.

The lampshade is attached to a coolie-shape lampshade frame, or can be slipped over an existing lampshade. If using a metal lampshade frame, bind the top ring with cotton tape, overlapping the ends and sewing them securely together.

A stunning trimming, such as the marabou feathers used here, provides an element of fun.

Ruched lampshade
Swathes of organza caught at random on a plain lampshade give a contemporary approach to a retro style. Use silk organza because it drapes more fluidly than synthetic versions. Silk organza with metallic threads has been used here to make the most of the lamp when it is illuminated. Ideally, use a conical paper shade for this project.

Making a loose lampshade cover

1 Cut a strip of fabric that is twice the circumference of the top of the shade plus 3cm/1¼in for seam allowances, by the height of the shade plus 9cm/3⅝in. Press 1cm/⅜in under then 1.5cm/⅝in on one long edge for the lower hem. Machine or handsew in place.

2 Press 1cm/⅜in under then 3cm/1¼in on the upper long edge. Stitch close to the inner pressed edge.

3 Starting 3cm/1¼in from one end, fold the upper edge in 1.5cm/⅝in deep pleats 3cm/1¼in apart. Pin in place 2.5cm/1in below the upper edge. Slip the cover over the lampshade and check the fit, overlapping the short raw edges by 3cm/1¼in. Adjust the pleats if necessary.

4 Handsew the pleats in place 2.5cm/1in below the upper edge. With the right sides facing, stitch the short edges together, taking a 1.5cm/⅝in seam allowance. Neaten the seam with pinking shears, and press the seam open.

5 Slip the cover over the frame or existing lampshade and catch to the top ring with a few stitches. Sew a decorative trim or tie ribbon around the pleat stitching.

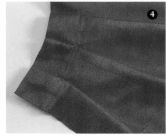
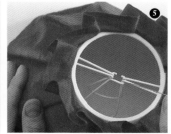

Making a ruched lampshade

1 *Fold a 1m/1¼yd square of silk organza diagonally in half and work on the fabric through both layers. Lay the fabric over the front of the lampshade with the fold 5mm/¼in below the lower edge; have the seam of the lampshade at the back.*

2 *Arrange the organza in random and irregular pleats, pinning the organza to the lampshade as you work. Pin the organza to the lampshade as far as the seam on one side and 5cm/2in from the seam on the other.*

3 *Catch the pleats to the shade with tiny handstitches. It is not necessary to sew all the pleats as the stiffness of the organza will hold the shape.*

4 *Trim the organza to 1.5cm/⅝in beyond the seam on both raw edges at the back. Fold under 1.5cm/⅝in on the second raw edge and fold and pin the organza in pleats along the seam. Handsew securely in place.*

5 *Cut off the excess fabric 2cm/¾in above and below the shade with pinking shears. Glue the raw edges inside the shade with all-purpose household glue.*

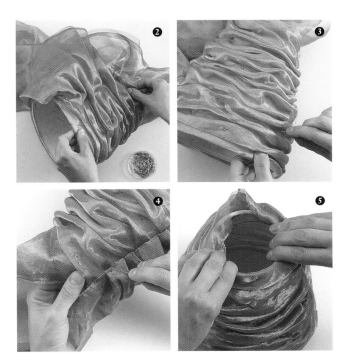

lanterns

Lend an exotic feel to a room with a flamboyant fabric lantern. Ideally suited to Eastern style decor, lanterns are inexpensive to create and can be embellished with beads and tassels. Instead of a lampshade frame, the lantern is supported by a utility lampshade ring which can be bought cheaply and in various sizes from craft suppliers.

Ribbon and paper lanterns

A very simple way to use remnants of ribbons is to cut them into lengths and wrap one end over a utility lampshade ring and handsew in position, enclosing the ring. Turn under the lower raw ends, either straight across or to a point, and sew in place, then attach a large bead to each ribbon end. Embellish inexpensive Chinese paper lanterns by sewing long streamers of fine ribbons to them. This is great for decorating a garden party as the ribbons will move in the breeze. It is easy to change the colour of a plain paper lantern by making a tube of coloured organza to slip over it. Sew on a few beads or sequins at random to catch the light. Catch the organza to the top of the lantern with a few discreet stitches.

This Moorish lantern will lend an exotic air to any decorative scheme. It looks particularly effective when made in rich-coloured silks.

Making a Moorish lantern

This shapely lantern is very effective if made from shot silk, as it will subtly change colour when viewed from different angles. Beads are sewn to the points but you could attach tassels instead if you prefer. Take 1cm/⅜in seam allowances throughout.

1 From fabric, cut six panels and six pediments (see diagrams below). Stitch the panels together in pairs along one long edge, ending the stitching at the lower dot.

2 Stitch all the panels together along the long edges, stitching two opposite seams between the dots for attaching to the lampshade ring. Press each seam open after stitching. Trim the seam allowance to 5mm/¼in at the lower edge and point to reduce the bulk. Turn the lantern right side out.

3 With right sides facing, stitch the pediments together in pairs, leaving the straight upper edges open. Snip the curves and clip the corners. Turn right side out and press.

4 Thread a fine needle with a double length of thread and knot the ends securely. Insert the needle through the point of the lantern and bring it out on the right side. Thread on four large beads then a small bead.

5 Pull the beads along the thread so the first large bead is against the lantern point. Insert the needle back up through the large beads to the inside of the lantern so the small bead rests on the last large bead. Repeat to fix the beads securely. Sew one large bead and a small bead to the point of each pediment. Tack the raw edges together.

6 With the right side of the pediments facing the wrong side of the lantern, stitch each pediment to a lantern panel, matching the notches. Press the seams open.

7 Slip the lantern through a 30cm/1ft diameter utility lampshade ring. Lift each pediment over the ring, positioning the seams with a 1cm/⅜in gap at the intersections of the ring.

8 Slipstitch the top of the pediments together edge to edge for 1cm/⅜in. Catch to the panel seams with a few stitches, enclosing the ring.

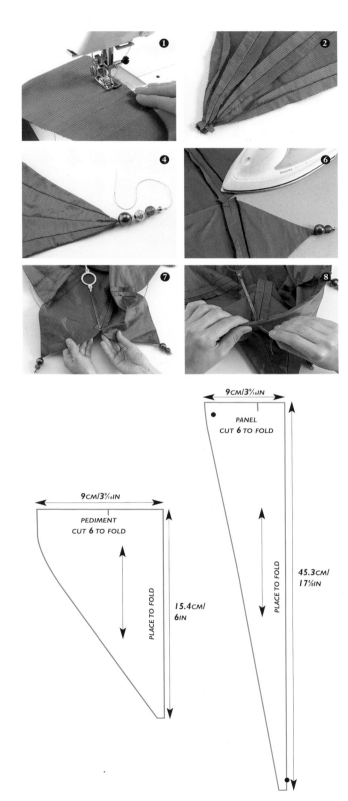

9CM/3⁹⁄₁₆IN

PANEL
CUT 6 TO FOLD

9CM/3⁹⁄₁₆IN

PEDIMENT
CUT 6 TO FOLD

PLACE TO FOLD

PLACE TO FOLD

45.3CM/
17⅞IN

15.4CM/
6IN

throws

An elegant throw provides a swift cover-up on shabby seating and can change the mood of a room, from summer to winter for example, as a sumptuous throw looks warm and inviting on a cold night. Velvet, chenille or fake fur fabrics can all be used, but fleece is also a good choice as it is washable and wears well.

A throw is a very simple soft furnishing project to create. Create an instant no-sew throw by using a bedspread, tablecloth or rug, or add finishing touches to a readymade throw by adding fringing or tassels to the edges. Drape the throw loosely over a sofa or chair. Alternatively, tuck it in or secure it in place with corkscrew pins.

For a throw that will cover your piece of furniture completely, measure the sofa or chair from the floor at the front to the floor at the back with a tape measure, following the contours of the furniture. Next, measure from side to side in the same way. Add 30cm/1ft to the measurements for each tuck in. For a single-layer throw, add a 2.5cm/1in hem on all edges. Alternatively, a small throw that drapes across part of a chair is very effective. If you need to join fabric widths, use flat felled seams on a single-layer throw or flat seams on a double-layer throw.

A double-layer throw is bagged out, or the edges are bound. Add seam allowances for bagging out. The two layers will need to be caught together, either by quilting, spot-quilting or just catching the layers with a few strong but discreet stitches. If the throw has fabric widths joined, catch the layers together along the seams.

There are many ways to decorate a throw. If you want to add decoration in just a few areas, put the throw in position and mark the best spots for showing off your handiwork. Large appliquéd shapes cut from felt are quick to apply with bonding web – felt does not fray, so you could highlight the design with a few bold embroidery stitches. Satin ribbons stitched in grid formation to an entire throw give a lovely shiny contrast on a matt-textured throw.

A bedspread makes a practical loose throw that can transform a sofa and instantly alter the mood of a room.

A row of eyelets or buttonholes along two opposite edges can be laced with cord for a nautical look.

Most fabrics are suitable for throws, but avoid stiff ones because they will not drape well. A double-layer throw can be made from two co-ordinating fabrics.

Making a double-layer throw

This small, vibrant throw is made from soft, fleece fabric in two colourways. It is spot-quilted with pretty mother-of-pearl buttons.

1 *Cut one rectangle from two fabrics 150 x 125cm/5ft x 4ft 2in. With the right sides facing, stitch the outer edges, taking a 1cm/⅜in seam allowance and leaving a 30cm/1ft gap to turn through. Clip the corners and turn the throw right side out. Press and slipstitch the opening edges together.*

2 *Smooth the throw out flat and pin the layers together. Use an air-erasable pen or pins to mark a grid of dots about 25.5cm/10in apart on the top layer. Spot-quilt the layers together at each dot, using a single twist yarn, threading on a 1.2cm/½in button and knotting the yarn on top. See the spot quilting technique in steps 3–4 on pages 200–201.*

wall hangings

There is often that favourite piece of fabric that seems just too good to cut up and make into something. The design may mean that it only looks its best if kept in one piece, or it may be an embroidery, a handworked quilt or painted silk scarf. Fabric can be framed but there is an easier way to display these treasured textiles.

Hanging the piece on a wall is an ideal way to show it off. To hang an embroidery or quilt, a length of touch-and-close tape can be handsewn to the back of the hanging at the upper edge. If attaching to a quilt, sew through the backing fabric and the padding so it is supported well but do not allow the stitches to show on the right side. Fix the hanging to a wooden batten attached to the wall. A hanging sleeve can also be attached to the back of the hanging. Cut an 11cm/4½in wide strip of fabric that is 5cm/2in shorter than the width of the quilt. Stitch a 1.5cm/⅝in deep double hem at each end. Press under 1.5cm/⅝in on the long edges. Pin the sleeve centrally to the back of the hanging just below the upper edge. Handsew securely in place, taking the stitches through to the padding of the quilt. Cut a wooden batten 2cm/¾in shorter than the sleeve. Insert the batten through the sleeve.

Making a wall hanging

The simplest way to display a length of fabric is to make a channel at the top and lower edge. A length of wood dowelling slotted through the lower channel will hold the fabric taut. A curtain rod threaded through the top channel can have decorative finials or tassels attached to the ends.

1 *Press under 1cm/⅜in then 1.5cm/⅝in on the long edges. Stitch close to the inner pressed edges.*

2 *Press 1cm/⅜in then 7cm/2¾in to the underside on the upper edge to form a channel. Stitch close to both pressed edges.*

3 *Press 1cm/⅜in then 2.5cm/1in to the underside on the lower edge to form a channel. Stitch close to the inner pressed edge. Cut a length of 1cm/⅜in thick wood dowelling 1cm/⅜in shorter than the width of the lower edge. Insert the dowelling into the lower channel. Slipstitch the ends closed.*

4 *Insert the curtain rod through the upper channel, check the length, allowing for finials at each end, and cut the curtain rod shorter if necessary. Fix on the finials. Attach the curtain rod to the wall using a pole support.*

photo frames

A treasured photograph needs a special setting. A padded photo frame is very effective and would make a delightful gift. Adapt the technique to make frames to your personal requirements by altering the shape and size. Although velvet can be difficult to sew, only a small amount of stitching is involved in covering the frame.

Making a padded photo frame

1 Cut two frames from thick card and one frame from 113g/4oz wadding (see diagram on page 249). Cutting along the solid lines, cut out the window on one card frame for the front. Stick the wadding to the front frame with fabric glue.

2 Cut two frames from velvet along the broken line: do not cut out the window (see diagram on page 249). Cut a facing from cotton fabric, cutting 5mm/¼in inside the outer solid line. Draw the window on the facing. Matching right sides, pin the facing to one velvet frame and stitch along the window outline. Cut out the window, leaving a 5mm/¼in seam allowance. Snip the curves. Press the facing inside.

3 Place the front frame wadding side down on the velvet frame. Adjust the seam allowance to lay on the underside of the front frame and pull the facing through to the back. Glue the facing to the underside of the frame then pull the outer edges smoothly over the underside and stick in place.

4 Cover the remaining card frame with the remaining velvet frame, gluing the raw edges onto the underside. With the wrong sides facing, slipstitch the frames securely together along the outer edges, leaving a gap at one side between the dots to insert a 12.5 x 10cm/ 5 x 4in photograph.

5 Cut two stands from velvet, following the broken lines. Press under 1cm/⅜in along the lower wide ends. With right sides facing, stitch the stands along the raw edges, taking 1cm/⅜in seam allowance, leaving the lower edge open. Clip the corners and turn through.

6 Cut a stand from thick card, cutting along the solid lines. Score across the dotted lines on the card stand with a craft knife. Bend the stand outwards along the scored line. Insert the card stand into the velvet stand. Slipstitch the lower edge closed. Glue the upper 4cm/1½in of the stand to the back of the frame.

garden canopies

Make the most of sunny days with a protective canopy in the garden. The canopy can be freestanding with a pole at each corner and cords tied to tent pegs, or it can have poles at each side of one end and be tied at the other corners to a building or to the branches of a tree.

Canopies can be freestanding or attached to walls or garden furniture.

The poles can be supported in flagstaff sockets fixed permanently into a concrete floor, or wedged in flower pots weighted with pieces of brick and gravel inside.

Although large, garden canopies are easy to make. The basic canopy as described opposite can be enhanced in many ways: add a zigzag or scalloped border at each end, or tie cascading ribbons from the eyelets for a celebration garden party, binding ribbons around the poles to continue the theme. The canopy can be made from wide bands of contrasting fabrics, or can have braid or coloured tapes sewn along its length.

Avoid stretchy fabrics and those that are very heavy; mediumweight canvas is a good choice. A sheer fabric canopy would look very pretty. A row of awnings made from deckchair canvas can be extremely smart especially if co-ordinated with garden seating.

Making a garden canopy

This canopy measures 1.45 x 2m/4ft 9in x 6ft 6in and is made from striped cotton fabric. It has metal eyelets at the corners and a smart border at each end. You can adapt the size to suit your own requirements.

1 Cut the canopy 150 x 261cm/4ft 11in x 8ft 6¼in from fabric. Press 1.5cm/⅝in under on the short edges. Fold 17cm/6¾in to the right side at the pressed ends to form a facing.

2 Stitch the side edges, taking a 2.5cm/1in seam allowance. Clip the corners and trim the seam allowance. Turn right side out. Press 1cm/⅜in under then 1.5cm/⅝in on the long edges. Stitch close to the inner pressed edges, continuing the stitching to the ends of the canopy.

3 Stitch close to the inner pressed edges of the facings, then 3.8cm/1½in from the first stitching.

4 Fix a 1.5cm/⅝in metal eyelet centrally between the stitched lines of the facings 2cm/¾in inside the long edges. If the canopy is to be freestanding, fix an eyelet halfway along the long, side edges to tie cord through.

5 Apply two coats of exterior paint or varnish to 2m/6 ft 6in long, 2cm/¾in diameter wood dowelling poles. Sand one end of each pole to curve the edges. Make a hole in the centre of the rounded ends with a bradawl, and hammer in a large nail, leaving about 1.2cm/½in of the nail standing proud to slot through the eyelets.

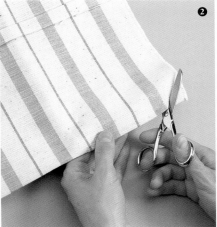

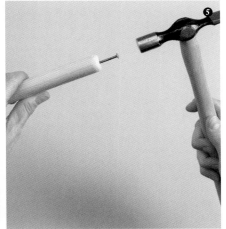

lined lampshade

Ready-made lampshades come in a limited range of fabrics. Making your own lined lampshade gives you far more freedom to create the right ambience in a room with some well-chosen lighting. Use a pale-coloured dress-weight lining inside the shade to reflect the light.

The lampshade needs a trimming at least 1cm/⅜in wide at the upper and lower edges to conceal the edges of the lining. Metal or plastic-coated metal lampshade frames are cheap to buy. Metal frames must be wrapped in tape. Light to mediumweight fabrics that drape well, such as silk, fine cotton, linen and crêpe, are recommended to cover the shade. Avoid stiff fabrics and fabrics that fray easily.

Making your own lampshades means you can include the lamps in the decorative scheme of a room. Choose new fabric or use remnants of fabric used elsewhere in the room.

Making a lined lampshade

A remnant of dupion silk was used to cover this 18cm/7in diameter drum lampshade frame. Keep the tape reel from unravelling as you bind the frame by securing it with an elastic band. A beaded trim and velvet ribbon are beautiful finishing touches.

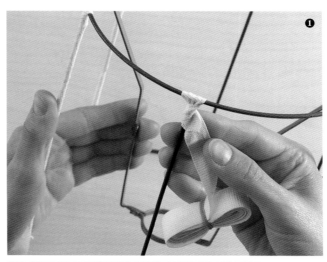

1 *To tape a metal frame, start at the top of one strut by binding the end of 1.2cm/½in wide white cotton tape over the top ring and around the tape end, securing it against the strut. Tightly bind the tape diagonally down the strut so each wrap of the tape slightly overlaps the previous one. At the lower ring, pull the tape through the last wrap. Cut off the excess. Repeat on all the struts except the last one. Tape the top ring starting at the last strut then work down the last strut and around the bottom ring.*

2 *Fold a square of fabric diagonally in half with right sides facing; it must be large enough to cover one half of the frame with at least a 4cm/1½in margin all round. With the folded edge parallel with the lower ring, lay the fabric over one half of the frame. Pin to the frame at the top and lower edge of two opposite struts. Adjust and re-pin the fabric to half of the frame at regular intervals, pulling the fabric so it lays taut and smooth.*

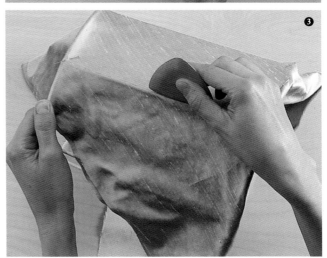

3 *When the fabric is free of wrinkles and lies evenly, mark the fabric along the centre of the pinned struts with tailor's chalk. Mark the position of the upper and lower rings. Remove the fabric, keeping the two layers pinned together. Cut along the fold.*

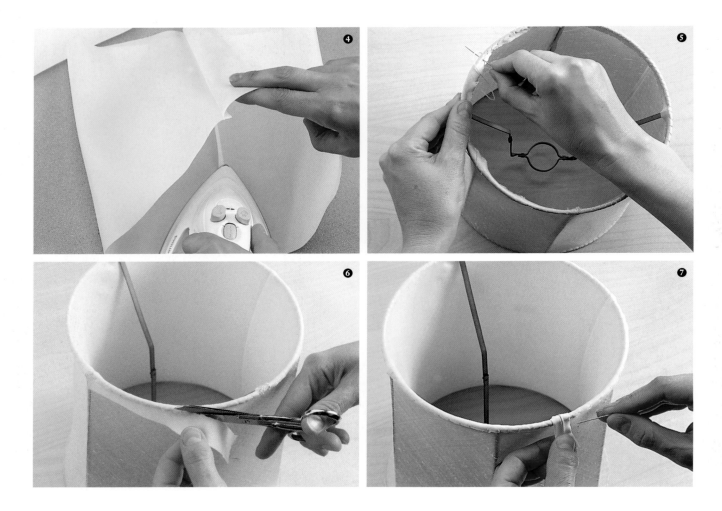

4 Stitch along the drawn lines, starting and finishing 2cm/¾in beyond the ring positions. Trim the seam allowances to 5mm/¼in. Press the seams to one side. Cut the upper and lower edges level with the ends of the seams. Fold, fit, pin and mark the lining fabric in the same way. Stitch 3mm/⅛in inside the drawn lines; this is because the lining should be smaller to fit inside the frame. Trim and press.

5 Slip the cover over the frame, right side outwards. Adjust the seams along two opposite struts. Pin the cover to the frame rings so the fabric is taut and smooth. Using double thread, oversew the cover to the rings with small neat stitches. Trim away the excess fabric close to the stitching.

6 Slip the lining into the frame with the wrong sides facing and match the seams, pinning in place. Snip the lining at the gimbals where they join the upper ring. Wrap the lining over the frame rings and re-pin so the lining is taut. Oversew the lining to the rings, taking care not to sew through to the lining inside the lampshade. The stitches on the outside will be covered with the trimming. Trim away the excess lining close to the stitches.

7 Cut a 2.5cm/1in wide strip of lining 14cm/5¾in long. Press lengthwise in half then in half again. Cut the strip in half. Slip one strip under a gimbal and pin the ends over the outside of the lampshade. Oversew to the upper edge. Cut off the excess strip and repeat on the other side. Sew the trimming to the upper and lower edges of the lampshade. If using a beaded trim, sew it in place first then sew a ribbon on top to cover the tape edge.

bordered throw

Make a sumptuous throw from luxurious fabrics to snuggle into on cool winter evenings. A soft chenille has been used to make this throw. A deep border of chocolate-brown dupion silk edges the throw with neat mitred corners.

Making a bordered throw

1 Cut a rectangle of chenille 133 x 98cm/4ft 4⅜in x 3ft 2½in. For the border, cut two strips of silk 156 x 23cm/5ft 1½in x 9⅛in and two strips 121 x 23cm/3ft 11⅝in x 9⅛in. Refer to the diagram below to cut the ends of the borders to points. Press 1.5cm/⅝in under on one long edge of each border.

2 With the right sides facing and matching the pressed edges, stitch the short borders between the long borders at the mitred ends, finishing 1.5cm/⅝in from the long raw edges. Clip the corners and press the seams open.

3 With the right sides facing, stitch the long raw edges of the border to the throw, pivoting the seam at the corners. Press the seam toward the border.

4 Pin the pressed edges along the seam, then press the border in half. Slipstitch the pressed edge along the seam.

Tip
Add a glamorous silk border to an inexpensive readymade throw by cutting it to size and following the instructions above.

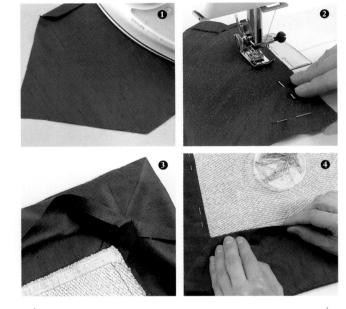

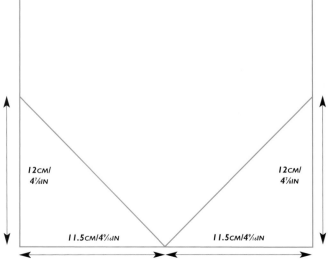

12CM/ 4⅞IN   12CM/ 4⅞IN

11.5CM/4⁹∕₁₆IN   11.5CM/4⁹∕₁₆IN

choux rosette picture hanger

Add a touch of opulence when displaying a favourite picture with a couture-style choux rosette with long tails to hang behind the picture. Silk suits the design, especially shot silk, as the hand-stitched ruching will catch the light and change colour in the shadows of the rosette.

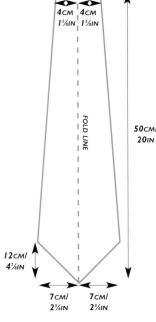

Making a choux rosette

Use fine bridal pins to pin the rosette so as not to mark the silk.

1 Cut a 9cm/3½in diameter circle of pelmet interfacing. Divide the circle into quarters with a pencil on the right side. Cut a 27cm/10½in square of fabric, i.e. three times the diameter of the circle.

2 Fold one edge of the square into pleats and, with right sides uppermost, pin the pleats to the circumference of one quarter of the circle. The pleats do not have to be equal in size. Handsew the pleats in place. Continue pleating the sides of the square onto the circle quarters.

3 Turn the rosette over and lift the edges of the silk over the edge of the circle for about 6mm/¼in. Catch in place, taking care not to take the stitches through to the silk on the right side.

4 On the right side, gently scrunch the fabric to reduce its bulk. Push pins through to the back of the rosette to hold the shape. Catch in place with tiny discreet stitches, taking the thread through to the back of the rosette. Cut a 10cm/4in diameter circle of silk to neaten the back. Pin to the back of the rosette and turn under the edges, then slipstitch in place.

5 Refer to the diagram to cut out the tails. Press 1cm/⅜in under at the narrow ends. Fold and pin lengthwise in half, with the right sides facing. Stitch the raw edges, taking a 1cm/⅜in seam allowance. Clip the corners, turn right side out and press. Sew to the back of the rosette, fanning the tails outwards. Sew a curtain ring to the back for hanging up the rosette.

4CM
1⅝IN 4CM 1⅝IN

FOLD LINE

50CM/ 20IN

12CM/ 4⅝IN

7CM/ 2¾IN 7CM/ 2¾IN

cafetière cosy

Keep the coffee piping hot with a neat padded cosy that wraps around a cafetière. The cosy is custom-made for an exact fit and has a pocket on the front to store a small spoon. Overlapping straps fasten the cosy with poppers.

Making a cafetière cosy

Measure the height of the cafetière from the base to just below the spout. Next, measure the circumference, passing the tape through the handle. Measure the distance between the inner ends of the handle for the depth of the straps.

1 Take 1cm/³⁄₈in seam allowances throughout. For the cosy, cut two rectangles of fabric and one of 112g/4oz wadding that are the height measurement plus 2cm/³⁄₄in by the circumference measurement less 1cm/³⁄₈in. Cut two rectangles of fabric and iron-on interfacing for the straps 8cm/3⅛in by the depth of the strap plus 2cm/³⁄₄in. Press the interfacing to the wrong sides of the straps to fuse them together.

2 Fold and pin the straps in half along their depth with the right sides facing. Stitch the upper and lower edges. Clip the corners, then turn and press the straps. Pin a strap to each end on the right side of one cosy.

3 Cut a rectangle of fabric for the pocket 13 x 7cm/5¼ x 2³⁄₄in. Press 1cm/³⁄₈in under then 2cm/³⁄₄in on the short upper edge. Stitch close to the inner pressed edge. Press 1cm/³⁄₈in under on the remaining pressed edges.

4 Wrap the cosy around the cafetière to check the fit. The straps should slip through the handle and overlap. Pin the pocket to the front of the cosy, and tack the straps and pocket in place. Stitch the pockets in position close to the side and lower edges, stitching back and forth a few times at the upper edge to reinforce them.

5 Place the cosy with the straps and pocket right side up on the wadding, then pin the remaining cosy on top with the right sides facing. Cut the corners diagonally to angle them. Stitch the outer edges, leaving a 10cm/4in gap in the lower edge. Carefully trim away the wadding in the seam allowance. Clip the corners and turn through.

6 Press the edges then slipstitch the opening closed. Topstitch 6mm/¼in from the outer edges. Attach two poppers to the straps, following the manufacturer's instructions.

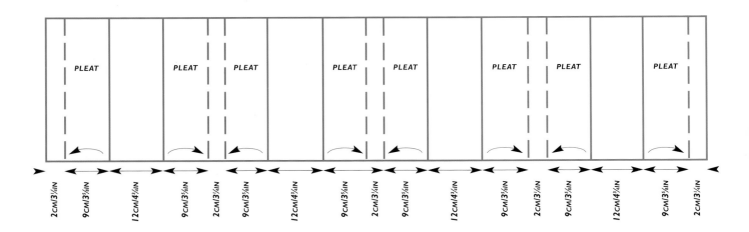

SHOE CADDY – POCKET STRIP PATTERN
(PAGE 164–5)

2CM/3/4IN · 9CM/3⅝IN · 12CM/4¾IN · 9CM/3⅝IN · 2CM/3/4IN · 9CM/3⅝IN · 12CM/4¾IN · 9CM/3⅝IN · 2CM/3/4IN · 9CM/3⅝IN · 12CM/4¾IN · 9CM/3⅝IN · 2CM/3/4IN · 9CM/3⅝IN · 12CM/4¾IN · 9CM/3⅝IN · 2CM/3/4IN

PLEAT · PLEAT · PLEAT · PLEAT · PLEAT · PLEAT · PLEAT · PLEAT

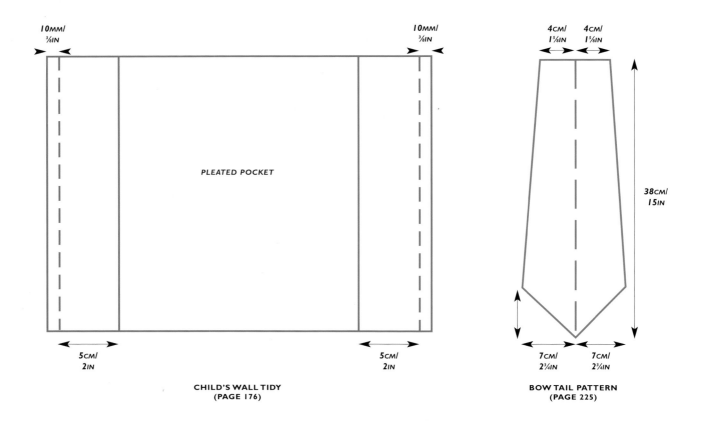

10MM/
3/8IN

10MM/
3/8IN

4CM/
1⅝IN

4CM/
1⅝IN

PLEATED POCKET

38CM/
15IN

5CM/
2IN

5CM/
2IN

7CM/
2¾IN

7CM/
2¾IN

CHILD'S WALL TIDY
(PAGE 176)

BOW TAIL PATTERN
(PAGE 225)

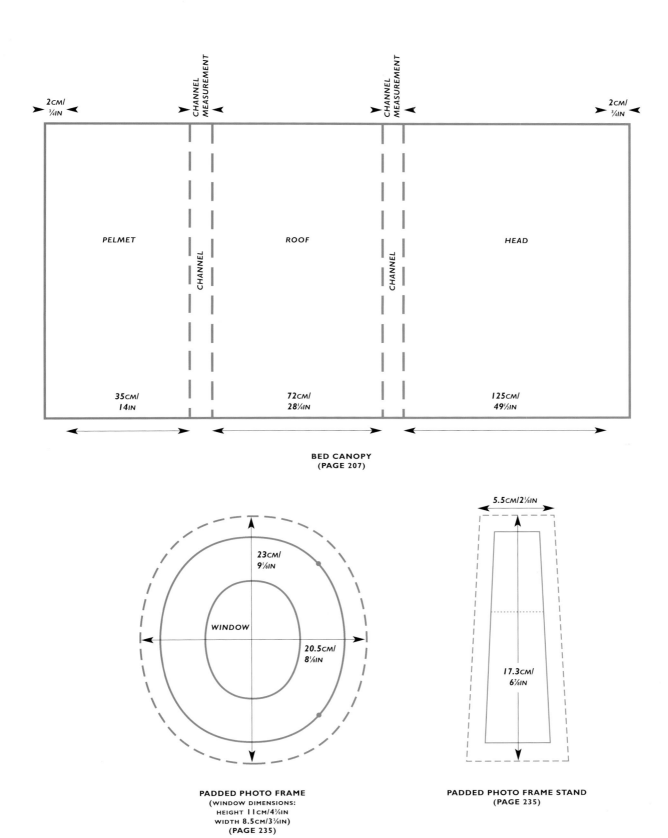

2CM/ ¾IN

CHANNEL MEASUREMENT

CHANNEL MEASUREMENT

2CM/ ¾IN

PELMET

ROOF

HEAD

CHANNEL

CHANNEL

35CM/ 14IN

72CM/ 28¼IN

125CM/ 49½IN

BED CANOPY
(PAGE 207)

23CM/ 9⅛IN

WINDOW

20.5CM/ 8⅛IN

PADDED PHOTO FRAME
(WINDOW DIMENSIONS:
HEIGHT 11CM/4⅜IN
WIDTH 8.5CM/3⅜IN)
(PAGE 235)

5.5CM/2⅛IN

17.3CM/ 6⅞IN

PADDED PHOTO FRAME STAND
(PAGE 235)

PLEASE NOTE: THESE PATTERNS ARE GUIDES ONLY AND ARE NOT TO SCALE

glossary

Appliqué
Fabric shapes applied to a background fabric by hand or zigzagged by machine.

Awl
A small pointed tool for piercing holes in leather.

Bagged out
Two pieces of fabric the same size, stitched all round and turned to the right side.

Batten
A strip of wood slotted into blinds to hold fabric taut, or attached above a window to hang a blind from.

Bias
A 45-degree angle on fabric. Bias-cut strips are used to make bindings and to cover piping.

Binding
Narrow strips of fabric bound around the raw edges of fabric to neaten them.

Bouclé
A yarn spun with a looped finish, either knitted or woven.

Bradawl
A small tool for piercing holes in wood for screws, nails and hooks.

Canopy
A fabric panel fixed above head height, for example above a bed.

Clipping
Cutting across the corner of a seam allowance to reduce the bulk of the fabric.

Dowel
A length of rounded wood inserted into blinds to hold the fabric taut.

Drop
The height of a curtain or table.

Drop-in seat
An upholstered board dropped into the frame of a chair.

Fabric grain
The lengthwise direction on a piece of fabric, parallel with the selvedges.

Facing
A panel or strip of fabric used to back a section of the main fabric.

Finials
Ornamental ends for curtain poles.

Flat felled seam
A strong seam that encloses the raw edges.

Flat seam
A single stitched seam, the most commonly used seam.

French seam
A double seam enclosing raw edges.

Gathering stitch
A long stitch, worked by hand or machine, that is drawn up to gather fabric.

Gusset
A strip of fabric inserted to make a three-dimensional item, on a box cushion cover for example.

Heading tape
Curtain tape that forms the heading on a curtain.

Housewife pillowcase
A traditional pillowcase with an internal flap to hold the pillow inside.

Interfacing
Layer of stiffening material applied to the main fabric to give it more body or to stiffen it.

Lambrequin
A fabric-covered pelmet that continues down the sides of the window.

Masking tape
A low-tack sticky tape for sticking items temporarily in place.

Mitring
A neat method of turning a corner by folding under the fullness of fabric diagonally.

Notch
A snip cut into the edges of fabric to match when stitching.

Oxford pillowcase
A housewife pillowcase with a wide, flat border.

Patchwork
A technique of joining fabric squares or shapes edge to edge.

Pelmet
A wooden or stiffened fabric border that conceals the top of a curtain or blind.

Pelmet shelf
A wooden shelf fixed above a window
to support a pelmet.

Pile
The raised surface of a fabric such as
velvet. Pile fabrics must have the
patterns cut in the same direction.

Pinking
Cutting fabric with pinking shears to
prevent fraying.

Piping
A fabric-covered cord used in seams.

Quilting
Two layers of fabric joined
together with wadding sandwiched
between them.

Roller blind
A stiffened fabric blind suspended from
a sprung roller.

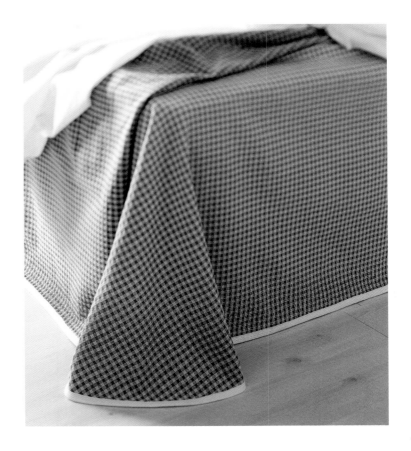

Roman blind
A fabric blind, stiffened with dowels,
that folds in pleats.

Satin stitch
A closely worked hand or machine
stitch that has the sheen of satin fabric.

Screw eye
A metal screw with a loop at the
head end.

Seam allowance
An allowance added to a seam.

Seam line
A marked or imaginary line to be
stitched along.

Selvedge
A woven, finished edge of a length of
fabric.

Squab
A thin cushion tied to the seat of a
chair.

Warp
The threads that run along the length
of fabric, parallel with the selvedges.

Webbing
A wide, woven braid, traditionally
made from hessian, used in upholstery.

Weft
The threads that run across a length of
fabric, at right angles to the selvedges.

Yarn
A spun or twisted thread for knitting
and embroidery.

Zigzag stitch
A machine stitch used for neatening
seams or for decoration.

index

A

appliqué 250

    pillowcases 192–3

    sheets 212–13

armchair covers 108–11

attic curtains 66–7

awls 250

B

back pockets (chairs) 107

bagged out 250

bags 154–5, 158–9

ballpoint needles 30

baskets (lined) 156–7

battens 250

bead-fringed runners 137

beads 24

beanbag chairs 101–3

beds

    bedding sizes 185

    canopies 206–7

    linen 182–219

    valances 196–9

bedspreads 202–3

beeswax 31

betweens needles 30

bias 250

    bias bindings 26, 44–5

    maker 28

    quilted table mats 140–1

bindings 44–5, 250

blind cord 26

blinds 68–71, 86, 251

blood stains 23

bobbins 39

bodkins 30

bolster bags 158–9

bonding web 47

borders

    curtains 64, 65

    tablecloths 129, 131

    throws 242–3

bouclé 250

bound-edge napkins 144–5

bows 224–5

box cushions 94–5

bradawls 250

braids 24, 25, 222–3

brocade 16

broderie anglaise 16

brushed cotton 20

buckram 20

bump fabric 20

bumpers (cots) 210–11

button thread 31

C

cafetière cosy 246–7

calico 20

candle wax removal 22

canopies 206–7, 236–7, 250

canvas 17

care of fabrics 22–3

case-headed curtains 60

cases (underbed) 163

casing 55, 60

chairs

    armchair covers 108–11

    back pockets 107

    beanbag 101–3

    deckchairs 104–5

    directors 106–7

chenille 17

chintz 17

    choosing fabrics

    bedding 184–5

    curtain 52

furnishing 16–19

    seating 90–1

    tables 126

choux rosette picture

    hangers 244–5

clipping 250

clothes covers 160–2

clothing envelopes 172–3

coffee stains 23

colour schemes 10–13

cord 24, 25, 46, 47

cord tidies 42, 43

corded hem napkins 138

corkscrew pins 30

coronas 208–9

cosy (cafetière) 246–7

cot bumpers 210–11

cotton 20

cotton sateen 21

cotton-covered polyester

    threads 31

covers

    armchair 108–11

    clothes 160–2

    dining chairs 120–3

    dressing table 142–3

    drop-in seats 96–7

    duvet 194–5, 216–17

    fitted table 148–9

    footstools 98–100

    headboards 205

    kitchen appliances 174–5

    lampshades 228–31,

      238–41

    seating 114–17, 120–3

    shelving 166–7

    tables 148–9

creating fabrics 13

crewel work 17

acknowledgements

The author would like to give special thanks to Steve Tanner for his superb photographs and attention to detail, Jack Britton for her beautiful styling, Karl Adamson for his excellent additional photography, and Jan Eaton, Gwen Diamond and Carol Hart for their practical advice and for making up many of the projects.

The author and publisher would also like to thank those who supplied materials and props:

The Dormy House for blank furniture e.g. screens, dressing tables, headboards and footstools. Available by mail order (telephone 01264 365808).

Scumble Goosie for blank furniture e.g. screens. Available by mail order (telephone 01453 731305).

3M for spray adhesive, available at good art and craft shops.

Offray for ribbons, available at good haberdashery shops and sewing departments.

Gütermann for threads, beads and sequins, available at good haberdashery shops and departments.

DMC for embroidery threads, available at good haberdashery shops and departments or by mail order (telephone 0116 281 1040).

Academy Costume Hire for antique shoes (telephone 020 7620 0771).

Bunny London, Unit 1, 22 South Side, Oxo Tower, London SE1 UK for children's clothes (telephone 020 7928 6269).

Crystal Franken, John Harmer, Robert and Georgina McPherson for lighting and flowers.

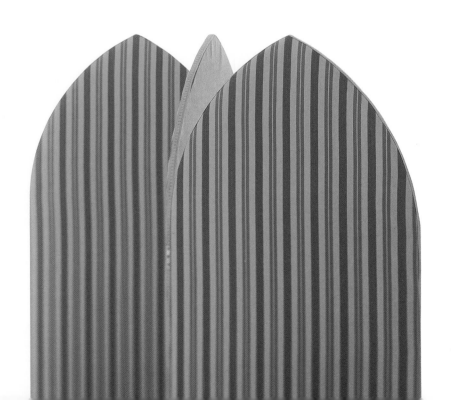